SHATTERING
THE MYTHS

SHATTERING THE MYTHS

Women in Academe

Judith Glazer-Raymo

The Johns Hopkins University Press

Baltimore and London

Johns Hopkins Paperbacks edition, 2001
9 8 7 6 5 4 3 2 1

The Johns Hopkins University Press
2715 North Charles Street
Baltimore, Maryland 21218-4363
www.press.jhu.edu

Library of Congress Cataloging-in-Publication Data will be found
at the end of this book.
A catalog record for this book is available from the British Library.

ISBN 0-8018-6641-3 (pbk.)

To Helen, George, and Judith

CONTENTS

PREFACE

Oh no no, you Angels, I say,
No hierarchies I pray.

Stevie Smith
"No Categories!"
(*Not Waving but Drowning*)

Although significant advances have been made since 1970 to enlarge women's representation in the academy, institutional leaders are reluctant to acknowledge the tenacity of policies that deter women's full participation. Administrators and policy analysts, in particular, share the view that problems related to women's equality have been largely resolved. Among the more salient issues affecting academic women are disparities with respect to men in almost every indicator of professional status—rank, salary, tenure, job satisfaction, and working conditions—across a range of institutional categories and types. In the context of a rapidly changing policy environment, I examine commonly held myths that view academic freedom and academic tenure as cultural artifacts of another era, fostering the growth of dual employment systems and sustaining glass ceilings and other barriers to women's advancement. I explore the impact of downsizing, restructuring, and policy termination on women's progress in the academy. I deconstruct the arguments of those who couch their critique of affirmative action and antidiscrimination policies in the language of flexibility, diversity, and scarce resources on the one hand and faculty productivity, merit, and accountability on the other. I propose strategies for demythologizing uncritical acceptance of women's status and for increasing women's participation and position in higher education. Throughout each chapter, I employ a feminist perspective in posing two questions: What role have legislative mandates, adopting new policies, and reallocating power structures played in the improvement of women's status? Conversely, what factors have inhibited their progress?

I use a critical feminist perspective to contrast the activism of the 1970s, the passivity of the 1980s, and the ambivalence and antipathy toward feminism in the 1990s. These waves of change have been accelerated by external forces—political, economic, and cultural—generational differences between women, and intellectual and ideological struggles within the women's movement and in the larger academic culture. My critique is informed by my experience in the academy as an administrator, researcher, community activist, teacher, mentor, and adviser. It also draws on the experience of women faculty and administrators as they articulate and reflect on the social, economic, political, and ideological contexts in which they work and the multiple influences on their professional and personal lives.

Using 1970 as my baseline, I begin, in chapter 1, with a personal and professional journey into the past and a reflection on the present in the context of the contemporary women's movement. At the outset, middle-class women of my generation adopted a liberal feminist perspective based on enlightenment principles of rationality, autonomy, and equality. In seeking to eradicate sexism and bias in the sixties and seventies and inspired by the civil rights movement, they looked to the state and the courts to ensure their constitutional rights of equality under the law. In describing the experiences of these "first-wave" feminists and the generations who followed, I go beyond a decontextualized account of events to consider what it has meant to witness and take part in those diverse experiences occurring at the juncture of social history, politics, and educational reform. Autobiography has enabled me to look more critically at the remarkable diversity of feminism in the 1990s, the role of ideology in policy formation and implementation, and the ambiguous status of the postmodern university.

In chapters 2 through 5 I trace women's progress in the past twenty-five years, drawing on data from national and regional databases, published and unpublished documents, and articles and commentary from a variety of sources. While researching these chapters between 1995 and 1997, I visited ten colleges and universities; conducted in-person, telephone, and electronic interviews with countless women and men; and participated in women's conferences, focus dialogues, and colloquia. In analyzing multiple policy decisions and interactions, I look beyond enactment of the statutes banning sex discrimination to their consequences for women during the past three decades. My research gained immeasurably from the work of feminist legal scholars who have raised important questions about women's ability to achieve sexual equality by assimilation into alienating institutional structures (Bartlett, 1994; Rhode, 1994). These scholars stress the importance of asking the "woman question" in conducting critical feminist analyses of governmental policies, thereby identifying the gender implications of rules and practices that might otherwise seem neutral or objective. They adopt a more activist view of feminists as agents of transformational social and political change. With women as the center of my inquiry, my goal has been to reveal the ironies and shatter the myths implicit in the prevailing social structures, political ideologies, and policy discourse. The cultural patterns that emerge represent the rich diversity of all women, including women of color. They affirm the significant impact of affirmative action policies but also reveal the intellectual, emotional, and psychic challenges that continue to confront women. In analyzing the ideologies underlying these policies, I trace the growing power and influence of the state, the courts, and the university in determining new policy directions.

In chapter 6, I advocate two strategies that have been used to implement change in the academy: gender bias commissions and feminist pedagogy. Both of these emerged as manifestations of the women's movement in higher education. I systematically study state and federal actions and institutional responses to affirmative action and equal employment laws and regulations, with particular emphasis on the development of campus commissions on the status of women. I also explore the development and uses of feminist pedagogy, and its embeddedness in feminist critique. I conclude by looking toward the future rather than the past. In reviewing the status of women at the close of the second millennium, I am concerned about the cultural, attitudinal, and structural constraints that inhibit women's progress and about the social backlash that threatens hard-earned gains. The corporate university dominated by patterns of managerialism also perpetuates gender hierarchies and reward systems rooted in credentialism and expertise. In presenting data, artifacts, and stories about women in academe, it is my intention to discard the mythic images that have been carried forward from earlier generations and to encourage women to become political actors at the center of the university.

ACKNOWLEDGMENTS

This book originated in conversations with women colleagues and students concerned about issues and trends confronting women in contemporary society. The preparation of a reader, *Women in Higher Education: A Feminist Perspective* (Glazer, Bensimon, & Townsend, 1993), provided the impetus for undertaking an in-depth investigation of women's role and status at the close of the second millennium. At the outset, I would like to acknowledge those who contributed to the book's development through their responses to my queries for data and my requests for interviews, their invitations to present papers and participate in symposia, and their willingness to provide feedback on various chapters.

I am grateful to Estela Bensimon and Betty Sichel for their collegiality and their invaluable comments on the manuscript at various stages of its development. I also thank Anna Neumann for her cogent comments on chapter 1 and the use of autobiography in scholarly research and Catherine Marshall for her helpful feedback on chapter 6. I appreciated the opportunity provided by James Bess to investigate feminist pedagogy and teaching motivation and thank him for engaging me in a dialogue on this topic. I am grateful to Michele Tokarzyck and the members of the Goucher College Colloquium for inviting me to present material from chapter 6 and for their helpful feedback. Judy Rogers and Dawn Person offered constructive critiques of earlier versions of my research on women's commissions at the 1995 annual meeting of the Association for the Study of Higher Education in Orlando and the 1996 annual meeting of the American Educational Research Association in New York City. Portions of the case study on feminist pedagogy in chapter 6 are excerpted from a paper presented by Betty Sichel and me at the annual meeting of the American Educational Research Association in San Francisco (Glazer & Sichel, 1994).

I am particularly indebted to two women for their research assistance: Ingebjorg McGrady, my graduate assistant, whose diligent efforts for two years provided me with innumerable resource materials; and my stepdaughter, Judith Sands, deputy law librarian for the New York City Corporation Counsel, whose indefatigable legal research contributed inestimably to chapter 3. I have gained many new insights into legal practice and the role of the courts in gender equity through the articles and briefs that she has located for me. I am also grateful to Kara Hone for her research assistance in 1996-97 and to William Sadler for his methodical work in preparing the statistical tables in this book.

I acknowledge the generosity and good will of several individuals who provided me with data, reports, and access to published and unpublished documents: Ann Ard, Eleanor Babco, Janet Bickel, Betty Chapman, Martin Finkelstein, Jean Finkford, Barbara Hoks, Carol Hollenshead, Debra Humphreys, Beryl Hunt, Helen Irvin, Mary Keese, Teresita Kopka, Sharon McDade, Jane Miller, Bernice Sandler, Liane Sorenson, Jane Stapleton, Myra Strober, Delores Thurgood, and Mark Westlye. Informative conversations were also held with Elizabeth Allen, Mae Carter, Barbara Curry, Martha Driver, Chris Golde, Ilene Harris, Sylvia Hurtado, Patricia Hyer, Sue Kaufmann, Diana Leonard, Anne Morey, Evelyn Patterson, Sue Rasmussen, Maryann Sagaria, Ann Shapiro, Esther Skirball, Sheila Slaughter, Ruth Sternglantz, Nancy Tobin, Barbara Townsend, Kelly Ward, and Gilbert Whitaker.

By prior agreement, I have sought to maintain the anonymity of those I interviewed, and thus throughout the book I do not identify them except in those cases where permission was granted to do so. Instead, I express my gratitude to the women and men with whom I spoke, those who arranged appointments for me preceding my visits to their campuses, and those who shared their time and their data so generously with me. Among this group are the many presidents, provosts, and vice presidents with whom I talked both in person and by telephone. Their interest and support have been most gratifying.

A grant from the Thanks Be to Grandmother Winifred Foundation and a one-year research sabbatical from my faculty position at the C. W. Post Campus of Long Island University enabled me to make site visits to various universities and colleges, and to meet with women faculty, administrators, and doctoral students, listening to and recording their stories and responses to my questions. I would like to thank Deborah Light, the TBTGWF president for her encouragement and support, and Geoffrey Berresford and the members of the C. W. Post Campus Research Committee for the grants they awarded me for preliminary research on this project. Research was conducted at many universities throughout the United States and at five libraries whose staffs I also acknowledge: New York University's Elmer Bobst and Law Libraries, the British Library, the New York Public Library, and the Elizabeth Schlesinger Library at Radcliffe College.

I owe a special debt to my editor, Jacqueline Wehmueller, who provided the initial impetus for undertaking this project and who has been entirely supportive at every step of its development. Finally, I thank my spouse, Robert Raymo, for his support and thoughtful comments throughout the research and writing of this book, and my children, Helen Glazer Marcus and George Glazer, for their inspiration and their love.

SHATTERING
THE MYTHS

1

THE PERSONAL AND
THE PROFESSIONAL

Becoming a Feminist

Feminists often say that we have to start with women's own experience if we are to understand how profoundly it influences our perspectives, values, attitudes, and role in society. "Beginning in women's experiences told in women's words was and is a vital political moment in the women's movement" (Smith, 1987). Those who criticize feminists like to say that making women's lives the focal point of our inquiry is a self-centered exercise that distorts the meaning of ideas and is overly subjective and irrational. In *Feminism without Illusions* (1991), Elizabeth Fox-Genovese comments that in looking back on her own life and the gap between the stories she was told and her own experience, she realizes that "education in feminism must include a measure of autobiography, if only to convince younger women that growing up as a woman, while it will never be easy, is possible" (p. 246). In *Writing a Woman's Life* (1988), Carolyn Heilbrun also examines her development as a writer, which in retrospect she views as inextricably linked to her development as a woman and a feminist. In reflecting on the use of a pseudonym, Amanda Cross, for her detective novel *Death in a Tenured Position,* Heilbrun observes: "As we age many of us who are privileged—not only academics in tenured positions, of course, but more broadly those with some assured place and pattern in their lives, with some financial security—are in danger of choosing to stay right where we are, to undertake each day's routine, and to listen to our arteries hardening. I do not believe that death should be allowed to find us in our tenured positions" (pp. 130–31).

My feminism evolved from an early awareness of the boundaries that compartmentalized the lives of men and women into public and private spheres. In describing the feminine mystique that alienates women from their domestic world, Betty Friedan identified three spheres of women's lives—

girlhood, motherhood, and personhood (1963). Twenty years later, Alison Jaggar redefined this mystique as derived from the fragmentation women experience in balancing sexuality, motherhood, and intellectuality (1983). Reflecting on my personal development, I would also include voluntarism as a defining characteristic of the feminist psyche of women who, like me, came of age in the 1950s. Our parents lived through the deprivation of the 1930s and 1940s, and we were the beneficiaries of their newfound postwar prosperity. Despite the periodic crises of the Cold War, we shared their expectations and optimism about the future.

In the fifties, single-sex private colleges and universities were the rule rather than the exception in the northeastern United States. I spent my freshman year at the University of Michigan but was disappointed in the quality of the undergraduate program, the emphasis on professional education, and the social milieu of fraternity and sorority life that enforced the separation of Jews and Gentiles. I transferred to Smith College, where expectations were high that we would master difficult subjects and challenging materials. The socialization process was entirely different from the coeducational midwestern university, with its emphasis on Greek key societies, football games, and beer parties. Smith had a decentralized residential structure that was self-governing and anti-elitist. As college women in the fifties, we were expected to abide by a curious combination of honor codes and strict rules, exemplified by residential house systems presided over by housemothers, unproctored examinations, nightly curfews, and compulsory attendance at weekly chapel chaired by the college president, Benjamin Wright. (Smith's board of trustees appointed its first woman president, Jill Conway, in 1975, three years after passage of Title IX.)

Although most of the teachers at Smith were women, an English major's exposure to women writers was minimal. Only Jane Austen, the Brontë sisters, and George Eliot were admitted to the canon. I briefly considered the possibility of attending law school after graduation, but Smith's high academic standards did not extend to equally high career expectations for its graduates. Whereas today's seniors are more concerned with grade point averages and LSAT, GRE, and MCAT scores, engagements and marriages preoccupied many of the women of my acquaintance, particularly since most of the men we knew were either serving in the military or seeking graduate school deferments. Our professors were formidable scholars who challenged us intellectually but who remained remote, intimidating figures with whom we rarely communicated outside of class.

For women of my generation, the fifties' version of success meant marrying the professionals we hoped to become, followed by motherhood, volunteer work, and at some point in the distant future, personhood. Our values mirrored those of our peers in "the family-centered, consumer-oriented, Freudian American world of the 1950s" (Rich, 1976, p. 25). We were the silent generation who left urban America for newly built suburban communities, assimilating into the dominant upper-middle-class WASP culture. We became the new conservatives—disciplined, ambitious, and using our newfound wealth to accumulate the badges of success for our families and ourselves.

I soon gravitated toward parent-teacher activities within the community, using voluntarism as a mechanism to liberate myself from gender constraints in acceptable ways. This decision turned out to be fortuitous, stirring my lifelong interest in education. In 1963, the mother of two young children and living in suburban Westchester County, New York, I was president of our local Parent-Teacher Association (PTA) when I was asked to run for what we traditionally referred to as "the woman's seat" on our local school board. I won that election by twenty-six votes, entering public life more by chance than by design. Our district was a bedroom community, and the four men on the board commuted to New York City daily. That left me the sole member who was available to sign checks, attend meetings, and represent district interests during school hours. I first served as district clerk and later as vice president and president. This progression of events enabled me to build a power base in the community and to expand my knowledge and understanding of the field of education. In due course I focused my attention specifically on educational policy making.

Social and Political Activism

My educational career evolved from community activism and school board politics to public relations, development, continuing education, and higher education administration at the State University of New York (SUNY) College at Purchase and at Westchester Community College. From there, it went to higher education scholarship, consortia management, and teacher education at New York University, St. John's University, and, ultimately, the C. W. Post Campus of Long Island University. Along the way, I secured the requisite credentials—a master's degree in media ecology and a doctorate in higher education administration, both at New York University. Although my experiences were not unique, they occurred when higher education and the workplace were being transformed. Many conflicts and challenges awaited women in the sixties, the seventies, and the eighties in their quest for access, acceptance, and recognition in male-dominated professions.

In 1963, our district began long-range planning that involved construction of one of the first middle schools in the state, the redesign of its curriculum, merger negotiations with several contiguous districts in Harrison and Port Chester, and attempts to gain support for a regional high school. This was an exciting decade in American education: President Lyndon Johnson and the Congress initiated an ambitious program of federal support through passage of the Elementary and Secondary Education Act of 1965. Head Start, Upward Bound, Title I, and economic opportunity programs held great promise for addressing the needs of economically and educationally disadvantaged students. New York State adopted a school aid formula based on weighted average daily attendance that decreased reliance on property taxes and opened a new funding source for growing districts like ours, with weak industrial bases of support.

I was vice president of the Blind Brook Board of Education in 1967 when the local newspaper announced that a new SUNY campus dedicated to the arts would be built on property in the neighboring district of Purchase. For several years, we had sought approval from New York State to build our own high school rather than send our children to a school in the village of Port Chester. In some ways, the ensuing debate was a classic case of neighboring communities separated by boundaries of class. Port Chester was the main village in the Town of Rye, a factory town bordered on the north by Greenwich, Connecticut, and on the east by the Byram River and the old Boston Post Road. The Town of Rye (now the village of Rye Brook) was a community of postwar developments built in the 1950s and 1960s, with an autonomous, union-free school district. Its residents were professionals and corporate executives, most of whom commuted to jobs in other parts of the county or in New York City.

The Ridge Street School (kindergarten through ninth grade) had become a center for educational innovation and a symbol of community identity for residents of Rye Town, who resented being compelled to pay tuition to send tenth through twelfth graders to the neighboring Port Chester High School. Meanwhile, the state was exerting pressure on the school boards in Rye Town and Port Chester to merge the two districts. This proposal threatened the growing town's identity and had little popular support in either jurisdiction. To overcome state intransigence, Rye Town residents organized citizens' committees, circulated petitions, researched the state's education laws, and sought surrogates to plead the district's case in Albany.

The commissioner of education, James E. Allen Jr., was a man of great influence whose power derived from his close relationship with Governor Nelson Rockefeller and the board of regents, which made policy for all education in New York State. He was a formidable opponent for our small, unincorporated town, and in retrospect he taught me my first lessons about the arbitrariness of educational politics in a public policy arena. To Allen and the regents, we were minor players in a much larger game to consolidate New York's union-free school districts into larger entities. They had been persuaded by James Conant, the former president of Harvard University and latter-day school reformer, that high-school size was critical in determining curricular and student diversity and academic quality. Working through intermediaries, he raised the specter of the loss of state aid (almost 50% of our budget) and denial of accreditation for any school built without state approval.

By the time the construction of Purchase College was announced in 1967, our board was ready for a confrontation with the commissioner and the regents. Millard Collins, the board's president at the time and an IBM executive, was able to secure a meeting for us with Samuel Gould, chancellor of the SUNY system, which was by then the largest multicampus system in the United States. Encouraged by Gould's receptivity, I drafted a proposal for a regional high school for the arts and humanities in our district, one that would give our students their own high school, establish a link with the new liberal arts college, and offer admission to tuition-paying students from other Westchester County districts. My proposal was enthusiastically reviewed within the state education department and endorsed by two women who were instrumental in gaining its approval in Albany—Vivienne Anderson, director of the state's Division for the Arts and Humanities, and Catherine Bloom, director of the Arts in Education program of the JDR 3rd Fund. The president of Purchase College, along with the Westchester Council for the Arts and the Westchester Regional Education Center, which was initiating its own arts and humanities project, added their endorsements.

Social and political events in the late sixties emboldened communities such as ours to mount a more militant opposition to state-imposed mandates. The Port Chester Board, with which we were slated to merge, refused to take our high-school students any longer, leaving us bereft of a long-term alternative and forcing us to negotiate tuition contracts with other school boards in Valhalla and Mamaroneck. Interest groups began to coalesce around the options of district autonomy or district merger. In 1969, the year I was elected president of the board (the first woman to hold that post in our district), educational and political power brokers in New York State were preoccupied with three significant events: the passage of the Taylor Law giving public school teachers the right to bargain collectively and enhancing the status of the New York State United Teachers (NYSUT); the decentralization of the New York City Board of Education into thirty-two autonomous school districts following the Ocean Hill–Brownsville crisis and subsequent teachers' strike—a conflict that ultimately magnified the power of Albert Shanker and the United Federation of Teachers (UFT) in New York City; and the seizure of the City College campus and subsequent student riots at other CUNY campuses as well as at Columbia and New York Universities.

Demands for a student voice in governance, for minority access, and for ethnic studies programs led to the early adoption of open admissions by the City University of New York's board of higher education, the inauguration of statewide higher education opportunity programs in both public and private colleges and universities, and preliminary proposals for need-based student aid. One result of these tumultuous events was the appointment by Rockefeller, the legislature, and the regents of a state commission on the quality and financing of public education. The Fleischmann Commission conducted hearings and developed ambitious recommendations for changing the school financing formula to eliminate reliance on property taxes, equalize per capita spending, and establish a set of professional and innovative "lighthouse" schools to serve the complementary functions of exemplary teaching, teacher training, and applied research (New York State Commission, 1973, p. 188). The groundbreaking recommendations of the commission's three-volume report, released in 1971, were deemed too costly to implement. But the report focused public attention on the need to link educational excellence with innovation and diversity of purpose, in designing ten model schools to be administered jointly by SUNY, CUNY, and the state's regional boards of cooperative educational services (BOCES). These elements were embodied in our district's high-school proposal.

In assessing the rapid changes in 1969 and 1970, I recall the impact of state intervention in municipal affairs. The governor's staff, the regents, the mayor, and legislative leaders all sought to resolve escalating educational crises. Age-old rivalries between upstate and downstate factions quickly reached a boiling point, making our modest proposal to build a new high school appear rather benign in comparison to New York City's political embarrassments. Commissioner Allen and his deputies ultimately retreated from their intransigence, giving us tacit approval for a district referendum. This experience in grass-roots diplomacy marked a turning point for me. It reinforced my belief in the importance of timing and collaborative team-work as well as the vagaries of educational policy making in a politically charged environment. I also recognized that as the first woman school board president in my district's history, I had to overcome male reluctance to break with tradition. That leadership position at a critical point in the district's expansion was instrumental in my growth as an educator.

Tenacity, willpower, timing, and luck culminated in the completion of Rye Town's Blind Brook High School in 1973. I had obtained a foundation grant of $115,000 for our district from the Arts in Education program of the JDR 3rd Fund. This grant enabled our staff between 1969 and 1972 to conduct needs analyses of area resources; to design and phase in an interdisciplinary, team-taught curriculum for kindergarten through twelfth grade (K–12); to initiate professional staff development; and to build the new high school as a laboratory for integrating the arts and humanities. We now take for granted the arts-in-education concept, but it was an innovative idea in 1969, as was our decision (not entirely successful) to build one of the nation's first open-plan high schools. Shortly thereafter, Allen left New York State for a position in the Nixon administration, and his deputy, Ewald Nyquist, proved more conciliatory and sympathetic. Having played a pivotal role in resolving the high-school issue, I retired from the board in 1972, seeking new challenges. It had preoccupied my time for nine years to the point that when we finally received the approval we had long sought, one of the local papers wryly observed that it should be called "The Judy Glazer High School."

The Study and Practice of Higher Education

My job at Purchase College came about through serendipitous circumstances and demonstrated once again the randomness of events in shaping women's careers in the early days of the women's movement. By 1970, as president of the school board, I was approached by the president of Purchase, Abbott Kaplan, to serve as a community relations adviser, assisting him and his staff on the political and educational framework of Westchester County and working in a newly established office of continuing education to develop outreach programs that would bring together the community and the university. This position was my entry into the field of higher education. At that stage in my life, it did not occur to me that there might be a glass ceiling for women. I was then serving my third term as an elected public official, and the president of a new college had personally invited me to become part of his staff, including me in academic planning for the new college and giving me confidence in myself as a neophyte administrator. The timing of my entry into higher education was indeed propitious. By June 1970, congressional hearings were focusing national attention on sex discrimination in higher education, and universities with federal contracts had begun to collect comparative data on women faculty and staff.

The faculty and deans assembled by President Kaplan were a remarkably talented group, each one prominent in a different branch of the performing and visual arts or in the humanities and sciences. Purchase was then the wealthy enclave chronicled by Stephen Birmingham in his book, *Our Crowd* (1967). It was populated by scions of German Jewish families and by investment bankers, newspaper publishers, and political and civic leaders who dwelled in secluded country estates and played golf at its exclusive country clubs. A few years earlier, Pepsico had built its world headquarters on the grounds of the Blind Brook Polo Club, and now a master plan was being developed for a $200 million college of the arts to be built on five hundred acres of pristine farmland in the shadow of Westchester County Airport. The State University Construction Fund commissioned a group of eight architects, led by Edward Larrabee Barnes, to build a new campus for the arts. An ambitious project, the campus boasted a new museum designed by Philip Johnson and a multitheater performing arts center to serve the entire region. In 1971, Purchase became the first college campus to be the subject of an architectural exhibit at the Museum of Modern Art.[1]

In 1973, I left Purchase to become assistant dean for community services at Westchester Community College. Although these two colleges were part of the same SUNY system, they had widely divergent missions and loci of control. The community college was a satellite of county government, a semi-autonomous organization deriving two-thirds of its budget from the state and the county, which also appointed its board of trustees. Westchester was then enjoying a building boom; several multinational corporations had opened headquarters in its towns and villages—IBM, Pepsico, Texaco, Union Carbide, and General Foods among them. My job at the community college, which was to run the adult, noncredit and off-campus programs, brought me into contact with business and government as well as with school districts, community organizations, and even prison populations. In contrast to Purchase's intellectual atmosphere, the organizational culture of the community college was mired in politics and devoid of scholarly interest. It was

---

1. The exhibit had its own catalogue raisonée with an introduction by Nelson A. Rockefeller. See *Architecture for the Arts: The State University of New York College at Purchase* (New York: Museum of Modern Art, 1971).

a major letdown, and I soon realized the necessity of a Ph.D. for an administrative career in higher education.

In 1975, therefore, I enrolled in New York University's higher education administration doctoral program. Neither the department in which it was housed nor the program itself had a woman faculty member. Most of the classes were held in the late afternoon and early evening for a large cohort of part-time students who were also full-time administrators pursuing doctorates in order to move into senior management positions. For commuting students, who were juggling professional, personal, and academic commitments, socialization into the campus culture was fragmented and happenstance. Unlike the typical academic route to advancement, from faculty member and department chair to dean, this cohort followed a different route, beginning as administrators and only later moving into full-time teaching and research.

My pursuit of the doctorate was achieved with some element of personal sacrifice. The year it was granted—1981—was also the year of my divorce, after twenty-seven years of marriage. Moving between supportive work and unsupportive home environments added another layer of conflict at a critical time. I was caught in the proverbial double bind experienced by women of my generation, wanting to take advantage of opportunities but at the same time risking family disapproval and the alienation of friends whose lives followed more conventional paths. Taking on burdens that the present generation is less likely to assume, I was in the awkward position of going to graduate school while my daughter was in college, my son was finishing high school, and my husband was at the peak of his professional career. While he was improving his tennis game, I was writing term papers, attending classes, and gaining work experience. In contrast, educated women are much more likely today to delay marriage and family until their careers are well under way. Women have a different set of problems—a higher cost of living, the need for two household incomes, a scarcity of full-time professional positions—within a culture that encourages them to balance multiple roles with grace, style, and minimum sacrifice.

By 1975, the year I started my coursework, the national mood had grown pessimistic and the electorate disaffected, following the Watergate scandal and President Nixon's subsequent resignation. Having worked on Nixon's reelection campaign in 1972, I felt betrayed by the turn of events and resolved to direct my energies toward completing my degree. My determination was reinforced by the realization that barriers to women's participation in higher education appeared to be crumbling as a consequence of affirmative action laws and regulations and subsequent changes in admissions, employment, contracting, and resource allocation. My daughter, Helen, benefited from the pressures placed on men's colleges and universities, after Title IX was passed, to expand their commitment to the education of women. In 1972, she was admitted to Yale University (which had initiated coeducation in 1968) as a member of the last freshmen class subject to a women's admissions quota. During her freshman year, with women students demanding "1,000 female leaders"—a response to the promise of its president, Kingman Brewster, to male alumni in 1968 that even though Yale was admitting women to its undergraduate college it would continue to graduate one thousand male leaders each year—the Yale Corporation finally approved a sex-blind admissions policy. Meanwhile, the faculty and board of trustees at my alma mater, Smith College, under pressure to admit male students, voted down coeducation on two occasions. This clash in values between advocates of single-sex colleges and coeducation became a key factor in the controversy surrounding affirmative action.

My scholarly interest in the politics of higher education was piqued by events in New York City, where the board of the City University of New York (CUNY) was engaged in a major confrontation with Albany over its free tuition policy. Having worked at SUNY for several years, I was intrigued by the contrast in missions between the two systems and their complex relationship to state and local government. Established in 1948 to provide greater access to returning World War II veterans, SUNY had the distinction of being the nation's newest and largest public university system, whereas CUNY remained its only municipally supported university. In 1976, I joined the staff of the Wessell Commission, appointed jointly by Governor Hugh Carey and the New York state legislature in a typical maneuver to move the locus of educational policy making from the statehouse to more neutral terrain. Members of the staff were given six months to write background papers, conduct interviews, and propose recommendations for the future financing and governance of public and private higher education. My interest in CUNY's modified status as a state-operated university gave me a timely dissertation topic on the relationship among open admissions, student aid, and tuition policies in New York City and State. From my service on the commission, I gained valuable firsthand knowledge about the politics of higher education that I put to good use in the next stage of my career at New York University.

For six years, I helped to develop and administer two interuniversity consortia when universities were becoming increasingly dependent on state resources. The first consortium was designed by the presidents of CUNY, Columbia, Fordham, NYU, and the New School for Social Research; the

Carnegie, Ford, Mellon, and Sloan Foundations provided funding. It brought into uneasy alliance graduate deans of arts and sciences and graduate faculty in six academic disciplines, for the development of cooperative Ph.D. programs. My role as associate director was to generate grant proposals, persuade reluctant faculty and deans to collaborate in joint academic ventures, and prepare background papers and reports. Given that consortia operated at the margins of university life, even with generous foundation support, we soon became content with small victories. Within two years, however, the veneer of cooperation eroded, and the doctoral consortium dissolved, despite state entreaties that too many doctoral programs of questionable quality were being offered in New York State.[2]

I then moved to another soft-money (externally funded) project in the NYU School of Education. This was the New York Alliance for the Public Schools, a coalition of business, civic, and educational organizations whose goal was to bolster New York City's failing public school system. As the alliance's first director, I worked with a consortium of education deans and faculty from NYU, CUNY, Fordham and St. John's Universities, and Teachers College at Columbia University. Having attended public schools in New York City, this project enabled me to revisit the school system of my youth. I was dismayed by the profound changes wrought during the intervening years. I had served almost a decade on a suburban school board where every member was directly accountable to the taxpayers in the district, so the politics of the board of education at 110 Livingston Street appeared byzantine by comparison. The city's decentralization plan, which seemed to hold so much promise in 1969, had added thirty-two new layers of bureaucracy to its elementary and intermediate schools but had kept the high schools under the direct control of the central board.[3] After spending eighteen months preparing a grant proposal for a curriculum leadership program for the 114 high-school principals and seeing the grant for $430,000 through to completion, I had expected to be appointed project director. But the political realities of working with the New York City Board of Education derailed that expectation, and I decided to leave the world of soft-money jobs and enter academic administration.

2. See Glazer (1982).
3. An edited transcript of a retrospective seminar on decentralization fifteen years after its inception that I convened with Dick Netzer, the dean of public administration at New York University, can be found in Glazer (1983). Participants in addition to Dean Netzer included Sandra Feldman, Albert Shanker, Max Rubin, and Lois Wilson.

My next position was as associate dean in the School of Education at St. John's University. Among the more satisfying aspects of my deanship was the opportunity to work closely with local schools in designing professional development programs for parochial and public school teachers who were mainly female. Another involved a funded project that I initiated at the request of the alliance, an interuniversity Mentor in Education program designed to attract minority high-school students to teaching careers. I became acutely aware of two separate spheres, faculty and administrative, each with divergent interests and priorities, and with little communication between them. Senior administrators reinforced this divergence by claims on our time and energy that made it almost impossible to maintain research interests or to teach more than an occasional evening course. My scholarly interests conflicted so deeply with these expectations that to move forward on an irrevocable path in administration, I realized, would foreclose other options that might prove more rewarding.

In 1988, a fortuitous telephone call from Helen Green, then dean of education at Long Island University, informed me about the availability of a tenure-track faculty position at the C. W. Post Campus in Nassau County. I joined one of the largest teacher education programs in the state. In 1996, I was elected vice president of the postsecondary division and executive board member of the American Educational Research Association.

All of these experiences have evoked a more scholarly interest in the gendered construction of the academy, the ways in which the policy environment impedes women's ability to eradicate barriers to their advancement, and the relationship between feminism and professionalism in higher education and the larger society. This book, therefore, is not only a journey in self-understanding but also an opportunity to explore women's role and status in the academy at the close of this defining decade of the twentieth century.

Social Reform and Feminist Politics

In tracing the growth of the women's movement in the United States, Buechler (1990) observes that after gaining full suffrage for women in 1919, the National Women's Party turned its attention to passage of the Equal Rights Amendment (ERA), keeping alive the flame of women's rights for the next four decades in the face of generally hostile public opinion that caused significant structural strain within the party's ranks. The party's continued activism in support of the ERA during the Kennedy-Nixon campaign in 1960 prompted Kennedy to appoint the Committee on Equal Employment Opportunity and the Presidential Commission on the Status of Women. In 1961, he also issued Executive Order No. 10925, calling on federal contractors to "take affirmative action to ensure that the applicants are employed, and that employees are treated during employment, without regard to their race, creed, color, or national origin" (Skrentny, 1996, p. 7).[4]

The presidential commission was perceived as a diversionary tactic by Kennedy and his lieutenants, who subscribed to the belief that the ERA would lead to the severance of labor laws that protected women from workplace abuses. Consequently, he named Esther Peterson, director of the Women's Bureau, as chair of this commission. Although the commission succeeded in derailing the ERA movement in the early sixties, its 1963 report highlighted discriminatory practices toward women and a clearly articulated platform around which feminists could organize. One immediate result was the passage in 1963 of the Equal Pay Act as an amendment to the National Fair Labor Standards Act, the first major piece of federal equity legislation for women. As the civil rights movement gained momentum and visibility, media attention galvanized educators to protest the violence directed against African Americans during the struggle to achieve school integration. Betty Friedan published *The Feminine Mystique* in 1963, calling on women to develop their own identities and paths to fulfillment. Many of us felt that she was talking about us—married women with children, living the life of middle-class suburban housewives, doing good works, but experiencing "the problem with no name."

In 1964, President Lyndon Johnson gained approval for the landmark Civil Rights Act, finally giving the force of law to the 1954 Supreme Court decision in *Brown v. Board of Education*. Progress was slow, and resistance was high. As black militancy grew, women also mobilized to pursue an equal rights strategy with greater vigor. Three pieces of legislation signed by Johnson became central to achievement of equal rights for women and minorities: Title VI of the Civil Rights Act of 1964 reaffirmed equal employment opportunity guarantees and bars against racial or ethnic discrimination in any programs or activities receiving federal assistance; Executive Order No. 11246

---

4. Affirmative action policy originated in the American labor movement as a clause in the National Labor Relations Act of 1935, meaning that employers would be required to cease discriminatory practices against union members or organizers and take "affirmative action" in behalf of victims of discrimination. See Skrentny (1996) for a historical analysis of affirmative action policy in the United States.

(1965) mandated a continuing program of equal employment in all federal departments and agencies; and Title VII of the 1964 Civil Rights Act prohibited discrimination based on race, sex, religion, color, and national origin. As part of the Civil Rights Act, Johnson also abolished Kennedy's Committee on Equal Employment Opportunity, establishing the Equal Employment Opportunities Commission (EEOC) to enforce the act's provisions in public and private organizations. Under Title VII, complainants would have 180 days to file charges alleging discrimination and the right to appeal adverse EEOC decisions in the federal courts.

State commissions on the status of women founded on the national model soon created a network of politically experienced women with significant organizational skills, the result of years spent on boards of the League of Women Voters, the Parent-Teacher Association, the Junior League, business and professional women's clubs, and other civic associations. In New York State, for example, Governor Nelson Rockefeller established a Women's Unit within his executive offices, reporting directly to his chief of staff and creating within the state the expectation that remedial action would be taken to remove vestiges of sex discrimination. Politicians saw the benefits of this network as a means of extending their political power bases to a larger pool of college-educated, articulate, and informed women who could be encouraged to support collective concerns and to develop a heightened group consciousness. These early advocates for women's rights found their own consciousness raised by their efforts to gain access to traditional male occupations. Their increased labor force participation in the 1960s became a pivotal factor in promoting women's common cause and contemporary feminism. Issues of economic equality and social justice became the basis for feminist theorizing and feminist activism, as manifested in campus commissions and women's studies programs (see chapter 6).

The civil rights, women's liberation, and student protest movements coalesced in the late 1960s and eventually collided with the status quo. The political infighting between the moderate and conservative wings of each political party often made it difficult to define what Republicans or Democrats really stood for, particularly since both parties were mired in the undeclared Vietnamese war, from which there seemed no easy escape. The symbiotic growth of these two movements, civil rights and feminism, brought new pressure on two presidents who were ideologically polar opposites—Lyndon Johnson and Richard Nixon—to include women as a protected class in federal affirmative action policies. For forty years, the National Women's Party had focused its energies on passage of an ERA, following its victory in winning approval for women's suffrage in 1919. In 1966, angered by the documented inaction of the EEOC in responding to charges of sex discrimination, feminists led by Friedan and other women activists joined forces to organize the National Organization for Women (NOW), moving their cause beyond regular government channels into the larger public policy arena. The heat generated by pressure from women's organizations prompted Johnson to issue Executive Order No. 11375 one month prior to the presidential election in October 1968. This amendment to an earlier order stated that "it is desirable that the equal employment opportunity programs provided for in Executive Order 11246 expressly embrace discrimination on account of sex." It mandated that federal contractors take affirmative action in the recruitment, hiring, employment, compensation, and training of employees regardless of sex, and file compliance reports of affirmative cooperation. For the first time, universities with federal contracts would be forbidden from discriminating on the basis of sex in employment.

In 1968, the disastrous riots at the Democratic convention in Chicago had precipitated Johnson's decision not to run for reelection, ceding the nomination to his vice president, Hubert Humphrey. Nixon was the ultimate victor, and his foreign policy soon became the target of antiwar demonstrations. The contemporary women's movement, which had been gathering momentum throughout the 1960s, became increasingly radicalized and confrontational. Militant feminists adopted Shulamith Firestone's *The Dialectic of Sex* (1970) as their manifesto—a far cry from Friedan's *Feminine Mystique*. No longer content with working at the margins of society, they rejected gender and race-neutral policies and allied themselves more directly with marxist and socialist feminism. Women of color formed Black, Chicana, and Puerto Rican caucuses, issuing their own demands for an end to racial, economic, and political repression. They also rejected the assimilationist ideology of equal rights feminists, whom they identified as mainly white, middle class, and privileged. As Teresa de Lauretis observed in writing about antifeminist theorists, the debates, internal divisions, polarizations, and conflicts that developed between political activists and academic feminists were defined in the seventies as "opposition between theory and practice which led, on the one hand, to a polarization of positions either for theory or against theory in nearly all cultural practices and, on the other, to a consistent, if never fully successful, effort to overcome the opposition itself" (1990, p. 264).

A new organization, the Women's Equity Action League (WEAL), took a more moderate position, seeking to work through the legal system in gaining equity for women. Bernice Sandler, who later founded the Project on the Status and Education of Women under the aegis of the Association of American Colleges and Universities (AAC&U), worked with WEAL in planning the strategy for enforcing Johnson's Executive Order No. 11375. On January 31, 1970, WEAL filed the first class-action sex discrimination complaint against all universities and colleges in the country, asking the Department of Labor to conduct a sweeping compliance review of all higher education federal contractors (Sandler, 1997b, p. 3). Press coverage of WEAL's legal action elevated its profile with women faculty, who began to collect institutional data on women's employment. As chair of the newly formed WEAL Legal Action Committee for Federal Contract Compliance in Education, Sandler filed charges against 250 institutions, including the Universities of Wisconsin, Minnesota, and Chicago, as well as the state systems of California, New Jersey, and Florida (p. 3). Thus began a strategy to use regulatory agencies and the courts as a means of ending sex discrimination.

A higher education subcommittee chaired by Representative Edith Green (D-OR) held congressional hearings in June and July 1970, generating more than twelve hundred pages of testimony documenting massive and persistent patterns of discrimination against academic women. Following acrimonious congressional debates on the issues and the wide distribution of this testimony to professional organizations, educational leaders, and the members of Congress, and with strong support from women's organizations, an omnibus higher education bill was approved by Congress in November 1971. Title IX, which was part of the omnibus legislation, banned sex discrimination in all programs and activities of educational institutions, including postsecondary education, that received federal grants and contracts. The act mandated that goals and timetables be adopted for admissions, hiring, promotion, and tenure, and granted compliance responsibility to HEW and OCR (Kaplin, 1985). It also extended Title VII to employees in public and private higher education and the Equal Pay Act to executive, administrative, and professional employees (Sandler, 1997b). WEAL now prodded HEW to adopt an affirmative action plan comparable to the Philadelphia Plan, which had set hiring goals for minority workers on government contract construction projects in the 1960s. With his reelection campaign against George McGovern in full swing, Nixon directed the EEOC to issue Revised Order No. 4, requiring all contractors to develop "an acceptable affirmative action program," including a workforce analysis of its employment of women and minorities. In October 1972, one month before the presidential election, the Department of Labor sent nondiscrimination guidelines to twenty-five hundred colleges and universities with federal contracts, requiring them to issue goals and timetables and to make good faith efforts to appoint women and minorities (Ripley, 1972, p. 20).

Feminist consciousness and expectations were significantly elevated by these rapidly unfolding events. The mood of women in academia was exuberant, combative, and overly optimistic as they organized teach-ins on sex discrimination, workshops on equal employment opportunity guidelines, and investigations of the economic status of women faculty, administrators, and students. But finding unassailable barriers and impatient with bureaucratic delays, they soon adopted civil rights tactics and organized coalitions, task forces, and commissions to press for institutional compliance. On the national level, WEAL joined NOW, the National Educational Association (NEA), the Association of Women in Science, and the Federation of Professional Women in filing three major lawsuits against HEW, accusing it of inaction in ending sex discrimination under Title IX. Within two years, $23 million was being withheld from Cornell, Columbia, Duke, Michigan, and Vanderbilt universities.

These events sparked my interest and prompted my active participation in feminist politics. In 1970, I had been introduced to a group of liberal Republican women who were organizing around issues of pay equity, women's rights legislation, and state passage of the ERA. One of our first goals was to organize the New York State Women's Political Caucus (NYSWPC), mirroring the National Women's Political Caucus (NWPC), as a bipartisan organization to lobby for women's legislation and to support women candidates for public office. We also organized a countywide group, Women for Honor and Integrity in Government (WHIG), which I chaired, to support candidates for state office, take positions on women's issues, and lobby for sex equity legislation. As a school board member and president, I had always viewed myself as apolitical. Party labels, party platforms, and party affiliations were frowned upon in our community, which prided itself on the civic-mindedness of its residents and the board's avowed nonpartisan approach to governance. Although the conflict between politics and education was difficult to resolve, the energy and optimism of feminists and their commitment to social and economic change generated enthusiastic participation.

As a means of building a statewide network of women committed to an equal rights agenda, we lobbied for the nomination of women to elected and appointed positions as legislators, judges, and board members but had limited success. We participated in consciousness-raising groups, which, as Catherine MacKinnon has noted, represented "many women's first explicit contact with acknowledged feminism" and the origin of "feminist method and practice" (1989, p. 84). The purpose of these consciousness-raising groups was not self-analysis. Instead, they helped define an agenda for political action based on our mutual interest in improving the personal and professional status of women, working through the political process, and articulating our positions on a variety of women's issues—voluntarism, the environment, women's health, public education, child care, and juvenile justice. A strong undercurrent running through these sessions was to move this grassroots organization of women as far as possible from the women's club image of political "gofers" who stuffed envelopes, baked cakes, and poured coffee at political meetings. In seeking more substantive roles as district leaders and lobbyists for women's causes, we confronted overt gender bias and covert resistance from men as well as women, who viewed feminism as subversive and threatening. Consciousness-raising groups tended to be loosely structured and self-selecting as women increased their commitment to economic and social change. Although I had worked with men and women in obtaining state approval for a high school in our school district, this was my first experience with women-centered activities since my undergraduate years at Smith. To paraphrase MacKinnon, consciousness raising helped to validate our actions and to create a feminist community by redefining what counted as verification and giving "both content and form to women's point of view" (1989, p. 87). This was an exhilarating time for women in politics, and although we were optimistic about our eventual success, we were also hampered by a lack of resources and limited access to the male power structure.

The ERA as Turning Point

At the same time that it was debating the omnibus higher education bill, Congress was also approving action on the ERA (in 1971 in the House, and in 1972 in the Senate). Ratification by two-thirds of the states became a new rallying point for feminists. Acts and orders that had been passed in the sixties were being revised to include women as a protected class and, belatedly, to include education as an employer. As one of the founders of the NYSWPC in 1971, I spent many hours helping to form bipartisan coalitions to gain passage of the ERA in New York State. The New York State and New Jersey legislatures both ratified the national ERA in 1972, meaning that statewide ERAs would be submitted to referenda by 1975. We confidently predicted they would pass.

Phyllis Schlafly, who started organizing New Right women in 1964, during the Barry Goldwater campaign, was an early and vocal opponent of the ERA. Choosing family values as its theme, the New Right mounted a state-by-state campaign to defeat the amendment. Every state organization endorsed the ERA. As a result, we were stunned by its resounding defeat in New York by a margin of 57 to 43 percent in November 1975. A well-organized campaign by the state's Right-to-Life Party and Conservative Party had overwhelmed the efforts of a pro-ERA electorate. Failing to obtain ratification in two-thirds of the states, the ERA was buried forever during the Reagan administration. By 1983, its opponents had gained significant momentum and visibility, and the public mood had changed. A *New York Times* poll reported that only 48 percent of women thought it should be re-submitted for ratification, while the majority concurred that equal rights could be achieved without a constitutional amendment.

The anti-ERA forces had successfully persuaded a skeptical electorate that the ERA—and, parenthetically, the feminists who promoted it—threatened traditional American family values, effectively defusing the equal rights principle on which the amendment was based.[5] I encountered Schlafly only once, in 1972 at the NWPC convention in Houston, and I could not fail to be impressed by her sharp political instincts and ability to garner support for her position. As moderates, we thought we represented the forces of reason and good will but failed to take seriously the power of the family values argument and the single-mindedness of Schlafly and her followers. The ERA's defeat seriously damaged the women's movement, destroying its momentum and its potential to foment social change. It also served as a warning to feminists that factional disagreements among aggrieved groups and duplicitous rivalries within the feminist camp threatened its viability as a movement. Eventually, this resulted in feminist disaffection with the Republican Party, giving the Democrats a new source of strength that when combined with overwhelming minority support, helped elect Bill Clinton to the presidency in 1992 and again in 1996. Men, who controlled all fifty state legislatures in 1982 when the ERA was defeated, had persuaded women to work against an amendment that few of them wanted or viewed in their self-interest. This disastrous episode became a defining moment for the contemporary women's movement, negating many of its earlier advances and severely under-

5. See Melich (1995) for an excellent analysis of Phyllis Schlafly's central role as the leader of antiratification forces opposed to the ERA. See also Berry (1986) for an analysis of the ERA's defeat.

mining its vigor. Having been drawn into feminist politics by the promise of equal rights legislation, I soon discovered that implementation would be difficult. Believing in the justice of our cause, women like myself were dismayed and frustrated by the ability of gatekeepers to successfully defend the status quo. Conservatives had won a major victory that closed a portentous chapter in the struggle for women's rights.

In 1976, after the defeat of the ERA referendum in New York State and the legislative decision not to bring it to a vote a second time, I was a Republican district leader in my community, actively engaged in feminist causes, doing educational consulting, and working on a state commission while pursuing my Ph.D. in higher education. From my attendance at district meetings with local politicians from the Town of Rye and the village of Port Chester, I realized that feminism and local politics belonged to separate worlds. Although community action had been an important part of my life, I resigned from my district leadership as well as several countywide boards in 1978. I did this with some misgiving, because I thoroughly enjoyed the political mayhem of campaigning and of advancing the policy agenda. In the course of my working day, however, virtually every decision maker was a white male within the educational establishment and the unelected power structure of business and government officials. Disheartened by the failure of the ERA and the rightward movement of the Republican Party and aware that party labels were becoming increasingly meaningless, I re-registered as an Independent. Many women found that as our professional careers took hold, the pragmatic path of academic feminism supplanted the more confrontational route of political activism.

Academic Feminism

Three of the earliest studies of women academics show how deeply embedded are the cultural myths that define women's personal and professional lives. They also reveal the difficulties that women scholars faced in combining marriage, motherhood, and academic careers in the first half of this century. Glazer and Slater (1987), in their study of women's entry into the professions between 1890 and 1940, explore the radical disjunction between professional scholarship and domestic responsibilities. Tracing the academic careers of nine women who acquired substantial reputations in their fields, they describe the "strategies of superperformance, separatism, innovation, and subordination [that] were so pervasive and so influential for future generations of professionals" (p. 211). Superperformers exercised indefatigable determination to be recognized as the equals of men in their professional roles and as wives and mothers. Separatists placed greater importance on successful professional careers than on marriage and motherhood, establishing single-sex communities for women who would be socialized "to accept the virtues of professionalism and scholarship over marriage." Innovators removed themselves from direct competition with men by developing feminized specialties such as social work, public health, and primary teaching. Because subordination meant accepting positions of lesser rank in male-dominated fields, women characterized as separatists and innovators chose not to directly challenge male-dominated universities and colleges but to build their own homogeneous academic enclaves. These communities were meritocracies in which admission was based on acceptable norms of intelligence, social class, and race as conditions for membership. In their efforts to balance professional and personal demands and gain equal status with men in the public sphere, early feminists readily accepted these norms.

Jessie Barnard, in *Academic Women* (1964), discusses one of the most persistent cultural myths affecting women's status in the university—that women prefer teaching and service to research and scholarship. In her long career as a sociologist, she did much to perpetuate this myth, drawing on a body of psychological and sociological research that characterized women as passive, emotional, and nurturing. She attributed women's inferior status in academic rank, salary, and working conditions to their noncompetitive natures, their marriage to other academics, and their lack of interest in status and prestige. Describing her own experience, she asserted that "the future career of any married academic woman depends very largely on her husband" (p. 231). Speaking from a privileged position and without reticence, she attributed her success to "a devoted retinue of helpers": "There is Mary, our cleaning lady, who takes four buses to come to our home now that we live in Wellesley and has never failed me unless public transportation stops running. I have a baby sitter, Lowell, who comes for a short time in the late afternoon about four times a week and helps with the dinner and the children's baths. Finally, this year we have Peggy, who comes in every morning for an hour after the whole family leaves for school. She puts the breakfast dishes in the dishwasher, does the beds and the laundry, and then disappears" (p. 239).

That this revelation appeared in the same year the Civil Rights Act was passed shows how much the sensibilities of women have changed in the past three decades. It calls to mind the experience of the women in Glazer and Slater's account, who were expected to adhere to the values of superperformance in juggling marriage, motherhood, and professional careers.

A year after the publication of Barnard's study, Helen Astin undertook the first survey of women doctorates to learn more about their career development, their patterns of career choice, their occupational achievements and rewards, and their work participation (1969, p. 8). Not surprisingly, she found that sex discrimination was widespread; women's attrition rates were high; and tenure policies affected women more negatively. Thus, she concluded: "Women, however highly talented and well educated, tend not to be as successful (if success is measured by large salary and high position) in their professional lives as men" (p. 91). Referring to Barnard's arguments that women were by nature "less competitive than men, more inclined to be submissive, accepting, and sympathetic" and were "satisfied with lower pay and position," Astin conceded that "even the most capable, ambitious, and well educated woman will usually choose husband and children over career if conflicts arise between these two areas of her life" (p. 92). In Astin's view, although salaries and working conditions were problematic, by far the biggest dilemma for women professionals, besides earning the doctorate, centered on their family situations, in particular "the difficulties of finding and keeping domestic help." She notes, "Not only is such help hard to find, but it is also costly, especially since the expenses incurred are not tax deductible. In some cases, the wife's being employed represents such a drain on finances that it is more sensible if she does not work. The loss to society that results from this paradoxical situation may be a serious one" (p. 110).

Thus, as academic feminists focused their attention on the absence of women in positions of intellectual authority and in the taught curriculum, their early research continued to portray women as ambivalent about their professional roles. By the late 1960s, spurred on by the women's movement and the rhetoric of radical feminists, women academics became increasingly assertive in demanding representation on decision-making committees, equity in salaries and benefits, reforms in hiring and tenure policies, and such quality-of-life improvements as women's health clinics and campus childcare.

Unfortunately, as I demonstrate in the course of this book, these issues remain largely unresolved. The theoretical implications of feminist practice emerged gradually from the polemical discourse and writings of women who adopted the ideologies of radicalism, marxism, and socialism, as well as liberalism. Feminists applied these ideologies to scholarly analyses of the traditional canon, with a view to transforming knowledge in their fields and subfields. Liberal feminists challenged sex discrimination and the sexual division of labor within their institutions, demanding improvements in women's professional status. Radical feminists viewed theory and practice as intertwined and continually evolving from women's lived experiences in a patriarchal society (Rowland & Klein, 1996, p. 9). The feminist poet Adrienne Rich captured the mood of radical feminists, challenging them to redefine the "male-created, male-dominated" university as a woman-centered place "in which women shape the philosophy and the decision making though men may choose to study and teach there" (1979, p. 155). When she originally published "Toward a Woman-Centered University" in 1974, Rich declared that equal rights was merely the beginning of women's quest to transform their institutions. Twenty years later, when I commented on the essay after a reading of her memoir, *What Is Found There* (1995), she responded with a smile: "We never did reach that point, did we?"[6]

Continuing education for women began as an extension of the formal curriculum rather than an integral component of degree programs. One specific step taken by many institutions was to inaugurate reentry programs for women preparing for new careers. I recall the euphoria of designing continuing education courses for adult students as well as the opposition we encountered in gaining acceptance of women's studies minors in the traditional curriculum. I also recall the surreptitious and clandestine meetings held in coffeehouses and off-campus centers, the orchestrated briefings on Title IX legislation, and the difficulties that women's committees encountered in collecting data on the status of women and minorities on their campuses.

Women's studies courses, originating as isolated offerings in sociology, anthropology, history, art, and literature, were eventually integrated into the curriculum. Through this incremental process, feminism became a scholarly endeavor, the academic manifestation of the women's movement reinterpreted as new paradigms of disciplinary knowledge. Women's commissions and task forces undertook thorough inventories of the campus community and formulated equity-based and issue-oriented action agendas on salaries, promotion and tenure, fringe benefits, and child care (see chapter 6). Meanwhile, women faculty concentrated on their scholarship, conducting critiques of classical theories that challenged the traditional canon, constructing new theoretical frameworks that incorporated women's work and women's experiences, and challenging male colleagues to rewrite programs to include feminist theories. As Kramarae and Spender demonstrate in their anthology of women's writing, a knowledge explosion in every discipline resulted from this creative infusion of women's scholarly activity throughout

6. The poetry reading of excerpts from Rich (1995) was held at New York University in fall 1995.

the seventies and eighties (1992). Women's studies courses originated in research universities in the late 1960s, and by 1995 the National Women's Studies Association listed more than six hundred certificate, undergraduate, and graduate degree programs.

Although many women faculty professed an interest in the ERA, prochoice legislation, and campus-based childcare, their main preoccupation became teaching, research, and career advancement within the academy. Women administrators soon recognized that without the protection of tenure their positions were too tenuous to jeopardize by involvement in overt political activities, and they turned their attention to incremental changes within their institutions. To be taken seriously within the academy required following a traditional career path. They did not think about shattering glass ceilings in the seventies—that metaphor would not enter the academic lexicon until the mid-1980s.

As a school board member in the 1960s, I was well aware of the educational system's gender-based hierarchy: virtually all suburban school systems in Westchester were run by men, whereas women made up the majority of the teaching, clerical, and support staff. Rich (1979) describes the complex and often bitter process through which women gain status in their universities. Those women, whom we sometimes dismissed as "Queen Bees," learned that to ensure their survival, they must "vote against other women, absorb the masculine adversary style of discourse, and carefully avoid any style or method that could be condemned as irrational or emotionally charged" (p. 138). The experiences of women faculty and administrators reported throughout this book provide definitive evidence that gender neutrality is a fiction in the professoriate and in academic administration. Educated within traditions of female conformity, competent women have anticipated rewards, acceptance, and recognition for their conscientious work and their acceptance of institutional norms. Instead, they have soon come to realize that as women, it is difficult to escape the roles into which they are typically channeled and that have shaped their identities.

Title IX and Affirmative Action

Not until July 21, 1975, three years after Nixon signed the omnibus higher education act, did the federal government finally implement Title IX. Earlier that spring, the Committee for Affirmative Action–Universities had collected more than fifteen hundred signatures on a petition calling on President Gerald Ford to fulfill his promises to enforce equal rights laws. Under pressure from Republican neoconservatives, who alleged that affirmative action meant reverse discrimination against white males, Ford had delayed any action on Title IX, a tactic that infuriated women's organizations that had enthusiastically supported the 1972 education amendment. Following the publication of this petition in a full-page advertisement in the *New York Times* on April 6, 1975, Ford (now a candidate for reelection in 1976) hastened to sign the regulation that June. But the damage had been done. Impatient with congressional efforts to amend Title IX and with federal foot-dragging by HEW on enforcement of the new regulation, academic feminists allied themselves with the two teachers' unions, the NEA and the American Federation of Teachers (AFT), to support his opponent Jimmy Carter, who had promised teachers an autonomous cabinet-level Department of Education (DOE). In 1976, following his defeat of Ford, Carter delivered on this campaign pledge, assigning responsibility for the enforcement of affirmative action statutes to the Office of Civil Rights (OCR), which he transferred from HEW to the new DOE. Equal expenditures for women's athletics aroused more controversy than any other aspect of these regulations among alumni, students, and admissions and athletics directors. The impact of Title IX on women's athletics is an interesting example of how high the stakes had become in higher education as women struggled to convert paper promises into viable programs and policies.

Women in Sports

In 1974, in my role as assistant dean for community services at Westchester Community College, women approached me from the newly organized Association for Intercollegiate Athletics for Women (AIAW) to cosponsor a conference on women in sports. Hundreds of women attended this event—athletes, sports writers, coaches, teachers, and students—to discuss the issues and formulate strategies for implementing Title IX. Founded in 1971, the AIAW experienced phenomenal growth throughout the decade. By 1979 the AIAW had 950 institutional members, as compared to its formidable rival, the all-male NCAA, with seven hundred members.[7] Recognizing the potential strength of this new organization, the NCAA, which then represented

---

7. An open letter to women in higher education, "A Commentary on Women's Athletics," is contained in *Project on the Status and Education of Women* (Fall 1980), 2–3. The Association of American Colleges published this newsletter, edited by B. Sandler, between 1971 and 1991. It provides an important historical record of Title IX, women's athletics, and sex discrimination issues.

only men's athletics programs, voted to incorporate women from Division II and III schools into their governance structure. This action sparked heated debate over the future status of women's intercollegiate athletics and the autonomy of AIAW. Within five years, however, the NCAA prevailed, and the AIAW was disbanded.

The experience of the AIAW demonstrates the complexity of women's dilemmas in male-dominated environments and the gender implications of athletics expenditures. It also shows the impact of external influences on institutional policy making. The federal Equity in Athletics Disclosure Act, signed by President Clinton in 1995, requires coeducational colleges and universities with intercollegiate athletic programs that also participate in federal student aid programs to prepare annual reports of gender-related information about their athletic programs. In implementing this and earlier requirements, the courts have applied the "proportionality rule," which asserts that the ratio of male to female varsity athletes must equal the ratio of male to female undergraduates. In formerly all-male institutions as well as in those with big-money varsity sports programs, this rule, one of three possible tests used by the courts in determining Title IX compliance, has provoked considerable rancor within coeducational institutions with a sizable commitment to intercollegiate athletics.

The most closely watched case charging sex discrimination in sports has been *Cohen v. Brown University*, a class action Title IX lawsuit brought by nine women students. It originated in April 1992, when Brown, which has thirteen varsity teams for women, cut off support for both women's varsity gymnastics and volleyball. In December 1992, on the basis of arguments made in the lawsuit, U.S. District Judge Raymond Pettine ordered Brown to reinstate these two sports to varsity status. He determined that by eliminating the two teams, women's participation had been reduced to 40 percent, even though they constituted 51 percent of the undergraduates. Brown subsequently filed an appeals brief as well as a revised gender equity plan. In a 2–1 decision, the First Circuit Court of Appeals affirmed the district court's determination "that the University violated Title IX in not effectively accommodating the interest and abilities of female student athletes" (Heckman, 1997, p. 569). As Diane Heckman notes in her analysis of sex discrimination in academics and athletics since the passage of Title IX, the First Circuit Court rejected Brown's contention that Title IX was an affirmative action or quota statute. The court's decision asserted that the statute "is an anti-discrimination statute, modeled explicitly after another anti-discrimination statute, Title VI" (cited by Heckman, p. 571). In 1996, Brown asked the Supreme Court to overturn the appellate ruling, but in April 1997, the court denied this request, in effect allowing the current interpretation of Title IX to stand.

The stakes in this case were so high that many organizations, institutions, and individuals filed briefs in Brown's behalf. Among these were five higher education associations, including the American Council on Education, the Association of American Universities, the American Association of State Colleges and Universities, and the National Association of State Universities and Land-Grant Colleges, all of which have been historically strong advocates of affirmative action and nondiscrimination; forty universities and state systems; eight coaching organizations; forty-nine Republican members of Congress; and the state of Colorado, which had lost a similar case in the 1980s (Naughton, 1997a, p. A45). Following the court's decision, the National Women's Law Center, a women's advocacy organization, filed charges with the Office of Civil Rights against twenty-five universities it alleges have violated Title IX by failing to give sufficient support to women's athletics (Naughton, 1997b, p. A39).

Donna Lopiano was one of the speakers at our 1975 conference on women in sports and is now head of the Women's Sports Foundation. After the Brown decision, she commented that in women's Division I sports programs, "The glass is half empty and half full." Although the number of women in college sports has increased fourfold since the 1970s, only 37 percent of those who compete in Division I collegiate sports are women, and only 9 percent of Division I members are in compliance with the proportionality rule (Naughton, 1997a, p. A39). In a fifteen-year review of women's participation in intercollegiate sports since the advent of Title IX, Acosta and Carpenter found significant disparities between women and men in coaching positions: in 1977, women accounted for 90 percent of the coaches of women's teams, compared to only 48.3 percent in 1992; although the number of head coaching jobs for women's teams increased by 812 since 1982, women held only 181 of these jobs by 1992, compared to the 631 held by men. Men are also more likely to be paid higher salaries: by 1995-96, the median Division I institution paid the head coach of a men's team 44 percent more than a woman in the same position (Naughton, 1996, p. A35).

Backlash against Women

Throughout the 1980s, the appointment of conservative judges to the federal bench and the election of conservatives to Congress resulted in new legislation threatening the status of women in academia. (Chapter 3 provides examples of the growing body of case law relating to sex discrimination in tenure, pay equity, and sexual harassment.) Symptomatic of the changing policy environment was a proposal by Senator Orrin Hatch (R-UT) to limit the scope of Title IX only to those programs receiving direct federal aid. Although he withdrew this bill under pressure from women's groups in his home state of Utah, in 1984 the Supreme Court ruled in *Grove City College v. Bell* that Title IX did not have the broad institutional coverage assumed by previous administrations. This decision proved to be a major setback for sex equity, narrowing the interpretation of Title IX from nondiscrimination in all educational programs and activities to only those receiving federal aid. Since the sole federal support received by Grove City College came through student financial aid, only that program was covered (Project on Status and Education of Women, 1984).

The Civil Rights Restoration Act, which was passed in March 1988, reinstated provisions of Title IX affected by the Grove City decision, increasing the motivation of affirmative action officers to revisit their programs. This act prompted a second round of women's commissions and presidential mission statements reiterating institutional commitments to student diversity. It made it easier for women and minorities to file complaints with the OCR and to sue for retroactive pay adjustments and changes in the workplace. The Civil Rights Act of 1991 amended Title VII, reversing several Supreme Court decisions and addressing other problems arising in employment discrimination: it extended compensatory damages for victims of intentional discrimination based on race and national origin to also include sex, religion, and disability; and it permitted punitive damages against organizations with more than five hundred employees (Leap, 1993, p. 26). Between 1988 and 1995, 347 Title IX complaints were filed and seventy-eight compliance reviews were initiated by the OCR (Grant & Curtis, 1996).

By the end of the Reagan-Bush administration, the conservative discourse had become more insistent, moving rapidly from policy reform and modification to policy dismantling and termination. In higher education, those years were marked by institutional retrenchment, attacks on affirmative action, and public backlash against women and minority activism. By 1990, feminist scholars had retreated into their academic enclaves and professional associations, concerning themselves with the development of their disciplinary specializations and moving away from grass-roots and community activism. They read different journals, attended different conferences, and adhered to different agendas than those of community and grass-roots activists. Alienated by conservative ideologues and corrupt politicians and preoccupied with their personal and professional activities, they failed to monitor affirmative action and nondiscrimination policies. Meanwhile, events in

California, Texas, and other states raised important public policy questions about the court's willingness to uphold the constitutionality of gender and race preferences.

Susan Faludi, a journalist with the *Wall Street Journal*, characterized the antifeminist backlash as "the loss of collective spirit" that had energized an earlier generation of women, a sense that the feminist revolution may have asked women to pay too high a price for their aspirations. Her extensive critique, *Backlash: The Undeclared War against American Women* (1991), revealed the depth of gender bias in societal institutions. It also prompted some rather inflammatory rhetoric on the part of conservative women scholars, who accused feminists of being captives of "the backlash myth" and of finding the glass half empty when it was "three-quarters full" (Sommers, 1994, p. 242). In her research funded by three conservative foundations and entitled *Who Stole Feminism? How Women Have Betrayed Women*, Sommers distinguishes between equity feminists (herself included) and gender feminist academics (the opposition), whom she categorizes as overzealous extremists with an ideological agenda that threatens American ideals. Her assertions that "women have attained parity in economic status" and that academic feminists are "imposing a narrow political agenda, diluting traditional scholarly standards, and using up scarce resources" (p. 86) are rooted in cultural myths that do not hold up, as I have found in my analyses of national data. Neither does her justification of the glass ceiling as a manifestation of women's lower motivation, part-time workplace experience, and household and childcare responsibilities.

Underlying the debate between equal rights and cultural feminists are questions about "the validity of normative constructions of gender in the light of behaviors and qualities that contradict the rules, to point up rather than resolve the contradictions, to articulate a political identity for women without conforming to existing stereotypes about them" (Scott, 1990, p. 145). Cultural feminists firmly reject the liberal standard of equality for masking the intersection between sex, race, and social class discrimination, marginalizing both women and minorities, and reinforcing a standard of white heterosexual maleness (Eisenstein, 1994). Dissension among feminist scholars and theorists threatens to undermine the scholarly achievements of academic women, excluded from full participation based on their perceived difference but included with the expectation that they will readily adapt to existing institutional norms and accommodate their differences. The idea of female-friendly policies and programs is not considered in the laws or policies they produce or by those who lead our institutions. In writing on "the myth of post-racism," Eisenstein explores how antigovernment discourse had been institutionalized during the Reagan-Bush era through policies that substituted individual rights for equal opportunity and made the dismantling of affirmative action the centerpiece of that process (1994, p. 40). Meanwhile, women outside the academy criticize academic feminist discourse as inaccessible and irrelevant in resolving the real-life problems of poor women, minority women, and Third World women. Younger women who gained access to professions that were previously closed to an older generation and who are able to live alternative lifestyles with impunity repudiate what they view as artificial distinctions between motherhood and personhood.

The early civil rights movement had gained much of its cohesiveness from the leadership of Martin Luther King Jr. and other African Americans. But the diverse and often conflicting views of the movement's adherents began to compete for leadership positions and the ability to influence policy makers. Similar changes transformed the women's movement into a diverse and loosely connected polity characterized by generational, demographic, and political differences. It was no longer possible to easily define the meaning of a feminist perspective or to assume that feminists who espoused similar epistemological positions could agree on the consequences of their theorizing. The successful passage of Proposition 209 in California, which rescinded affirmative action policies and programs, portrayed women as victims of their own success. It also signified the need to rethink the tactics of women's resistance to political conservatism and their commitment to social justice and cultural diversity.

The context of women's struggle for equity has altered significantly in the past two decades as women have achieved greater economic, political, and professional status. The women's movement is very much alive, despite the rhetoric of antifeminists. Ample proof of its vigor can be seen in the many coalitions and networks representing women's interests on a range of issues and concerns. Some of the more prominent of these include the Feminist Majority Foundation, the National Women's Policy Institute, the National Council for Research on Women, the National Abortion Rights Action League, and numerous professional organizations representing women's interests. Professional journals, such as *Signs, International Women's Studies Forum, Feminist Studies, Gender and Society,* and *Hypatia* have been publishing women's scholarship since the seventies and eighties. All the same, it is not uncommon to hear younger women dismiss the movement as no longer viable. Its context has been significantly altered in the past twenty-five years in response to cultural, economic, and political changes on the part of diverse constituents. In 1990, I participated in the first symposium on women in higher education held at the Association for the Study of Higher Education (ASHE) annual meeting. The session was well attended, and we were commended for our courage in presenting research papers on feminism. Even though it is now more common to be invited to offer a feminist perspective on an academic theme, women in the field of higher education continue to be reticent about characterizing their research as feminist.

The affirmative action movement has now come full circle. In my classes as well as in my visits to universities to meet with women faculty and administrators, younger women often express concern about being perceived as affirmative action candidates, asserting that it is time to move on to other subjects and problems. Others indicate that inequities and constraints continue to deter their progress. Women of color complain that they are often perceived as tokens within their schools. Most women, irrespective of color, express concern about the pledge of New Right ideologues to dismantle Johnson's civil rights and educational legislation under the guise of balanced budgets and family values.

Affirmative Action under Siege

The debate over affirmative action is being fought on legal and theoretical grounds, and the policy cycle has shifted from implementation to termination. Two resolutions approved by the University of California's board of regents on July 20, 1995—calling for the elimination by 1997 of race, religion, sex, color, ethnicity, and national origin as criteria for admissions, hiring, and contracting on its nine campuses—have become the blueprint for a fundamental conflict. The position of women, including women of color, will be directly affected by its outcome. In announcing the resolution, the governor, Pete Wilson, proclaimed: "Merit, not the color of one's skin or gender, should be [government's] guiding principle."[8] In a separate executive order, the governor, who is also a member of the board of regents, stated that all government agencies, including California's three public higher education systems, should be prepared "to end preferential treatment and promote individual opportunity based on merit."[9] These actions laid the groundwork

8. Letter from Governor Pete Wilson to Howard Leach, chairman, University of California Board of Regents (June 1, 1995).
9. Executive Order w-124-95 to End Preferential Treatment and to Promote Individual Opportunity Based on Merit; issued by Governor Pete Wilson (April 1995).

for the successful California Civil Rights Initiative (CCRI), or Proposition 209, an amendment to California's constitution that prohibits public higher education and other state and local governmental agencies from using race or gender in employment, admissions, or public contracting. In language similar to federal equal opportunity statutes, it affirmed: "The state will not use race, sex, color, ethnicity, or national origin as a criterion for either discriminating against, or granting preferential treatment to, any individual or group in the operation of the state's system of public employment, education or public contracting."

Several organizations attempted to overturn this amendment following its approval in November 1996 by a 10 percent margin (55–45). A year later, the Supreme Court refused to hear a challenge to its constitutionality brought by the American Civil Liberties Union, the People for the American Way, the Lawyers' Committee for Civil Rights, and other national organizations representing women and minorities. It let stand the earlier ruling by the Court of Appeals for the Ninth Circuit Court, which covers ten western states, including Hawaii and Alaska. By September 1997, the three California state systems—the University of California, the state colleges, and the community colleges—conceded that they had abandoned most of the preferential practices banned by Proposition 209. The freshman class of 1998 in the UC system, the first to be admitted under the new rules, showed an increase in the percentage of Asian Americans (35.4%) but declines in the percentage of African Americans, Latinos, and Native Americans, particularly in the flagship campuses at Berkeley and Los Angeles (Bronner, 1998, p. A28).

On November 5, 1997, voters in Houston, Texas, defeated a measure similar to Proposition 209 that would have prohibited affirmative action in its hiring and contracting. A heavy minority vote against that measure as well as less inflammatory campaigning for its passage contributed to its defeat. It also followed another publicized ruling the previous April. In *Hopwood v. University of Texas Law School*, the U.S. Court of Appeals for the Fifth Circuit, with jurisdiction in Texas, Louisiana, and Oklahoma, had declared that an admissions policy designed to overcome segregation by giving preference to African-American and Latino applicants had denied four white applicants "equal protection of the laws" guaranteed by the Fourteenth Amendment. It ruled that the law school "may not use race as a factor" in admissions. The Supreme Court subsequently declined to rule on the constitutionality of race-based preference systems in university admissions, thus letting stand its 1978 decision, *Bakke v. University of California Board of Regents*, which "has been widely interpreted as allowing or even encouraging affirmative action as a means of insuring racial diversity in universities" (Verhovek, 1996, p. A1). The Texas decision banning the use of affirmative action in admissions and financial aid decisions, which has been upheld on appeal and extended to all public universities in that state, indicates a changing policy climate in higher education's efforts to eliminate both sex and race inequality. Expressing concern about the decline in minority enrollments under the new rules, the Texas Board of Regents announced in May 1998 that it would appeal the *Hopwood* decision.

The Center for Individual Rights, which had brought the Hopwood case against the University of Texas, in October 1997, also initiated a class-action suit on behalf of two white students who were denied admission to the University of Michigan. This suit differs in two respects from the Texas claim: it is directed against undergraduate admissions policy, and it seeks to hold university administrators personally liable for civil rights violations under Title VI of the Civil Rights Act (Lederman, 1997a, p. A27). Moreover, it occurs at a time when twenty-six states are considering measures to restrict affirmative action policies and programs. These events presage new chapters in the nation's twenty-five-year pledge to uphold affirmative action. They have prompted a series of public statements and newspaper endorsements of affirmative action by educational leaders, among them the presidents of sixty-two research universities, six of whom were chancellors of UC campuses. They have also led to the formation by President Clinton, in 1997, of an advisory panel on race relations chaired by an African-American historian, John Hope Franklin.

Piscataway Township Board of Education v. Taxman (No. 96-479), involving two women teachers, a New Jersey school board, a coalition of civil rights organizations, and the federal courts, demonstrates the uncertain future of affirmative action as public policy. It also reinforces Eisenstein's invocation of "the myth of racialized gender" in its use of affirmative action litigation as a wedge issue, pitting white and African-American women against each other. In 1989, the Piscataway board in the interests of affirmative action retained Debra Williams, the only African-American teacher in the high school's business department, while dismissing Sharon Taxman, one of several white teachers. Both teachers had been hired on the same day and had similar qualifications. Taxman subsequently filed a complaint citing reverse discrimination. In August 1996, the U.S. Court of Appeals for the Third Circuit upheld a lower court ruling that prohibited any consideration of race in employment under Title VII unless undertaken as a remedy for actual discrimination. Unwilling to pay the damages awarded to Taxman by the Court of Appeals, the Piscataway board appealed to the Supreme Court. When the court agreed to hear the case, the media speculated that a woman, Justice Sandra Day O'Connor, could be the pivotal vote and that "the future of affirmative action may well be in her hands" (Greenhouse, 1997, p. A1). Its relevance to higher education was clearly evident in a brief filed by the American Council on Education (ACE) and twenty-four other higher education organizations, in which they urged the Supreme Court "not to prohibit colleges from using racial preferences to promote diversity" (Lederman, 1997a, p. A28). The National Association of Scholars, which disputed the ACE claims that achieving racial diversity was a compelling state interest, expressed an opposing view. Ultimately, a civil rights coalition prevailed, and the Black Leadership Forum raised $300,000 of the $433,500 needed to settle the case out of court.

The passage of Proposition 209 rescinding affirmative action in California and the consideration of comparable legislative proposals by other states and the Congress are ominous signs of a growing antifeminist and antiminority movement. Two proposals patterned after Proposition 209, which would have barred race and gender preferences in all public higher education, were debated and ultimately defeated in the Congress—the Civil Rights Act of 1997 and the Riggs amendment to the Higher Education Act of 1998. Rejected by a vote of 249 to 171, the anti-affirmative action amendment sponsored by Representative Frank Riggs (R-CA), would have barred federal support to public colleges and universities that granted preferential treatment in admissions "based on race, gender, or ethnicity" (Burd, 1998, p. A35). The Supreme Court's rejection in 1997 of the appeal on the constitutionality of Proposition 209 also sent negative signals regarding the judiciary's commitment to affirmative action. President Clinton's adoption of a centrist position in 1996, mirroring much of the liberal Republican message of the 1970s, is another marker in the rightward movement of public policy makers. Ethnic politics has replaced feminist politics, and women in academe now operate from different sets of assumptions than they did in the 1970s or the 1980s about what has been achieved and what remains to be done.

My professional career in academia, begun in mid-life, reflects the advances made by many women in the 1970s and 1980s. A closer analysis of the movement of women into higher education during the past twenty-five years shows that we were aided in our quest by political events, economic growth, and demographic change on an unprecedented scale. It is also evident that the grass-roots activism of both the women's movement and the civil rights movement have been superceded by a series of debates on equality and social justice and that we run the risk of dissipating hard-earned gains in a more conservative political climate. In this overtly feminist critique of higher education, my concern is with the issues that continue to deny women full economic, political, and social equality.

2

THE ACADEMIC PIPELINE AND THE ACADEMIC LABOR MARKET

Women's economic participation in the paid workforce has been rapid and visible throughout the latter half of this century. When viewed in historical perspective, this phenomenon has resulted from a combination of factors—social, economic, political, and personal—that have played an important role in the entry and advancement of women in higher education as students, faculty, and professional staff. To examine the magnitude of women's progress in the professoriate by rank, field, and institutional type, I have used the 1970s as my baseline. During that decade, the Equal Employment Opportunity Act and Title IX were enacted, and several earlier laws and executive orders were extended to protect women in both public and private higher education. In analyzing data from the past twenty-five years, I have explored the relationship among antidiscrimination laws and regulations, women's increased presence in traditionally male occupations, and institutional and disciplinary norms. Recognizing the difficulties of generalizing from databases that treat women as a variable, if at all, I extended the scope of my inquiry through site visits and interviews with women faculty. I investigated several persistent problems relating to the academic pipeline and academic labor market; the dimensions of women's absence or presence in academic disciplines; and three salient denominators through which women's progress can be measured—degree attainment, postgraduate employment, and academic status.

Women in the Workforce: An Overview

Economists mark World War II as a watershed in women's workforce participation, one result of wartime shortages caused by the military mobilization of American males, with the consequent demand for women in the labor market. Passage of the Servicemen's Readjustment Act of 1946 (the G.I.

Bill), followed by other scholarship and fellowship programs under the National Defense Education Act in 1957, ushered in an unprecedented expansion of higher education. As new colleges were founded, multicampus systems for public higher education were built. Women enrolled in greater numbers, spurred on by economic needs and new societal attitudes. By 1970, women constituted more than half (52.3%) of the resident population of the United States, 16 years and older, a proportion that has changed imperceptibly in the past twenty-five years.[1]

By the mid-1960s, the civil rights movement and the passage of equal employment legislation raised women's expectations concerning their participation in the workforce. Women's college enrollment rates expanded steadily throughout the 1970s and, by 1980, were consistently higher than men's. Between 1980 and 1994, women's participation increased from 6.2 million (51.9%) to 8.1 million (55.4%), an average annual growth rate of 2.1 percent, for a 30 percent increase (Gerald & Hussar, 1995, p. 12). The National Center for Educational Statistics (NCES) projects that women will maintain their 55 percent enrollment share up to the year 2005 (ibid.). Women are 52 percent of all full-time and 59 percent of all part-time students, and they represent 55.8 percent of all undergraduates, 55 percent of all graduate students, and 41 percent of all first professional students (Babco, 1997, p. 3).

Access to higher education also led to greater participation by women in the labor force. According to Bureau of Labor Statistics trends in workforce participation, only 50.1 percent of women ages 25 to 54 were in the workforce in 1970. By 1993, however, 75.3 percent of women in this cohort were working or seeking employment. By 1994, 60.2 million women were in the paid labor force, accounting for six of every ten women in the working-age population.[2]

Many explanations are offered for women's lower economic status, some of them based on fact and others on societal attitudes about the appropriate roles for women: women are more likely to work part time, to be in unskilled or semiskilled occupations, to have fewer years of experience, and to be less productive than men. Labor statistics belie the myth that women work for

1. These data are derived from the U.S. Department of Commerce, Bureau of the Census, *Current Population Reports*, cited by Kopka & Korb (1996), 2, 3.
2. See Herz & Wootton (1996). An annual almanac of women in the workforce, published by the Women's Research and Education Institute, it is an excellent compendium of socioeconomic and demographic data on women's employment, health, economic security, military and political participation. See also Kopka & Korb (1996), 54, 55.

other than economic reasons or that they are less committed, motivated, or hardworking than men. In 1994, the Women's Bureau of the Department of Labor undertook a national survey to determine how working women feel about their jobs. About 250,000 women responded to the "Working Women Count!" questionnaire, expressing a consensus for change regarding equitable compensation, erosion of health care benefits, affordable child care, the difficulties of balancing work-family roles, and limited opportunities for professional advancement.[3]

In 1997, the Bureau of Labor Statistics also reported that after almost two decades in which the pay gap between men and women had narrowed, it was widening again. Women's median earnings, which increased from 62 to 77 percent between 1979 to 1993, declined to 75 percent in 1997. Women economists attribute this trend to a variety of circumstances, including the anti-affirmative action backlash; the recent overhaul of the federal welfare system, which has brought more women into the workforce at the low end of the pay scale; and the likelihood that more men than women will earn bonuses and overtime pay (Lewin, 1997). Since retirement benefits are linked to salary levels, women who experience pay inequities can also anticipate lower social security and retirement pensions. Because of salary disparities, at least 6 percent of employed women, regardless of race or ethnicity, hold two or more jobs (46% of all multiple job holders) in addition to having disproportionate burdens of homemaking, childbearing, child rearing, and elder care (Herz & Wootton, 1996, p. 55). Women federal workers continue to have lower average salaries in almost every occupational series, including engineering, physical and life sciences, mathematics and computer sciences, economics and psychology (Babco, 1996, p. 186). Babco notes that even though "women dominate in most of the health-related occupations, only in the nurse, occupational and physical therapist categories [do] women earn more than men" (p. 187).

The experiences of mothers and fathers in the U.S. labor force illustrate the differences in family demographics for men and women (Galinsky & Bond, 1996). Although seven out of ten mothers with children under the age of 18 are now employed, 23 percent of these are in the "contingent workforce" compared to 4 percent of men, owing to their greater likelihood of holding

3. Sherlock (1995, Winter–Spring), 6–8, contains an interview with Robert Reich, President Clinton's first-term secretary of labor and a discussion of "Working Women Count," a national survey conducted in 1994 by the Women's Bureau of the Department of Labor. See also Department of Labor (1995, March).

part-time jobs. Employed mothers are also more likely to have lower hourly wages and fewer fringe benefits, such as health insurance, paid vacations, and Family and Medical Leave Act (FMLA) of 1993 coverage. The Teachers Insurance and Annuity Association (TIAA-CREF) estimates that only 9 percent of American women 40 years and older receive or expect to receive retirement benefits from their employers, partly because women are more likely to serve as primary caretakers of children and elderly parents, opting out of the workforce "an average of 11½ years over a lifetime compared with 16 months for men," and partly because they are in the contingent workforce (TIAA-CREF, 1997, p. 8). In an account of the experiences of mothers and fathers in the workforce, Galinsky and Bond (1996, p. 80) observe: "By their own self-reports, employed mothers are more stressed, coping less effectively with their lives, more burned out by their jobs, less satisfied with their marital relations, and less satisfied with themselves as parents." Furthermore, women feel better about their work and themselves when they enjoy greater autonomy, more control over their work schedules, reasonable job demands and greater job security, more equal opportunities for advancement, more access to flexible time/leave benefits and dependent care benefits, more supportive supervisors and a family-friendly workplace culture, and spouses or partners who take more responsibility for family work.

The attitudes, values, and experience of contemporary American women in the workforce are the backdrop against which I examine the status of women faculty in American universities. How do they fare in terms of preparation for academic work, compensation, tenure, working conditions, and job satisfaction? Is gender equity still a viable goal, and what alternative scenarios are suggested by these data?

The Pipeline Myth: Women's Degree Attainment

Women's progress through the academic pipeline is closely related to several factors: disciplinary field of concentration, institutional and departmental affiliation, mentoring or sponsorship, geographic mobility, and race or ethnicity. These realities belie the persistent myth of the paucity of qualified women, a recurrent refrain in the background of debates about affirmative action and gender equity in academe. Business-oriented concepts being applied by educators and employers contribute to the perception that graduate schools produce Ph.D.s for an academic labor market, which is highly selective, market driven, and concerned with workloads and productivity in research. Each year, however, the academic pipeline expands to accommodate the increasing number of women degree recipients in practically every discipline and professional field. From a review of national databases, institutional evaluations, report recommendations, and women's commission documents, I report my findings on enrollments and degree completion for women students, postdoctoral academic employment by field, and the dual employment track for part-time and non-tenure-track faculty.

Enrollments

Higher education enrollments increased by 60 percent between 1970 and 1994, from 8.6 million to 14.3 million (Snyder, Hoffman, & Geddes, 1996, p. 182). Women and part-time students accounted for much of this growth. Between 1970 and 1994, the total number of women students increased from 3.5 to 7.9 million (+44%), while the number of men students rose from 5.0 to 6.4 million (+8%). Two factors accounted for this rapid growth—the growing number of part-time women students attending two-year colleges and the large proportion of reentry adult women students. For example, between 1975 and 1978, the U.S. Census Bureau reported that the proportion of women students aged 25 to 34 grew 187 percent, and the number of women over the age of 25 in two-year colleges nearly tripled. Women's graduate enrollments grew five times as fast as men's throughout the 1970s, and by 1980 women students outnumbered men at both the undergraduate and graduate levels. Between 1984 and 1994, women full-time graduate students increased by 62 percent compared to a 25 percent increase for men, whereas women part-time graduate students increased by 30 percent compared to 8 percent for men. By 1994, women were 55.2 percent of all students (compared to 40.7% in 1970), 55.7 percent of all undergraduates, and 57.3 percent of all graduate students.

Degree Completion

The number of degrees awarded to women has increased significantly since 1970. In 1994, women were awarded 935,089 undergraduate degrees, or 55.7 percent of the total, a figure equal to their enrollment ratio and representing an increase from 43.2 percent in 1970 (Snyder, Hoffman, & Geddes, 1996). They earned 59.5 percent of all associate degrees, compared to 42.9 percent in 1970, and 54.6 percent of all bachelor's degrees, compared to 43.2 percent in 1970. Since 1982, women's share of bachelor's degrees has exceeded 50 percent. Sizable growth has occurred in two fields in particular, business management and health sciences, which now account for 22 percent and 6 percent, respectively, of all bachelor's degrees awarded. At the graduate level, women also experienced a steady increase in degrees awarded, earning 57.3

percent of all graduate degrees: from 39.7 percent of all master's degrees in 1970 to 54.5 percent by 1994 and from 5.2 percent of all first professional degrees in 1970 to 41.2 percent by 1994. In specific terms, women received, by 1993–94, 43 percent of all J.D.s, 41 percent of all M.D.s., 38.5 percent of all D.D.S./D.M.D.s, and 46 percent of all M.B.A.s.

Equally impressive are the doctoral statistics. Because in most fields the Ph.D. is the terminal degree for faculty, these data, when analyzed by discipline, unequivocally refute the pipeline argument—that not enough women candidates qualify for tenure-track positions. NCES data show that between 1960 and 1970, women received only 11.7 percent of all doctorates. From 1970 to 1980 their share more than doubled to 29.7 percent, and from 1980 to 1990 it grew to 36.6 percent (see table 1).

By 1994, women had increased their share to a record 38.4 percent.[4] When foreign students are excluded from the totals, as shown in table 2, the percentage of U.S. women Ph.D.s jumped to 47 percent.[5]

Data from the Survey of Earned Doctorates, compiled by the Doctorate Records Project of the National Research Council, show that women earned a record number of Ph.D.s in 1995 (16,333), nearly ten times the number earned in 1965 (1,760), increasing their representation from 11 to 39 percent in three decades. Meanwhile, the number of men doubled from 14,580 in 1965 to 25,277 in 1995, while their representation among all Ph.D.s decreased proportionately, from 89 to 61 percent (p. 4). This decline occurred between 1976 and 1995, when men experienced a relative stasis in doctoral degrees awarded (from 25,262 to 25,277) at the same time that women's participation jumped from 7,684 to 16,333. Much of this shift resulted from the decline in male U.S. citizens earning doctorates (from 20,427 in 1976 to 14,909 in 1995) and a doubling in the number of male non-U.S. citizens earning doctorates

4. These data are derived from U.S. Department of Education databases, especially *Digest of Educational Statistics* and *Integrated Postsecondary Education Data Systems (IPEDS) Completions Surveys* (selected years). See also Henderson et al. (1996). This report presents a summary analysis with tables of data collected by the Survey of Earned Doctorates, sponsored by five federal agencies (NSF, NIH, NEH, USDE, and USDA) and conducted by the Doctorate Records Project of the National Research Council.

5. In Gerald & Hussar (1995), the National Center for Educational Statistics gives projections based on low, intermediate, and high estimates of national data. It forecasts a continued increase in the number and proportion of undergraduate and graduate degrees awarded to women, also predicting that the number of degrees awarded to men will increase at the undergraduate and first-professional levels but not at the master's or doctoral levels.

Table 1 Ph.D. Awards by Field, Year, and Sex (All Graduates)

Field of Study	1969–70			1979–80		
	Total	Women	% Women	Total	Women	% Women
All fields	29,866	3,976	13.3	32,235	9,672	29.7
Education	5,894	1,196	20.3	7,940	3,521	44.3
Engineering	3,681	24	0.7	2,507	95	3.8
Humanities	2,778	739	26.6	2,825	1,201	42.5
Life sciences	3,289	469	14.3	3,636	946	26.0
Mathematics	1,236	96	7.8	724	100	13.8
Physical sciences	4,312	235	5.4	3,089	384	12.4
Psychology	1,668	372	9.6	2,768	1,166	42.1
Professional fields	3,137	358	11.4	5,901	1,385	23.5
Social sciences	3,861	487	12.6	3,225	874	27.1

during that period (p. 134).[6] For women doctorates, however, the growth rate has been continuous for both U.S. and non-U.S. citizens (p. 135).

Women of Color: Enrollment and Degrees

The proportion of American college students who are minorities increased from 15.7 to 24.6 percent between 1976 and 1994. For the past two decades, the growth in enrollments among women of color has been significant, from 8 to 14.1 percent between 1976 and 1994, compared to an increase from 7.7 to 10.5 percent for men. They represent 14.7 percent of women undergraduate students and 9.7 percent of women graduate students. African-American (6.5%) and Latina women (4.2%) exceed the percentage of men in these cohorts; Asian men and women students are equally represented (2.8%). By 1995, racial and ethnic minorities received almost 14 percent of all Ph.D.s awarded to U.S. citizens—more than 16 percent each

6. See Henderson et al. (1996). According to the 1996 *Summary Report* of the Survey of Earned Doctorates, in 1993 foreign students were clustered in science and engineering where they earned one-third of all Ph.D.s. The increase in number of degrees awarded to non-U.S. citizens (with temporary or permanent visas) accounted for 64 percent of the annual increases for all Ph.D.s from 1985 to 1995; 90 percent of these students enjoy university support compared to 75 percent of American doctoral candidates. China, India, Taiwan, and Korea account for 55 percent of these students, more than 70 percent of whom are in three fields—engineering, physical and life sciences. Almost twice as many men (39%) as women (20%) are among the cohort of non-U.S. citizens.

Table 1 (*continued*)

Field of Study	1989–90			1993–94		
	Total	Women	% Women	Total	Women	% Women
All fields	39,235	14,372	36.6	43,939	16,855	38.4
Education	6,937	4,000	57.7	6,983	4,224	60.5
Engineering	4,788	434	9.1	5,992	665	11.2
Humanities	2,519	1,231	48.9	3,114	1,578	50.7
Life sciences	3,826	1,439	37.6	4,544	1,849	40.7
Mathematics	862	163	18.9	1,157	253	21.9
Physical sciences	4,109	809	19.7	4,655	1,010	21.7
Psychology	3,391	1,956	57.7	3,709	2,300	62.0
Professional fields	8,367	2,932	35.0	10,035	3,616	36.0
Social sciences	2,992	987	33.0	3,640	1,313	36.1

Source: U.S. Department of Education, National Center for Education Statistics, *Digest of Education Statistics*, and Integrated Postsecondary Education Data System "Degree Completion" surveys.

in education and engineering and from 9 to 13 percent in the remaining broad fields (humanities, social sciences, life sciences, and physical sciences). African Americans, Latinos, and Native Americans earned most of their doctorates in education and the social sciences, whereas Asians earned most of their degrees in life sciences and engineering. Women of color received 25 percent of all first professional and 29 percent of all doctoral degrees awarded to women. African-American and Puerto Rican women earn more doctorates than their male cohorts (51.4% and 55.4%, respectively). For all other ethnic groups, women earn fewer Ph.D.s: whites (43.4%), Asians (26.7%), Native Americans (45.3%), Mexican Americans (42.7%), and other Hispanics (36%).

Characteristics of Women Ph.D.s

These gains for women despite unequal university support can be attributed to several factors: greater access to graduate and professional schools and male-dominated programs; the availability of scholarships, fellowships and research grants; a larger critical mass of women baccalaureates pursuing academic careers; and a relative stasis in U.S. male doctoral enrollments. The national data also highlight other differences between the doctoral experience of women and their male cohorts: women are less likely to obtain a doctorate in the same field as their baccalaureate degree (51% compared to 58% of men) but are more likely to have a slightly older median age (35.6 compared to 33.2 years), and to be unmarried (48.5% compared to 41% of men).

Table 2 Ph.D. Awards by Field, Year, and Sex (Excluding Temporary U.S. Residents)

Field of Study	1980–81			1989–90		
	Total	Women	% Women	Total	Women	% Women
All fields	28,636	9,605	33.5	30,593	12,734	41.6
Education	7,307	3,564	48.8	6,360	3,761	59.1
Engineering	1,595	67	4.2	2,505	301	12.0
Humanities	2,420	1,066	44.0	1,506	991	65.8
Life sciences	3,429	977	28.5	3,115	1,203	38.6
Mathematics	555	97	17.5	459	87	19.0
Physical sciences	2,610	315	12.1	2,906	585	20.1
Psychology	2,861	1,252	43.8	3,286	1,951	59.4
Professional fields	5,158	1,410	27.3	6,721	2,591	38.6
Social sciences	2,701	790	29.2	2,291	843	36.8

They rely more extensively on personal resources (46%) and less on university support (44%) as compared to men, who obtain 58 percent of their funding from university sources (teaching or research assistantships). The ability to garner institutional support may contribute to men's lower median time to complete the degree (ten years) compared to women's (twelve years) and may influence their plans to pursue postdoctoral research (29% for men versus 23% for women). In the sciences, Ginorio emphasized the need to "warm the climate for women in academic science," through the formation of networks, peer groups, and mentoring support in doctoral science programs and through greater access to postdoctoral fellowship opportunities. She notes that although postdoctoral fellowships are essential for women whose goal is academic science, they can become "revolving holding pens for increasingly frustrated [female] graduates who cannot find permanent positions" (p. 15).

Fields of Study

Women earn the majority of doctorates in three broad fields of study: psychology (62%), education (60.5%), and humanities (50.7%) (see table 3). They earn fewer doctorates in six other broad fields: life sciences (40.7%), social sciences (36%), professional fields (36%), mathematics (22%), physical sciences (21.7%), and engineering (11.2%). Policy analysts frequently specify science and engineering fields as problematic for women, who earn only one-third of these doctorates compared to 52.2 percent of non-science doctorates (Henderson et al., 1996). As shown in table 3, women obtain an

Table 2 (*continued*)

| Field of Study | 1993–94 | | |
	Total	Women	% Women
All fields	32,385	15,217	47.0
Education	6,380	3,921	61.5
Engineering	2,807	405	14.4
Humanities	2,540	1,328	52.3
Life sciences	3,299	1,409	42.7
Mathematics	596	146	24.5
Physical sciences	3,000	661	22.0
Psychology	3,544	2,210	62.4
Professional fields	7,434	2,963	39.9
Social sciences	2,667	1,098	41.2

Source: U.S. Department of Education, National Center for Education Statistics, *Digest of Education Statistics*, and Integrated Postsecondary Education Data System "Degree Completion" surveys.

almost equal percentage of doctorates in professional as in academic fields and subfields. They earn the majority of Ph.D.s in four out of ten academic fields: area/ethnic studies (51.6%), foreign languages (60%), letters (57.7%), and psychology (62%); and the majority of Ph.D.s in five out of sixteen professional fields: education (60.5%), health sciences (57.2%), home economics (74%), library/archival sciences (69%), and public affairs (54.1%). Changing patterns of gender composition are evident in some disciplinary specializations. For example, in the social sciences, women earn the majority of Ph.D.s in anthropology (61%) and sociology (51%) but half as many in political science (27.8%) and economics (24.3%). In the sciences, they earn almost twice as many Ph.D.s in the life sciences (40.6%) as in the physical sciences (21.7%). In the latter field, they obtain more than twice as many degrees in chemistry (28%) as in physics (12.3%) or geology (17%).

Psychology: A Feminized Field

The changing educational pipeline in psychology provides an interesting case of a field that has undergone significant shifts in gender composition since the 1970s. The Task Force on the Changing Gender Composition of Psychology (1995) examined societal, disciplinary, and demographic trends in psychology, including patterns of men's and women's involvement in both the educational pipeline and the workplace. It viewed the 1970s and 1980s as

Table 3 Doctoral Degrees by Field, Year, and Sex

Field of Study	1969–70			1979–80		
	Total	Women	% Women	Total	Women	% Women
All fields	29,866	3,976	13.3	32,235	9,672	29.7
Professional						
Agriculture/Natural resources	734	31	4.2	991	112	11.3
Architecture/Environmental design	11	1	9.1	79	13	16.5
Business/Management	603	10	1.7	796	115	14.4
Communications	17	0	0	193	72	37.3
Computer/Information science	107	2	1.9	240	27	11.3
Education	5,894	1,196	20.3	7,940	3,521	44.3
Engineering/Engineering technology	3,681	24	0.7	2,507	95	3.8
Health sciences	357	58	16.2	786	351	44.7
Home economics	116	83	71.6	192	146	76.0
Law	35	3	8.6	40	4	10.0
Library/Archival sciences	40	16	40.0	73	38	52.1
Parks/Recreation	97	0	0	21	8	38.1
Protective services	—	—	—	18	3	16.7
Public Affairs	—	—	—	353	127	36.0
Theology	200	3	1.5	1,319	77	5.8
Visual/Performing arts	734	142	19.3	655	242	36.9
Total professional	**12,626**	**1,569**	**12.4**	**16,203**	**4,951**	**30.6**
Academic						
Area/Ethnic studies	86	9	10.5	145	50	34.5
Foreign Languages	869	290	33.4	549	315	57.4
Letters	1,205	373	31.0	1,501	691	46.0
Liberal/General Studies	140	21	15.0	106	24	22.6
Life Sciences	3,289	469	14.3	3,636	946	26.0
Mathematics	1,236	96	7.8	724	100	13.8
Multi/Interdisciplinary studies	—	—	—	295	94	31.9
Philosophy/Religion	564	55	9.8	374	77	20.6
Physical sciences	4,312	235	5.4	3,089	384	12.4
Psychology	1,668	372	9.6	2,768	1,166	42.1
Social sciences	3,861	487	12.6	3,225	874	27.1
Total academic	**17,230**	**2,407**	**14.0**	**16,412**	**4,721**	**28.8**
Not classified	10	0	0	—	—	—
Grand total	**29,866**	**3,976**	**13.3**	**32,615**	**9,672**	**29.7**

Table 3 (*continued*)

Field of Study	1989–90			1993–94		
	Total	Women	% Women	Total	Women	% Women
All fields	39,235	14,372	36.6	43,939	16,855	38.4
Professional						
Agriculture / Natural resources	1,215	243	20.0	1,278	296	23.2
Architecture / Environmental design	94	28	29.8	161	50	31.1
Business / Management	1,123	277	24.7	1,450	403	27.8
Communications	269	125	46.5	345	171	49.6
Computer / Information science	592	90	15.2	813	125	15.4
Education	6,937	4,000	57.7	6,983	4,224	60.5
Engineering / Engineering technology	4,788	434	9.1	5,992	665	11.2
Health sciences	1,594	853	53.5	1,985	1,136	57.2
Home economics	297	214	72.1	365	272	74.5
Law	471	203	43.1	81	16	19.8
Library / Archival sciences	35	23	65.7	45	31	68.9
Parks / Recreation	30	17	56.7	116	46	39.7
Protective services	36	12	33.3	28	11	39.3
Public Affairs	486	264	54.3	527	285	54.1
Theology	1,181	163	13.8	1,635	225	13.8
Visual / Performing arts	830	366	44.1	1,054	469	44.5
Total professional	**19,978**	**7,312**	**36.6**	**22,855**	**8,425**	**36.9**
Academic						
Area / Ethnic studies	114	54	47.4	155	80	51.6
Foreign Languages	505	296	58.6	888	533	60.0
Letters	1,257	692	55.1	1,344	776	57.7
Liberal / General Studies	29	18	62.1	119	46	38.7
Life Sciences	3,826	1,439	37.6	4,544	1,849	40.7
Mathematics	862	163	18.9	1,157	253	21.9
Multi / Interdisciplinary studies	298	108	36.2	235	78	33.2
Philosophy / Religion	430	117	27.2	528	145	27.5
Physical sciences	4,109	809	19.7	4,655	1,010	21.7
Psychology	3,391	1,956	57.7	3,709	2,300	62.0
Social sciences	2,992	987	33.0	3,640	1,313	36.1
Total academic	**17,813**	**6,639**	**37.3**	**20,974**	**8,383**	**40.0**
Not classified	1,444	421	29.2	110	47	42.7
Grand total	**39,235**	**14,372**	**36.6**	**43,939**	**16,855**	**38.4**

Source: U.S. Department of Education, National Center for Education Statistics, *Digest of Education Statistics,* and Integrated Postsecondary Education Data System "Degree Completion" surveys.

a time of expanding opportunities in psychology but the late 1980s and 1990s as a period of change with potentially negative implications for the profession's prestige. The proportion of degrees in psychology awarded to women exhibited tremendous growth at all levels. Between 1970 and 1991, women's share of bachelor's degrees in psychology rose from 43 to 73 percent, and it is now the most popular undergraduate major. The proportion of women students in psychology master's and doctoral programs increased by almost one-third to 68 percent of all enrollments by 1993 (Pion et al., 1996, p. 514).

In analyzing distribution trends of men and women across individual subfields, the APA Task Force found that the number of women doctorates in three health service provider subfields—clinical, counseling, and school psychology—grew by 52 percent between 1981 and 1991; 29 percent fewer degrees were awarded to men in the same subfields. As a result, women were now 64 percent of new Ph.D.s in these subfields (Task Force, 1995, p. 10). The three applied subfields (developmental, educational, and industrial-organizational) increased only slightly for women but declined for men, except in industrial/organizational psychology, which had always been—and continues to be—a male-dominated specialty (ibid.).

By 1991, one-third of all full-time employed psychologists were women, a number almost equally distributed among higher education (34%), non-profit institutions (33%), and self-employment or private businesses (35%). Attention may be drawn, however, to an interesting phenomenon: although the percentage of psychologists increased by 68 percent between 1973 and 1991, neither women nor men fared well in academia, where their proportions declined from 45 to 26 percent for women and from 43 to 28 percent for men (Task Force, 1995, p. 15). As in other professional fields, women psychologists are less likely than men to occupy managerial or administrative positions, and they are more likely to teach in two-year colleges or schools (41%) and to be relegated to part-time or non-tenure-track positions. In the early 1970s, women psychologists constituted 9 percent of full professors, 14 percent of associate professors, and 25 percent of assistant professors. Although their numbers have quadrupled in the past two decades, women psychologists are still only 25 percent of all full professors, 27.4 percent of associate professors, and 30.3 percent of assistant professors. Worse still, women with temporary status as instructors, adjuncts, or lecturers constitute 63 percent of all psychologists (Pion et al., 1996, p. 522). Access to major journals is a primary source of communicating and disseminating research. An examination of citation rates for the five major APA journals noted that by 1991, the percentage of women authors increased by at least 30 percent, but women editors continued to be in the minority (15%, or three APA journals). A higher percentage of women held associate or consulting editorial positions (p. 523).

Postgraduate Employment

Similar patterns can be seen between women's increased labor participation and degree attainment in fields other than psychology. By 1993, 90.3 percent of all women with doctorates were in the workforce, compared to 80.3 percent of women with baccalaureates. The proportion entering academe is lower than two decades earlier for both men and women (54% in 1995 versus 60% in 1975) (Henderson et al., p. 19). More women than men plan to teach (60% versus 49%), however, and twice as many men than women plan to enter business and industry (27% versus 13%). So, too, for engineers (61%) and physical scientists (47%), who are more likely to pursue nonacademic employment than are those holding doctorates in the humanities (85%) or professional fields (73%). Although women have consistently entered the professoriate in greater proportions than men, their actual numbers have exceeded men only since 1992. Undoubtedly, women are in the doctoral pipeline, and their numbers show signs of continuing to increase throughout the 1990s. How do these trends translate into their participation on college and university faculties?

The Changing Status of Women Faculty[7]

In 1970, there were 2,525 postsecondary institutions and 450,000 instructional faculty, 23 percent of whom were women (Snyder, Hoffman, & Geddes, 1996, p. 175). By 1993, the establishment of more than one thousand new colleges and universities over twenty-three years brought the total of post-

7. Affirmative action laws and regulations provided impetus for collecting and analyzing faculty data by gender and for disaggregating the totals by gender, race, and ethnicity for public and private institutions as well as by Carnegie classification. Three sources of data are used here: the *Digest of Educational Statistics* (Snyder & Hoffman, 1996), which began publication in 1968 and has disaggregated data by gender and race since 1972–73; the annual economic reports of Committee Z of the American Association of University Professors (AAUP) published annually in the official AAUP bulletin, *Academe,* and reported by gender for its member institutions since 1974–75; and the analyses of the 1993 National Survey of Postsecondary Faculty (NSOPF) conducted by the Office of Educational Research and Improvement (OERI); see Zimbler (1994). A 1992 survey of 31,354 faculty in 974 institutions, it provides the basis for a national faculty profile consisting of data on their professional background, status, and roles, distribution among categories of institutions and academic ranks, workloads, compensation, and attitudes toward their work.

secondary institutions to 3,632. As shown in table 4, the total number of faculty by 1993 had more than doubled to 933,373: 38.7 percent female and 61.3 percent male; 59.6 percent full time and 40.4 percent part time; 71 percent in public and 29 percent in private institutions; 69.4 percent in four-year and 31.6 percent in two-year colleges. Of the 554,903 full-time instructional faculty, 33.5 percent were women, compared to 24.3 percent in 1975. Despite these gains, they held more full-time than part-time positions only in private four-year institutions (45.6% compared to 41.8%) and were in the majority compared to men only in private two-year colleges (52%) (p. 229).

Between 1975 and 1993, the percentage of women faculty had grown proportionately at every rank: from 9.6 to 17.2 percent of full professors; from 17 to 30.3 percent of associate professors, from 28.8 to 42.2 percent of assistant professors; from 41.4 to 51.2 percent of lecturers; from 40.6 to 49.4 percent of instructors; and from 33.2 to 41.1 percent of faculty with no academic rank (see table 5). Faculty of color accounted for 13.5 percent of full-time faculty and 12.5 percent of part-time faculty. However, more men than women are full professors, particularly at research and doctoral universities. Conversely, more women are assistant or associate professors.

It is worth noting that the proportion of women has grown much faster at lower ranks than among senior faculty. Twenty-two percent of full-time women faculty are non-tenure-track (NTT), bringing the percentage of faculty with either part-time or non-tenure track status to 62.4 percent (National Education Association, 1996). In short, less than two-fifths (37.6%) of all women faculty in higher education are on the tenure track. Because women are more likely to be either NTT or PT (part-time) faculty, academic jobs for the growing numbers of women doctorates may be more limited than optimistic NCES forecasts would indicate (Gerald & Hussar, 1995) (see table 6).

Computer forecasting affords the opportunity to estimate the time it will take for women to reach parity with their male counterparts. An empirical analysis of AAUP faculty data by gender and rank in 109 Category I institutions determined that, based on the rate of increase between 1975 and 1988, it would take women in research universities ninety years to achieve equal representation with men and until 2149 for women to reach parity with men as full professors (Alpert, 1990). The APA Task Force on Women in Psychology estimated that at the current rate, women psychologists would not reach parity with men across all academic ranks until the year 2200 (Pion et al., 1996, p. 522).

In attempting to discern why women are "disproportionately represented at two- and four-year institutions, within the lower ranks, in nontenured

Table 4 Employees by Primary Occupation, Employment Status, and Sex (Fall 1993)

	Full Time and Part Time				Full Time				Part Time			
	Total	Men	Women	% Women	Total	Men	Women	% Women	Total	Men	Women	% Women
Total, all employees	2,643,453	1,276,502	1,366,951	51.7	1,811,541	867,618	943,923	52.1	831,912	408,884	423,028	50.9
Professional staff	1,713,478	945,089	768,389	44.8	1,054,629	594,109	460,520	43.7	658,849	350,980	307,869	46.7
Exec./Admin./Managerial	146,899	84,537	62,362	42.5	140,790	81,723	59,067	42.0	6,109	2,814	3,295	53.9
Faculty	933,373	571,308	362,065	38.7	554,903	368,403	186,500	33.6	378,470	202,905	175,565	46.4
Instruction & research asst.	203,958	120,996	82,962	40.7	—	—	—		203,958	120,996	82,962	40.7
Nonfaculty professionals	429,248	168,248	261,000	60.8	358,936	143,983	214,953	59.9	70,312	24,265	46,047	65.5
Nonprofessional staff	929,973	331,413	598,560	64.4	756,910	273,509	483,401	63.9	173,065	57,904	115,159	66.5
Technical/Para-professional	186,844	74,763	112,081	60.0	145,318	60,365	84,953	58.5	41,526	14,398	27,128	65.3
Clerical & secretarial	445,521	52,107	393,414	88.3	358,202	33,699	324,503	90.6	87,319	18,408	68,911	78.9
Skilled crafts	65,036	60,779	4,257	6.5	61,834	58,579	3,255	5.3	3,202	2,200	1,002	31.3
Service & maintenance	232,572	143,764	88,808	38.2	191,556	120,866	70,690	36.9	41,016	22,898	18,118	44.2

Source: U.S. Department of Education, National Center for Education Statistics, Integrated Postsecondary Education Data System "Staff" surveys.

Table 5 Full-Time Faculty by Academic Rank and Race/Ethnicity

A. Fall 1993

Academic rank	All Faculty		White, Non-Hispanic		Black, Non-Hispanic		Hispanic	
	Total	% Women	Total	% Women	Total	% Women	Total	% Women
All ranks	554,903	33.6	471,442	33.2	25,850	47.9	17,907	41.9
Professors	159,072	17.2	142,435	16.6	4,564	34.0	3,523	30.3
Associate professors	122,789	30.3	106,438	30.0	5,352	42.0	3,866	38.8
Assistant professors	131,152	42.2	105,474	43.2	7,724	50.6	4,880	46.0
Instructors	69,859	49.4	57,425	49.5	4,783	55.8	3,590	47.6
Lecturers	13,762	51.2	11,305	51.2	840	55.0	446	53.6
Other faculty	58,269	41.1	48,365	43.7	2,587	59.3	1,602	46.0

B. Fall 1985

Academic rank	All Faculty		White, Non-Hispanic		Black, Non-Hispanic		Hispanic	
	Total	% Women	Total	% Women	Total	% Women	Total	% Women
All ranks	464,072	27.6	417,036	27.1	19,227	45.6	7,704	30.4
Professors	129,269	11.6	119,868	11.3	2,859	28.0	1,455	17.1
Associate professors	111,092	23.3	100,630	23.0	4,201	38.2	1,727	25.9
Assistant professors	111,308	35.8	97,496	35.8	5,895	50.4	1,968	33.1
Instructors	75,411	42.6	66,799	42.2	4,572	53.9	1,798	36.5
Lecturers	9,766	47.8	8,477	47.7	631	51.8	251	53.4
Other faculty	27,226	38.4	23,766	38.9	1,069	56.1	505	40.6

C. Fall 1975 and Fall 1980

Academic rank	Fall 1975		Fall 1980	
	Total	% Women	Total	% Women
All ranks	377,157	24.3	395,992	26.4
Professors	87,188	9.6	104,857	10.2
Associate professors	88,286	17.1	97,195	20.4
Assistant professors	106,245	28.8	96,868	34.8
Instructors	76,761	40.6	30,754	51.7
Lecturers	5,219	41.4	6,257	46.3
Other faculty	16,458	33.2	60,061	36.1

Table 5 (*continued*)

A. Fall 1993 (*continued*)

Academic rank	Asian or Pacific Islander		American Indian/ Alaskan Native		Unknown Race		Nonresident Alien	
	Total	% Women	Total	% Women	Total	% Women	Total	% Women
All ranks	25,671	25.3	2,016	38.5	1,111	30.2	10,906	22.9
Professors	7,083	11.3	353	19.5	165	20.0	949	9.9
Associate professors	5,529	20.2	285	31.9	169	20.7	1,150	17.4
Assistant professors	7,650	30.5	434	51.4	376	34.0	4,614	21.2
Instructors	2,329	47.8	617	36.0	224	30.8	891	32.1
Lecturers	560	54.1	56	48.2	25	40.0	530	39.1
Other faculty	2,520	33.2	271	49.8	152	40.1	2,772	26.4

B. Fall 1985 (*continued*)

Academic rank	Asian or Pacific Islander		American Indian/ Alaskan Native	
	Total	% Women	Total	% Women
All ranks	18,370	19.2	1,735	19.7
Professors	4,788	8.2	299	11.7
Associate professors	4,130	16.4	404	14.1
Assistant professors	5,469	22.5	480	16.3
Instructors	1,806	38.8	436	29.8
Lecturers	360	41.1	47	38.3
Other faculty	1,817	20.6	69	33.3

Sources: (**A**) U.S. Department of Education, National Center for Education Statistics, Integrated Postsecondary Education Data System "Staff" survey, Fall 1993. (**B**) U.S. Department of Education, National Center for Education Statistics, *Digest of Education Statistics*. (**C**) U.S. Department of Education, National Center for Education Statistics, *Digest of Education Statistics*.

Note: Data for 1975 are not comparable with later years. In fall 1975, if an institution reported all faculty as instructors, the data were tabulated in that rank. In future years, if an institution reported all faculty as instructors, these individuals were tabulated as "other faculty." Data for 1975 and 1980 are not available by race/ethnicity.

Table 6 Employees by Primary Occupation, Employment Status, and Sex (Fall 1993)

	Totals			% of Grand Total Men			% of Grand Total Women		
	Grand Total	% Full Time	% Part Time	Total	Full Time	Part Time	Total	Full Time	Part Time
Total, all employees	2,643,453	68.5	31.5	48.3	32.8	15.5	51.7	35.7	16.0
Professional staff	1,713,478	61.5	38.5	55.2	34.7	20.5	44.8	26.9	18.0
Exec./Admin./Managerial	146,899	95.8	4.2	57.5	55.6	1.9	42.5	40.2	2.2
Faculty	933,373	59.5	40.5	61.2	39.5	21.7	38.8	20.0	18.8
Instruction & research asst.	203,958	0	100.0	59.3	0	59.3	40.7	0	40.7
Nonfaculty professionals	429,248	83.6	16.4	39.2	33.5	5.7	60.8	50.1	10.7
Nonprofessional staff	929,973	81.4	18.6	35.6	29.4	6.2	64.4	52.0	12.4
Technical/Paraprofessional	186,844	77.8	22.2	40.0	32.3	7.7	60.0	45.5	14.5
Clerical & secretarial	445,521	80.4	19.6	11.7	7.6	4.1	88.3	72.8	15.5
Skilled crafts	65,036	95.1	4.9	93.5	90.1	3.4	6.5	5.0	1.5
Service & maintenance	232,572	82.4	17.6	61.8	52.0	9.8	38.2	30.4	7.8

Source: U.S. Department of Education, National Center for Education Statistics, Integrated Postsecondary Education Data System "Staff" surveys.

and part-time positions, and in traditionally female departments" (Bellas, 1993, p. 62), I asked an African-American woman who has been affirmative action officer of a large urban research university for more than two decades to give me her perspective on hiring women faculty. She recalled some common pipeline arguments: "Not enough qualified women in our field. . . . We can't afford the best minority candidates and besides they wouldn't be happy here. . . . They expect us to find jobs for their husbands or boyfriends. . . . We interviewed a woman but she wasn't the faculty's first choice. . . . We don't hire from within and it is a good thing too. We search for the best in their field and they may not be women."

Finkelstein, Seal, and Schuster (1995) analyzed NSOPF-93 data on junior faculty (those with less than seven years of experience) and found signs that this trend may be changing.[8] Women constitute almost 41 percent of this cohort, making them one-third of junior faculty in research universities, 46 percent in doctoral universities, and 44.6 percent at comprehensive universities (p. 5). Reflecting their increased diversity, women of color constituted 37.7 percent of this cohort, a larger percentage than white women faculty, who are 34.4 percent of the "new academic generation" (p. 7). The largest increases have been in social sciences, fine arts, education, humanities, and health sciences and the smallest in agriculture and engineering, where only 4 percent of faculty are women. Other studies of junior faculty also note the higher percentage of women, mainly in nonscientific disciplines, among new hires (Blackburn & Lawrence, 1995; Trautvetter, 1995).

Faculty Roles

Women continue to spend significantly more time teaching than men (58% versus 46%) and much less time in research (16% versus 27%). The likelihood that they teach in community colleges and less selective institutions, where greater value is placed on classroom instruction, may account in part for this situation, as demonstrated by Blackburn and Lawrence (1995) and Finkelstein, Seal, and Schuster (1995). The NSOPF-93 survey showed a lower degree of satisfaction among junior female faculty, suggesting to Finkelstein et al. (1995) that in determining what constitutes fair treatment, either inequities have increased or faculty sensitivities are higher (p. 19).

8. These data are derived from a 1995 draft of *The New Academic Generation* generously provided by the authors, M. J. Finkelstein, R. K. Seal, and J. H. Schuster. See *The New Academic Generation: A Profession in Transformation* (Baltimore: Johns Hopkins University Press, 1998).

However, women faculty in both new and senior faculty cohorts reported less equity for women and minority faculty and far less job satisfaction than their male colleagues. For example, only 56.7 percent of senior women agreed somewhat or strongly that they were treated fairly in contrast to 84.3 percent of senior men, whereas 63.4 percent of new cohort women reported perceptions of fair treatment, compared to 81.7 percent of men (Finkelstein et al., p. 20).

In their study of women and minority faculty at a research I university, Olsen, Maple, and Stage (1995) found that women faculty shared similar values with male colleagues in their interest and commitment to research and scholarship. Even within the ranks of distinguished research professors, however, female faculty earned, on average, $27,000 less than male colleagues, leading them to speculate that job satisfaction had more to do with gender-based pay inequities than institutional support and recognition of scholarly productivity (p. 285).

The small number of Latina women faculty in the University of California's nine-campus system prompted one woman to comment wryly that "we should wear tiaras wherever we go." That the UC system has 78 percent white male faculty means that most committees are chaired by men and have little or no female representation. Latina women on these campuses believe they are victims of tokenism, are generally perceived as affirmative action candidates, and are expected to represent the interests of Latina students.

My own research and experience as a white woman who has taught in both research and comprehensive universities has confirmed the difficulties of balancing the demands of teaching, research, and service. In two-year and four-year colleges, faculty may have 12–15 contact-hour teaching schedules, large enrollments, and considerable student advisement and committee responsibilities. Teaching may be the major priority, but criteria for reappointment rely heavily on research potential and scholarly productivity. These conflicting demands undermine women's job satisfaction and allow few windows of opportunity for sustained research and publication during the academic year. A woman English professor teaching four sections of English composition with weekly writing assignments reported: "We are being offered an early retirement incentive and although I really enjoy teaching, my schedule is so heavy now that I am seriously thinking of accepting the package. I just don't have time to pursue my scholarship teaching four days a week, grading all those papers every evening and on weekends, doing class preparations, and working with students outside of class."

The Dual Employment Track

Women are doubly disadvantaged in assuming a disproportionate number of part-time and non-tenure track positions. This trend began in 1972 immediately after passage of the Equal Employment Opportunity Act and Title IX. In its quest for mechanisms that would expand opportunities for women, the Carnegie Council on Policy Studies in Higher Education (1975) made three well-intentioned recommendations that unwittingly encouraged the development of a dual track for men and women faculty: the appointment of "qualified women lecturers" who met institutional standards but had less substantial records of achievement in research and publication; the appointment of women as part-time and non-tenure-track teachers and administrators; and provisions for granting tenure and fringe benefits (or compensation in lieu thereof) for women hired as part-time faculty, reifying their lower status and legitimizing a dual hiring track. Within one decade, the academic labor market absorbed increasing numbers of PT and NTT faculty, and dual tracks became an accepted hiring strategy. Universities justified these schemes on three levels: they offered employment to teaching assistants, enabling them to attract first-rank graduate students and to provide them with stipends and teaching experience while meeting requirements for the doctorate; they maintained a modicum of flexibility and room for expansion or contraction in response to market demand; and they enabled management to make dual appointments of mid-level administrators who could teach one or two courses for departments lacking the requisite number of full-time tenure-track faculty to staff required courses.

The nature-nurture argument was used to justify part-time hiring as a creative approach enabling younger women to combine marriage, family, and career and to avoid the hardships of being the last hired and first fired in times of financial exigency. Part-time positions provided an expedient mechanism for responding to federal mandates. The economic and social implications of part-time employment were glossed over by provosts and deans eager to meet stated goals and timetables and to demonstrate their good-faith efforts by hiring more women for part-time positions. By 1976–77, four-year colleges and universities boasted one part-timer for every three full-time faculty. Although the proportion of full-time faculty had increased by only 9 percent, part-time faculty had grown by a startling 38 percent. The federal government and university employers put a positive spin on part-time employment, proclaiming that 1 million new jobs could be created through voluntary work sharing.

Data provided by the American Association of University Professors' (AAUP) Committee G on Part-Time (PT) and Non-Tenure-Track (NTT) Appointments, the NSOPF-93 survey, and the U.S. Department of Education's Integrated Postsecondary Educational Data System (IPEDS) all point to the increase of part-time and non-tenure-track faculty in the 1980s and 1990s. PT faculty constitute 17 percent of all faculty in the "Fortune 100" research universities, 26.4 percent in other doctoral and master's level universities, nearly 30 percent in comprehensive universities, 32.6 percent in liberal arts colleges, and 52 percent in community colleges. Fewer than 5 percent of PT faculty are on the tenure track; less than 10 percent are protected by collective bargaining agreements; and 79 percent are classified below assistant professor—67 percent as instructors and 72 percent as lecturers.

In AAUP member institutions, women constitute 43.2 percent of all PT faculty, a 54 percent increase in the past decade. Women in these institutions also constitute 45.7 percent of all NTT faculty. In contrast, men who are 62.3 percent of the faculty in AAUP institutions are also 56.8 percent of all PT faculty and 54 percent of all NTT faculty (Committee G, 1992). An NEA analysis of the NSOPF-93 data also found that in 1992, men and women NTT faculty were 22 percent or 110,227 of all full-time faculty in the United States and between 25 and 40 percent of all first-time junior faculty hires, with an alarming 40 to 45 percent filled by women (NEA, 1996). NTT faculty are in the lowest ranks: instructors (28%), assistant professors (25.4%), and lecturers (10%); more than two-thirds (68%) are in institutions that award tenure. The heaviest concentration of full-time NTT faculty is in research universities (39.5%), doctoral granting (18.5%), and comprehensive institutions (16.9%), where research is a higher priority and where women are less likely to be employed. They are less numerous in community colleges (12.3%) and private liberal arts colleges (7.8%) where women faculty predominate. PT faculty are also in the lowest ranks: more than 50 percent are instructors, and 27.6 percent are lecturers or have no title at all.

Contrary to the myth that NTT and PT faculty support continuing and adult education programs, the NSOPF-93 data show that the vast majority teach mainstream credit-bearing courses (90.7% of NTT faculty) compared to the 9.3 percent who teach only noncredit courses. Although it is argued that employing NTT faculty promotes flexibility of hiring in specialized, low enrollment fields and rapid responses to changes in the academic labor market, 53.8 percent taught between one and five courses in fall 1992, affording them a considerable presence relative to full-time faculty teaching loads. Institutions hiring women in these positions assert that the NTT's main responsibility is teaching, not research or service, but the AAUP's Committee

G found that applicant pools are often merged, and the differences in characteristics of those hired on or off the tenure track are not significant. Disciplinary differences indicate that they are most likely to be in the health sciences (28%), natural sciences (15.7%), and the humanities (12.5%), reflecting their presence in medical and professional schools and in soft-money projects. The AAUP views this phenomenon as evidence of a two-tier system in which faculty off the tenure track account for half of all new appointments.

The data are irrefutable. They show that in the past two decades, women's employment in NTT term appointments such as research and clinical nonteaching faculty, laboratory managers, and clinicians has predominated in research institutions, medical and professional schools, and soft-money projects funded with external grants and contracts where issues of diversity or academic freedom are unlikely to be raised. The cumulative impact of these data is to raise questions about the early optimism of liberal feminists that affirmative action would motivate academic institutions to lower employment barriers for women. As a young woman teaching English on two different campuses of one university stated: "For me being an adjunct is my version of 'temping,' which is why I don't stew a lot about my situation. If I think I'm not valued or I think I'm being abused, I leave and get another position. It's not difficult to get one-year appointments or adjunct assignments. Adjunct and contract work are available at this university or anywhere else. You just have to recognize that there are no tenure track appointments. Adjunct work is a choice. Adjuncts now paper all the schools in this university."

When I asked her how she came to receive an adjunct appointment, she responded:

> I was in the right place at the right time. They had hired someone with
> a doctorate and teaching experience to do the course but she didn't
> work out and in the middle of the term they called my doctoral advisor
> and I happened to answer the phone. I had already taught this course
> and offered to do it and they hired me. A committee of three faculty interviewed me; it was a pretty intense interview. I also function as an advisor for which I get paid extra. Even now, because of the exigencies of
> the budget, I don't actually know until the semester starts whether I
> have an appointment, although they tell me much earlier. It depends on
> two things—enrollments and money.

The AAUP underscores the economic advantage gained by postsecondary institutions that hire PT faculty, paying them much less than the prorated equivalent paid to full-time faculty for comparable work (Committee G,

1992). Three out of eight part-timers (38%) earned less than $20,000 in 1987; fewer than 50 percent earned as much as $30,000 in 1987; nearly one-third earned $40,000 or more. A female faculty member teaching major electives on an adjunct basis at an urban research university explained:

> Adjuncts get paid an hourly wage, that is, 45 contact hours @ x number of dollars per hour, or $2,500 to $3,000 per course. As an adjunct, I get paid 25 percent less to teach major electives than a full-time person would get. Let's face it. This is a buyer's market. If we quit tomorrow there would be another 5,000 people angling for our assignments. There is such a high level of unemployment now and no benefits. People live on credit card debt, and if you're a doctoral student, on student loans. I have friends who are $80,000 in the hole. They will never get out. Entry-level salaries for teaching jobs aren't even competitive with the public schools in this city. To live here entirely on adjuncting, I would have to teach five courses a semester. That would give me about $25,000 to $30,000 a year before taxes. I'd definitely need some other income. To compound the problem, we get no benefits, no health care, no perks at all.

Low morale among PT teaching and research assistants erupted into walkouts, grade strikes, and demonstrations at several research universities within the past year. When the University of California appealed a judge's decision in support of teaching and research assistants at UCLA, a strike was called at that campus and at Berkeley and San Diego. At Yale University, where teaching assistants have sought the right to unionize since 1980, the National Labor Relations Board (NLRB) filed a complaint against the university for its punitive action against teaching assistants (T.A.s) who held a "grade strike" in December 1996 (American Federation of Teachers, 1997, p. 3). A doctoral student teaching as an adjunct in the English and theater departments of an undergraduate college explained: "I'm completely out of the loop when it comes to departmental decision making or the life of the university in which I teach. I am always treated with respect but I am mostly invisible. Teaching evenings only compounds the problem. More women than men do this kind of work for a variety of reasons—can't move and this is the only job available, don't want to work full-time, can't get full-time teaching. The biggest abuses are salaries and lack of benefits." When I inquired why she continues to do this kind of work she replied: "I do have choices. I can leave teaching and go into some other field, something I might eventually decide to do when I finish my dissertation."

Several factors contributed to the expanded use of part-time and non-tenure-track faculty: the unprecedented expansion of higher education throughout the 1960s and 1970s, partly due to open admissions and other affirmative action policies; the consequent demands for remedial and development courses and services to meet the needs of new cohorts of underprepared students; the availability of federal and state monies for graduate and postgraduate research and development, scholarships and fellowships, and need-based student aid; and inflationary pressures to reduce budgetary commitments.

Since the Carnegie Council first recommended the use of part-time and non-tenure-track faculty, these proposals are being used to maintain a veneer of compliance with nondiscrimination regulations without the impediment of committing resources to pensions, health plans, office space, and related personnel costs. Hiring and promotion goals and timetables can be met by employing women and minorities to teach lower-division courses, to assist senior faculty with their research and teaching while fulfilling their doctoral requirements, to staff soft-money projects, and to fill non-tenure-track positions.

Observations on Data Trends

What do these trends mean? Are we moving inexorably toward a dual-track employment system in which a minority of full-time instructional faculty, supplemented by a large, temporary part-time workforce, bear the burden for academic standards? Will this structure lower the prestige and status of feminized fields, which already have higher proportions of PT and NTT faculty? And will women continue to bear the brunt of this inequitable and divisive policy? Analysts of these trends are not optimistic.

The AAUP observes that by denying professional status to PT and NTT faculty and exempting them from peer evaluation and other accountability measures, professional commitments to all faculty are diluted and the quality and stability of the professoriate are threatened (Committee G, 1992, pp. 44, 46). Bess (1997), too, in an extensive analysis of organizational conditions that accompany tenure versus contract systems in academic organizations and the associated motivational climate—the norms and values that they produce—argues convincingly that contract systems are coercive, hierarchical, and rule-based, whereas tenure systems are professional, peer-dominated, and built on trust, good will, and commonly held notions of collegiality. The American Federation of Teachers deplores this trend toward renewable term appointments. In its monthly publication, *On Campus*, the

AFT has noted the ominous parallel within the highly bureaucratized K–12 system, where school boards are seeking ways to circumvent moving probationary teachers into tenured positions. Although legislative action will be necessary to rescind tenure policies and implement three- or five-year renewable contracts, the debate has been ongoing since my own school board experience.

In 1997, two school boards in Suffolk County, New York, hired new teachers and teaching assistants on renewable contracts rather than tenure-track appointments, insisting that they sign due process waivers of their rights to file grievances in the event of dismissal. In both instances, court orders issued at the request of the statewide teachers' union, the New York State United Teachers (NYSUT) invalidated the waivers, ruling that only the state legislature can alter tenure and seniority provisions (Sandberg, 1997). Attempts by governors, legislatures, and state school boards to dismantle tenure laws for K–12 teachers have also been reported in California, Connecticut, Michigan, New Jersey, South Dakota, and Texas; these efforts are part of a political shift to the right, under the rubric of productivity, flexibility, and cost savings (Richardson, 1995). The drift into term appointments is part of a larger school choice and taxpayers' movement to privatize K–12 education, shift resources from public schools into voucher systems, and cut back on public school funding, with a potentially disproportionate impact on women, who comprise the majority of the teaching workforce.

Are there solutions to these problems? The AAUP recommends two kinds of faculty appointments: probationary and continuous tenure. It is not clear how much this differs from Caplow and McGee (1958) recommending a category of lecturer for those who choose teaching rather than research or, for that matter, how it differs from the Carnegie Corporation's experiment during the 1970s of promoting the Doctor of Arts as a nonresearch liberal arts degree for future college teachers (Glazer, 1993). The AAUP also advocates a tenure track for part-time faculty, now offered at only 9 percent of all institutions, a ceiling of 15 percent on NTT hires by an institution and 25 percent within a department, and long-term contracts that include benefits and tenure. At Long Island University, an adjunct faculty union affiliated with the Communication Workers of America is independent of the full-time faculty union affiliated with the AFT. Adjunct faculty who teach forty-eight hours are eligible for seniority status and in effect have de facto tenure. This system is potentially divisive, setting up dual tracks within departments and schools, placing heavier burdens on the diminished ranks of full-time faculty, and diverting resources from academic programs. It seems essential that better definitions be given for part-time appointments, including professional requirements, performance evaluation criteria, opportunities for conversion to tenure-track status, and inclusion in campus governance.

In reviewing data on enrollments, degree attainment, and women's participation in the professoriate, it is evident that affirmative action and nondiscrimination statutes have had a major impact on increasing numerical equity. Women students and degree recipients are becoming the new majority in academic and professional fields. If, however, we apply the proportionality rule that is now being used to assess resource expenditures in women's athletics, the gap between numbers of women students and women faculty is sizable. Coeducation in most previously all-male institutions has now been in effect for at least two decades. In such universities as Yale and Brown, women have surpassed men in undergraduate enrollments (60–40 at Yale, 51–49 at Brown). Yet, the adage "the higher the fewer" still seems peculiarly apt. Women's representation in the senior ranks of tenured faculty is below parity with men. That women are more likely to be in part-time or non-tenure-track positions is further evidence of a gender gap of major proportions in many disciplines and at many universities.

Two sets of claims within the academy will have long-range implications for women's progress: assertions of a "Ph.D. glut," which refers to the overproduction and underemployment of new doctorates in both academic and professional fields; and numerical evidence that PT and NTT faculty, many of whom are women, are becoming the new majority, as part of corporate restructuring within the university. Two sets of claims from the external environment will also affect women's status: the impact of external demands for greater accountability and productivity on the status and autonomy of the academic profession; and the negative impact of efforts to rescind affirmative action. Despite the public perception—some might say myth—that women have achieved parity with men, the data show that this is not the case for women in the professoriate. In a bureaucratized and commodified university organization dominated by corporate boards of trustees and regents, financial considerations often preempt academic ones. Although accountability and productivity are well-honed strategies for lowering costs in the corporate sector, they are grossly inconsistent with the values and attitudes associated with professionalism and faculty motivation.

The advent of a new generation of faculty with more women in its cohort may mean that barriers to women's entry into the professoriate are diminishing. But overall and gender-related percentages of tenured senior faculty have not changed significantly in the past decade. Some critics speculate that public negativism toward faculty may encourage state governing boards to demand greater accountability and productivity as measured by teaching contact hours and service to the institution and the community. In the past decade, this trend has contributed to stagnant salary growth, less research support, attacks on tenure and affirmative action recruitment, and fewer opportunities for job mobility. Its effect on women can be seen in their disproportionate representation in lower-paid fields and in less prestigious institutions, where the research-teaching dichotomy impedes career advancement, perpetuates salary discrimination and barriers to promotion, and reinforces the gender-based composition of departments and other units of the university. Ultimately, this trend reinforces disparate and dysfunctional structures and practices, as can be seen from my review of women's economic and tenure status.

3

LEVELING THE PLAYING FIELD

Tenure and Salaries

The playing field is not yet level for women faculty, who fare better in obtaining entry-level positions than in being equitably compensated or in earning tenure. These two interrelated problems contradict and undermine the stability and diversity of American higher education. It is ironic but perhaps not coincidental that as more women earn doctorates and enter the academic profession, the barriers are being raised, the criteria are being altered, and as shown in chapter 2, part-time and non-tenure-track positions are more prevalent. Tenure and salary equity continue to elude women, even though the federal courts have consistently maintained that amendments to Title VII and the Equal Pay Act "opened the door for college and university faculty" to seek redress when they thought their institutions had discriminated against them (LaNoue & Lee, 1987). As external forces encroach on institutional autonomy through budgetary, legislative, and judicial decisions, the faculty role in university governance also erodes.

Women Faculty and Tenure

Political attacks on tenured faculty are not new, but they have taken a more ominous turn in the past five years, becoming one of the most contentious policies to polarize higher education. Women faculty are not only less likely to earn full-time tenure-track positions, but twenty-five years after sex discrimination was originally banned, the proportionality rule so judiciously applied in athletics is inoperative in departmental hiring or promotion. Whether this rule would work in women's favor is a moot point. There is a serious disjuncture, however, between the educational pipeline and the university organization, making tenure an illusory target for many qualified women who are now choosing alternative professional careers. In an increasingly segmented academic labor market of full-time, part-time, and non-tenure renewable faculty appointments, the professoriate is becoming more stratified and the university more consumer-oriented. A woman faculty member who began her teaching career in 1980 with a soft-money position (while her husband began his career in the same field on a tenure-track line) but was able to work her way into a tenure-track position told me how "depressing" it was "to know that after fifteen years, the same problems are still being discussed at meetings. What bothers me is that women are being blamed for their inability to seize the moment when the problems are really more systemic. For example, in our business school, women are 54 percent of the students but only three or four of the faculty. Those women faculty never speak out on women's issues either by choice or because the business school's climate is not conducive to their active participation."

The 1995–96 AAUP salary survey of 2,200 member institutions reports that women are 33.5 percent of tenure-track faculty versus 66.5 percent for men, and that their tenure rate is only 48 percent of tenured faculty—no more than a 2 percent improvement in twenty years, and much lower than men who enjoy a 72 percent tenure rate (Committee Z, 1996). It is even more troubling, however, that 22 percent of full-time women faculty are teaching off the tenure track compared to 7 percent of men. The high variability of women's tenure status when compared to men's highlights the precarious relationship between the educational pipeline and the academic workplace. The 1996–97 AAUP survey data predict a "buyer's market" for the diminishing supply of tenure-track positions, with exceptions only in the status fields where market alternatives proliferate, such as law, business, engineering, and economics (Bell, 1997, p. 18).

By 1993, according to data compiled by the Commission on Professionals in Science and Technology (Babco, 1997, p. 154), four times as many men (169,200) as women (41,800) held full-time faculty positions in science and engineering (S&E), and twice as many men (55,300) as women (28,000) held part-time positions in these fields. These data also reveal that women faculty in science and engineering fields are more likely to be employed part time (40.2%) than full time (59.8%) compared to their male counterparts, three-fourths of whom enjoy full-time status (75.4%). Only 25.9 percent of women S&E faculty had been awarded tenure, compared to 51.4 percent of men. They were also less likely to be teaching in research and doctoral institutions, as compared to men (29% versus 43%) and more likely to be teaching in public, two-year colleges (36.5% versus 24.6%). When broken down by field, the percentage of tenured women doctoral scientists and engineers employed in universities and four-year colleges was much lower than their male coun-terparts: physical sciences (24.5% women versus 48.5% men), chemistry (18% women versus 59% men), environmental sciences (31.5% women versus 59.9% men), and biological sciences (25.8% women versus 61.8% men). In mathematics, women were more likely to obtain faculty positions in either undergraduate (24.4%) or master's level departments (22.3%) than in doc-toral ones (12.6%), accounting for only 6 percent of tenured mathematics faculty in Ph.D. programs (Babco, 1997, p. 196).

Tracing the changing tenure status of faculty by sex also revealed that be-tween 1987 and 1991, the overall tenure rate declined for both men (−0.5%) and women (−0.7%) in all S&E fields. Both men and women experienced slight increases in computer and information science, environmental sci-ence, and engineering. The only significant tenure rate increase for women was in agricultural science (+11%), whereas a large decrease occurred in chemistry (−16%) (Vetter, 1994, p. 137).

Tenure rates for women faculty in the humanities and social sciences fur-ther underscore gender disparities. Women, who account for one-third of all humanities faculty (n = 70, 100), have a 49.3 percent tenure rate as compared to men, 70.6 percent of whom are tenured (Vetter, 1994, p. 138). In the social sciences, where women account for 29.5 percent of all faculty, they have a 19.8 percent tenure rate (Babco, 1997, p. 145). The only three fields in which the majority of women faculty are tenured are English (53.4%), social work (66.8%), and health sciences (76%).

Tenure under Scrutiny

Tenure has become a moving target in higher education, and economists predict that as the tenure debate intensifies, its doom will be sealed within the next two decades. University presidents and boards of trustees are among its most vigorous critics and faculty its most ardent defenders. The Ameri-can Association for Higher Education (AAHE) and other organizations are conducting studies to eliminate, cut back, or restructure both the process and criteria for awarding tenure. The risk is great that in reforming the process and redefining the nature of faculty roles, tenure will become a mar-ket mechanism for further stratifying the professoriate.

Richard Chait, apparently an implacable enemy of tenure, views the AAUP tenure system as a cultural artifact of another era, a shibboleth reflect-ing outmoded views of academic freedom (Magner, 1997). He contends that faculty salaries tend to be lower as a result of tenure rules and that many faculty would be willing to trade flexible employment arrangements in exchange for higher salaries. In a speech at the 1997 AAHE Forum on Faculty Roles and Rewards, he offered little empirical data to support his claim that "term contracts and tenure share the same gene pool" (Chait, 1997a). Although it could be argued that men and women will both be affected by changes in tenure policy, his characterization of tenure as "the abortion issue of the academy—a controversy marked by passion, polemics, and hardened convictions" appears to frame it as a feminist issue (Chait, 1997b, p. 30). This may be colorful hyperbole, but there is little evidence to support his contention. The implication that a one- to five-year contract can provide a faculty member with the opportunity to engage in long-term research, to mentor graduate students and advise undergraduates, and to fulfill community and university service roles does not hold up under scrutiny.

In what has been called the largest antitenure wave in twenty-five years, at least twenty-three state legislatures are considering changes in tenure in public institutions. On one side are proponents such as Mathew Finkin, who argues persuasively that tenure is essential for the protection of academic freedom and the pursuit of scholarship (1996). He notes that institutions already have tremendous latitude in establishing faculty employment policies, which set the norms for research, teaching, and citizenship. Rank-and-file faculty cite institutional budgetary shortfalls and administrative overspending as more appropriate targets for cost containment. Other proponents cite its role as a catalyst for apprenticeship of new faculty, peer review, the production and dissemination of knowledge, and collegiality, arguing that without tenure, university governance would become the sole purview of professional managers to advise students, run departments, determine curriculum, and hire and fire faculty.

Tenure critics frequently cite the medical school model as proof of the viability of non-tenure-track employment arrangements. However, women faculty at medical and dental schools observe that doctors or dentists with clinical and research appointments are likely to be staff physicians at affiliated hospitals or to have lucrative private practices from which they derive their main sources of income. Similar arguments can be raised regarding lawyers who teach as adjunct faculty members and are frequently of counsel or partners in law firms, high-profile litigators, judges, or retired politicians. Their motivation may come from the prestige and visibility they gain from being associated with a particular institution, whereas the law school dean appreciates the value of their reputation and their practical knowledge of case law in a specialized field. Several women legal scholars who are also full-time tenured faculty members have made important contributions to the advancement of women's rights and the development of feminist legal theory. In their cases, it would be difficult to "decouple" their right to academic freedom and their right to tenure.

Candidates for tenure are generally required to have a terminal degree, typically a doctorate, although in the arts, for example, a master of fine arts degree is usually acceptable. The heretofore sacrosanct "Statement of Principles on Academic Freedom and Tenure" issued by the AAUP and the Association of American Colleges (AAC) in 1940 calls for a maximum period of probation not to exceed seven years, with service beyond that period constituting continuous appointment or tenure. In the 1960s, academic freedom and tenure were the employment standards in a burgeoning higher education system actively recruiting a new generation of faculty. Fritz Machlup, for example, wrote an impassioned defense of tenure in 1964 while serving as president of the AAUP and as the Walker Professor of Economic and International Finance at Princeton University. In placing the exercise of academic freedom above individual or institutional interests, he argued: "We want the teacher or scholar to be uninhibited in criticizing and in advocating changes of accepted theories, widely held beliefs, existing social, political, and economic institutions, the policies and programs of his educational institution or administration and governing board and in opposing infringements of academic freedom against any of his colleagues" (Machlup, 1996, p. 23). One hundred learned societies and professional associations endorsed the 1940 AAUP Statement of Principles on Academic Freedom and Tenure between 1941 and 1976 (AAUP, 1976).

By 1973, following a great upheaval in higher education, the AAUP-AAC Commission on Academic Tenure revisited the "Statement of Principles on Academic Freedom and Tenure" (AALS, 1994). The commission presented arguments for and against tenure, concluding that tenure "remains a major bulwark of both the academic freedom and the economic security of faculty members in higher education"—a means of attracting men and women of ability into the teaching profession, encouraging them to concentrate on their basic obligations to students and their disciplines, ensuring that judgments of professional performance would continue to be made on professional grounds, and creating an atmosphere favorable to academic freedom in research, the classroom, and the community for both nontenured and tenured faculty (AALS, 1994, p. 481).

A major shift occurred in the 1990s as professional schools, including schools of education, law, medicine, and business, reevaluated the dominant role of the arts and sciences in framing the tenure debate and conducted their own studies of faculty employment policies in relation to the demands of their changing fields. In designing standards for assessing research productivity, teaching effectiveness, and service within their professional communities, these schools have linked this process to broader efforts of accrediting and licensing agencies to redefine faculty roles and rewards in the professions.

One of the most influential documents emerged from the Carnegie Foundation for the Advancement of Teaching. In *Scholarship Reconsidered* (1990), Ernest Boyer proposed a paradigm for expanding the definition of scholarship to recognize and reward four dimensions: discovery, integration, application, and teaching. This approach resonated within the academy as institutions sought to respond to budget cuts, legislative mandates, and student needs. Admonitions that faculty workloads be increased, remedial programs be eliminated, and staffing be differentiated into clinical, part-time, and non-tenure-track positions, focused greater attention on the criteria for awarding tenure. Although Boyer and other critics referred to teaching and research as a "false dichotomy," evidence of the conflict between these two faculty roles has been endemic in a system that assigns greater status and prestige to those who do research than to those who teach, design curriculum, and collaborate with schools.

In its follow-up report, *Scholarship Assessed* (Glassick, Huber, & Maeroff, 1997), the Carnegie Foundation acknowledged the persistence of a dichotomy among research, teaching, and service as institutions continue to allocate different rewards for each aspect of faculty work: "Most college and university guidebooks implicitly suggest that different types of standards apply to different kinds of faculty work, leaving the impression that standards for research and creative work come from various disciplines; standards for teaching are institutionally defined, and standards for professional service vary so greatly by project and profession that hardly any guidance can be offered. This fragmented paradigm reflects the differential respect accorded research, teaching, and applied scholarship at most institutions. It also, we believe, helps perpetuate the hierarchy that places greatest importance on research" (pp. 22, 23).

In acknowledging the dichotomous and divergent functions of research, teaching, and service, the authors of this report express concerns that I heard repeatedly from women faculty in my visits to their campuses. In particular, junior faculty wondered about their prospects for earning tenure (1) when the standards and criteria are not clearly defined, (2) in departments and schools that are undergoing structural and programmatic changes, and (3) when grant support for research in "women's subjects" is being severely curtailed. One workload issue, for example, concerns service demands on junior women faculty. An affirmative action officer observed that "junior faculty women are caught in a double bind. Although service is given very little weight in tenure and promotion decisions, women and minorities will not be given adequate consideration if search committees, promotion and tenure committees and executive committees consist exclusively of white men. Because the vast majority of our faculty are white men, to have a woman and a minority on every committee greatly overworks women, particularly in the assistant and associate professor levels."

The Courts

Recent litigation reveals how the tenure debate is affected by nondiscrimination statutes and the judges who interpret them. From 1972, when nondiscrimination laws became applicable to faculty employment, until the Supreme Court's unanimous 1990 decision in *University of Pennsylvania v. Equal Employment Opportunity Commission,* the courts had been unwilling to interfere in the academic decision-making process. In their comprehensive review of case law on academic discrimination, LaNoue and Lee (1987) provide five case studies selected from more than three hundred judicial decisions handed down between 1972 and 1985. I draw on the work of LaNoue and Lee (1987), Leap (1993), and articles and briefs in discussing the experiences of women faculty who have sought to obtain redress through the courts. My purpose is not to analyze legal doctrine but to discuss the consequences of academic discrimination litigation as one route that women faculty have pursued to gain tenure and salary equity. LaNoue and Lee preface their case studies by noting that "when a lawsuit occurs, one of its most common forms is a claim that the institution has discriminated against an individual or class of faculty because of sex, race, national origin, religion, age, or handicap. The conflicts may be over hiring, promotion, tenure, salary, fringe benefits, pensions, or working conditions" (p. 23).

They segment the litigation process into ten stages, providing both a chronology and an analytical focus for examining changes in issues, actors, tactics, and impacts as the litigation progressed. Of the three hundred cases they analyzed, the majority were decided on procedural or jurisdictional grounds rather than on the merits, which they attributed to the court's reluctance to intervene in the academic personnel process. Their national survey of parties to these cases showed academic litigation to be a zero-sum game. Both winners and losers reported negative impacts on their finances, their personal and professional relationships, and most important, their careers. Only 20 percent of the plaintiffs won on the merits; more than half changed positions; a third changed careers or institutions; and several winners experienced retaliation. Most of the discrimination lawsuits were brought by women, the most common case being an individual white female suing a predominantly white institution. Women prevailed in only 9 of the 116 cases that were decided on the merits, however; class action plaintiffs won only 5 out of 12 cases (p. 24).

After scrutinizing recent judicial decisions in which the courts were asked to intervene, tenure critics may give inadequate attention to the anti-interventionist stance of the courts. In this context, they risk capitulation to affirmative action opponents who would remove legal safeguards that have made it possible for women to challenge discrimination in tenure decisions. Term appointments and other such alternatives may only compound an already contentious problem. For example, in 1984, in *Zahorik v. Cornell University*, the Federal Appeals Court of the Second Circuit declined to substitute its judgment in a tenure denial case, noting that more rigorous standards are applied by the courts in professional employment cases than in blue-collar cases, and reiterating "judicial deference to academic judgment and claims of academic freedom" (Gray, 1985, p. 34). LaNoue and Lee (1987) and Gray (1985) observed that as late as 1984, women pursuing tenure claims confronted courts reluctant to overturn tenure decisions and institutional reluctance to reveal the deliberations of tenure and promotion committees and documents, particularly with respect to the votes of individual faculty members and letters of recommendation. Leap also showed in his analysis of tenure discrimination cases from 1972 to 1992 that "rather than eliminating invidious discrimination against women and minorities in faculty positions, the passive stance taken by many state and federal courts appears to have exacerbated the problem" (1993, p. 182).

A recent examination of two decades of judicial decisions on tenure offers little cause for optimism (Leap, 1993). Leap's analysis of 103 tenure cases, 73 of which dealt with sex discrimination, revealed the judiciary's "almost inordinate degree of respect for the complex faculty personnel decisions that must be made by college and university administrators," the unwillingness of judges to challenge academic freedom claims "in the absence of convincing evidence of disparate treatment or impact," and the uphill battle of proving illegal faculty employment discrimination (p. 182).

In her analysis of "gender bias in academic robes," West (1994) also documents "the failure of law to promote change" in professional employment with special attention to the problems of applying Title VII to academic settings. She explodes the "unexamined myth of meritocracy," arguing that although judges may believe that standards for evaluating academic excellence are based on merit and that faculty personnel systems create a "legitimate meritocracy," the different value judgments of recruitment, promotion, and tenure committees "are based on highly subjective and personally idiosyncratic criteria" (p. 140). There is little evidence that academic politics, personal biases, and subjective evaluations will disappear if tenure is abolished, because admissions, hiring, and other manifestations of the selection process will continue to prevail in the current system. West concludes that universities have to provide women with remedies for either past or future discrimination, refocusing their energies from legal to institutional solutions, changing the ways they operate, hiring more women and considering for ladder appointments women colleagues filling nonladder appointments.

In a symposium on civil rights on campus, Swedlow also examines the myth of academic freedom which she asserts has evolved from another myth, the university as "a very special place surrounded by high walls that set it apart from the larger society and protect it from the influences of the larger society" (1994, p. 557). She argues that women "seeking to prove that they have been denied academic tenure in violation of Title VII have many obstacles to overcome" which include bringing suit against a small collegial community, responding to claims of academic privilege, and demonstrating in court that "her employer intentionally discriminated against her as an individual" (p. 558). In also noting the reluctance of judges to overrule or infringe upon academic privileges associated with the tenure system, she concludes that discrimination will continue to exist within the academy "as long as the courts allow the university to assert a privileged status and thereby refuse to honestly and fully evaluate what may be discriminatory employment rationales" (p. 558).

In *Penn v. EEOC*, Rosalie Tung, an Asian-American associate professor who, in 1984, had been denied tenure in the management department at the University of Pennsylvania's Wharton School of Business, filed an EEOC complaint claiming discrimination based on sex, race, and national origin. She alleged that after she rejected the sexual advances of her department chair, he had embarked on a campaign to destroy and defame her, filing negative letters with the personnel committee. She also contended that her research was as good or better than five male faculty who had received more favorable treatment, and that she was given no reason for tenure denial (Leap, 1993, p. 151). At the time, only one woman was tenured in the department, and in the entire business school, with more than three hundred faculty, only two faculty of color were tenured, both of them male. The university refused EEOC requests for peer review and related documents, asserting a First Amendment right of academic freedom against complete disclosure. When the Third Circuit Court of Appeals denied its claim and entered an enforcement order, the university appealed to the Supreme Court, which ruled unanimously that tenure review files were not protected by the First Amendment academic freedom privilege. In effect, the Court affirmed that access is allowed to all evidence that may be relevant in charges of academic discrimination and that ferreting out racial and sexual discrimination is a compelling government interest (Leap, 1993; Galle & Koen, 1993). Justice Harry Blackmun wrote in his decision: "Indeed, if there is a "smoking gun" to be found that demonstrates discrimination in tenure decisions, it is likely to be tucked away in peer review files. Any injury to academic freedom in addition to being remote and attenuated is speculative" (cited by Swedlow, 1994, p. 574).

Following the *Penn v. EEOC* decision, the majority of institutions responding to a survey of 1,325 U.S. colleges and universities stated that they planned to make use of peer review. As a result, they proposed clearer tenure and promotion criteria and other measures to strengthen their procedures (Galle & Koen, 1993, p. 22). In effect, this decision opened a sacrosanct policy to scrutiny, suggesting that the courts could intervene if they found the tenure process to be discriminatory.

The impact of *Penn v. EEOC* on tenure discrimination cases can be seen in another case, *Weinstock v. Columbia University,* in which a female assistant professor who taught chemistry at Barnard College from 1988 to 1994 and was denied tenure, was granted by court order access to her tenure dossier, the personnel files and tenure dossiers of Barnard and Columbia faculty, and the identities of members of an ad hoc committee who considered her candidacy. Recommended for tenure by the chemistry departments of Barnard and Columbia, the dean and president of Barnard, and a 3–2 vote of an ad hoc committee of faculty, she was denied tenure by the president of Columbia on the basis of a negative recommendation by the provost, Jonathan Cole. In ordering release of the requested documents, Judge John Keenan of the U.S. District Court asserted that "the peer review material itself must be investigated to determine whether the evaluations are based on discrimination and whether they are reflected in the tenure decision" (p. 7).[1]

1. *Weinstock v. Columbia University,* No. 95 Civ. 0569 (JFK) (S.D.N.Y. 1996) (LEXIS 16779).

Twenty tenure cases were cited in a report issued by the Boston University Faculty Council in 1996 (Leatherman, 1996). Two of these cases illustrate the problems encountered by feminists whose views are at variance with administrative attitudes toward their scholarship. Gillian Hart, an economist, and Seyla Benhabib, a political theorist, who were denied tenure at BU subsequently gained tenured positions at Berkeley and at Harvard. In each case, the faculty council report raised questions about the implications of administrative intervention in tenure decisions on faculty rights to academic freedom, citing President John Silber's speech to the board of trustees in 1993 describing the university's resistance to "political correctness and ideological fads," including feminism, deconstruction, and critical theory, in which he also emphasized that "we have not fallen into the clutches of the multiculturalists" (Leatherman, p. A21).

Three recent tenure denials illustrate the lack of adequate procedural safeguards for women who do research that goes against the grain. In April 1997, a panel of deans at Stanford University denied tenure to a historian, Karen Sawislak, despite the unanimous endorsement of her department (Wilson, 1997, p. A10). Also in April, Bonnie Honig, a political scientist at Harvard University, who conducts feminist critiques of traditional political theory, was denied tenure by President Neil Rudenstine. In this case, Professor Honig received an 18–6 departmental vote in support of her tenure bid. She was subsequently offered and accepted a tenured position at Northwestern University. A committee of fifteen women faculty urged Rudenstine to reconsider his decision, citing her growing reputation as a political theorist and Harvard's publicly stated commitment to gender equity (p. A11). Harvard, which did not grant tenure to a woman faculty member until 1948, awards tenure only at the level of full professor. The Committee for Equality of Women at Harvard, an organization of nearly two thousand Radcliffe alumnae originally organized by graduates of the classes of 1953 and 1958, has been lobbying for several years for an equal number of male and female tenured professors in the Faculty of Arts and Sciences. Despite their efforts, by 1997, women were still only 12.5 percent of tenured faculty at Harvard, compared to 13.3 percent at Stanford and 13.8 percent at Yale.

Shortly after Honig's tenure denial, a Yale University committee of deans and faculty also overruled its history department to deny tenure to Diane Kunz, a prolific scholar in international diplomacy. Following a second denial of the tenure decision, Kunz decided to take a leave of absence from academia. In her nine years at Yale, she published more articles and books than anyone else who had come up for tenure in the past thirty years.

She also bore four sons and adopted a daughter during the probationary period. In commenting on the tenure denial, she asserted that as women come up through the ranks, "the bastions are not falling" (Wilson, 1997, p. A10).

The high stakes of gender discrimination are also evident in *Wang v. University of California*. A woman who was denied tenure in the department of architecture at Berkeley alleged that the tenure committee had ignored positive comments about her by faculty and students and had misrepresented her record. The University of California settled the claim for $1 million, acknowledging that procedural errors had been made but denying Dr. Wang's allegations of sex and race discrimination (Sandler, 1996).

Another high-profile case, *Fisher v. Vassar College*, was the first major employment discrimination case since the Supreme Court's 1990 *Penn v. EEOC* decision. It was brought by Dr. Cynthia Fisher, a biologist at Vassar from 1977 through 1986, when she was denied tenure by the members of her department, which, although conceding the high quality of her scholarship and teaching, charged that after the completion of her postdoctoral studies in 1965, she had devoted nine years entirely to her family and personal life. While not specifically referring to the hiatus in her career as a negative factor, Vassar charged that during that time she "attended no meetings, belonged to no societies, and ceased all communications with colleagues in the scientific community" (cited in Klein & Pappas, 1995). After a three-week trial in 1994, Judge Constance Baker Motley ruled in Fisher's favor, finding Vassar guilty of simple sex discrimination based on her age and marital status, and awarding her $1 million in damages and attorneys' fees. Judge Motley's decision also provided a finding of gender disparity in salaries for junior women faculty.

In 1995, a three-judge panel of the Second Circuit reversed this decision, challenging Fisher's case of "sex plus marital status" discrimination. Judge Dennis Jacobs wrote in his legal opinion that "the biology department applied its standards in bad faith or applied more stringent standards to Fisher than to male candidates and single female candidates who had previously been granted tenure," having relied on collegiality as the primary criterion for its recommendation not to grant tenure. All the same, he rejected her claims of "sex-plus" discrimination (Klein & Pappas, 1995, p. 3). The twelve judges of the Second Circuit reheard the case in banc (as a whole) in June 1996. After an unprecedented one-year delay, they upheld Vassar's tenure denial by a split vote of 6–5. Indicative of the sharp divisions within the court, they issued five separate opinions. The majority held that the evidence was insufficient to show that Vassar actually discriminated against Fisher, provoking a dissenting opinion from Chief Judge John O. Newman (joined by three of the judges) in which he referred to the majority view as "bizarre" and flawed in its departure from established discrimination law and appellate court practice. In a separate dissent, Judge Ralph Winter (who is now chief judge-elect of the First Circuit) criticized the majority's "cut-and-paste analysis of Title VII decisions" (Alden, 1997). On January 20, 1998, the U.S. Supreme Court declined without comment to hear the Fisher case.

This case showed how difficult it was for women scientists seeking to combine marriage, family, and career to overcome occupational sex segregation and to earn professional recognition in a male-dominated field. In their analysis of *Fisher v. Vassar*, Klein and Pappas (1995) assert that universities, regardless of the outcome, should look on this case as an opportunity to revisit existing policies and procedures. They reiterate the hazards of judicial involvement in the "inherently subjective process of tenure review" and of reliance on "comparative evidence in proving discrimination" (p. 3). They also point out the potential impact of the Civil Rights Act of 1991, which amended Title VII and thus opened the door to jury trials in challenges to tenure decisions and to requests by plaintiffs for compensatory and punitive damages. Accordingly, they warn educational institutions to take appropriate steps to reduce the risk of potentially adverse and costly claims under Title VII (ibid.).

In her monograph on women in science, Vetter alluded to the "triple penalty of cultural, attitudinal, and structural impediments," which made it more difficult for women scientists to persevere in their professions (1992, p. 4). Consonant with the experience of Dr. Fisher, she identified the negative impact of marriage and family roles on hiring, promotion, and salaries in the sciences, particularly gaps in employment and relocation to accommodate spousal job changes. She also noted that one-third of all working scientists are women who have been in the scientific pipeline for many years but are still less likely to earn scholarly recognition—the most critical factor in tenure and promotion decisions. For example, in 1992, women scientists were only 4.2 percent of the 1,637 members of the U.S. National Academy of Science (p. 10). As of 1993, women were only 13.5 percent of all tenured faculty in science and engineering (n = 130,000) (Babco, 1997, p. 155). As I found in my research on both faculty tenure and faculty salaries, in the majority of academic and professional fields, women are less likely to gain tenure, receive recognition for their scholarship, be promoted to tenured full professors, and earn comparable economic rewards.

State Intervention

As higher education lost its most-favored status in the political arena in the 1980s and conservative state legislatures and governors pulled budget strings more tightly, academic tenure became a public policy issue. In a speech to the Boston Chamber of Commerce, James Carlin, a business executive and chairman of the Massachusetts Board of Higher Education, proposed eliminating or overhauling tenure and redistributing faculty workloads through the adoption of a dual-track career system of teaching and research professorships (Healy, 1997). Hostile politicians, seeking to hold the line on escalating budgets, criticized what they perceived as the high opportunity costs of faculty workloads. Putative abuses were held up to public scrutiny as the norm rather than the exception. By 1994, twenty-three states were exercising greater intervention into workload standards, productivity, and classroom contact hours. For example, Ohio adopted a law directing all faculty in its public universities to devote 10 percent more effort to undergraduate teaching (Committee C, 1994). At the same time, university administrators attempted to balance productivity mandates with reduced budgets and rising costs. In its analysis of faculty expectations, priorities, and rewards, the AAUP's Committee C on College and University Teaching, Research, and Publications observed: "Faculty feel caught in a ratcheting up of expectations to teach more, but continue to be evaluated primarily on publication, as these institutions continue to see faculty research as the road to institutional prestige and success" (1994, p. 36).

The "dead wood" myth also became fodder for critics of tenure, in which it was argued that faculty should not enjoy lifetime sinecures, particularly after the 1993 expiration of a federal regulation that exempted higher education from the Age Discrimination and Employment Act, a federal law ending mandatory retirement at age 70. This led to the specious argument that term appointments were actually beneficial to the institution because they brought fresh faces and new ideas into the college curriculum.

University Intervention

Until 1992, Bennington College had a policy of "five-year presumptive contracts" amounting to de facto tenure, unless it could be demonstrated that the faculty member's contribution "has markedly deteriorated or that he/she has substantially failed to perform the terms of the contract, or unless financial exigency or a change in educational policy requires its elimination" (Steiner & Zannoni, 1995, p. 98). In June 1994, the board of trustees declared financial exigency, and President Elizabeth Coleman terminated the services of twenty-six faculty, fifteen of whom were presumptively tenured. In a concurrent announcement, she announced that no new presumptive tenure contracts would be offered, compelling an AAUP investigating committee to conclude that "tenure no longer exists at Bennington College either as it is understood in the profession or as it was understood at Bennington" (p. 99).[2] The AAUP's Committee A on Academic Freedom and Tenure's investigation resulted in a strong censure of the college, which noted the absence of faculty participation in this change in educational policy: "Neither financial exigency nor program discontinuance can account for the disrespectful, petty, indeed vindictive and inhumane, manner in which the terminations were announced and carried out" (p. 101). A $3.6 million class action lawsuit filed by the aggrieved faculty is still unresolved.

Embedded in the tenure debate and in these legal actions are an important set of questions for women now entering the professoriate: What will be the impact of this hostility and rancor about tenure on the status of women and minorities? Is a market evolving in which faculty can exchange tenure for other more immediate benefits, or is that also a shibboleth? Can we design alternatives to tenure?

Recent attempts to change both tenure and salary policies at public universities have resulted in a revival of labor activism reminiscent of the 1960s and the early days of the civil rights and women's movement and casting doubt on the significance of the faculty's role in university governance. At the University of Minnesota, where the board of regents had sought to modify the tenure code to enable them to fire tenured professors whose departments were being eliminated or restructured, and to cut the base salary of individual faculty members for reasons other than financial exigency, a drive by faculty to unionize (defeated by a vote of 692 to 666 in February 1997) caused the administration to reconsider such drastic action. According to one faculty observer: "This debate, often furious, went on for over a year. It has been a battle between the faculty and the board of regents, with lots of pressure exerted by outsiders of many stripes: the governor, the business community, the media, the donors, the alumni, etc."

2. For the full text of the report, see Peter O. Steiner and Dianne C. Zannoni, "Academic Freedom and Tenure: Bennington College," *Academe* (March–April 1995), 81(2), 91–103. See also "The Meaning of Tenure," Finkin (1996), 3–65, which offers a comparative analysis of academic freedom and tenure in two cases—Rollins College and Bennington College.

A compromise agreement provided for the retraining and reassignment of faculty whose departments are terminated and for post-tenure reviews (PTRs) of all faculty. Post-tenure reviews despite faculty opposition are also being implemented in other state systems, including the State University of New York, the California State University, and the thirteen campuses of the University of Texas. A survey of one hundred public and private institutions has revealed that 72 percent of the respondents regularly review and evaluate tenured professors, either annually or at two- to five-year intervals (Arden, 1995, p. 39). Another analysis of its use confirmed its deployment in twenty-eight states that either have PTR or are considering it, mainly in the context of public sector demands for faculty accountability (Licata, 1997).

An untenured woman faculty member originally hired into a women's studies research center, with the understanding that her tenure would be decided within the center, related how the ground rules had changed in the four years since she arrived. Her story puts a human face on the tenure debate and how women preparing for tenure can find themselves in untenable situations not of their own making:

> Now there is only one tenured faculty member left in the center and the rest of us are untenured. So my tenure is being decided by eight to ten people in my department who had no say in my hire at all, and as a matter of fact are rather hostile toward the women's studies program. When I came, I was told not to worry about developing a book manuscript because all we require is three articles. At the time I thought that was really low but was actually pleased and that was a big factor in taking the job, because with three children I knew I would never make it in a really high-expectation scholarship place. Now I'm told we expect six publications. This all ties in with what I said earlier that junior women faculty aren't mentored by senior women who say they're mentoring us. Certain research projects that would have really contributed to my professional growth have been withheld from me because they wanted me to work on my publications, so that instead of helping me develop a multiproject approach, they sort of kept things away to give me time to write. On the other hand, they put me on a lot of committees. . . . I'm on a women's studies task force where I've spent two years, a waste of time because the senior people make all the decisions. I wish I'd known that three years ago because I wouldn't have put so much time and energy into it.

Her confusion about the hostility she encountered and the implications for her ability to earn tenure are mirrored in a study of twenty-three women professors engaged in feminist scholarship and women's studies at three research universities (Packer, 1990). In this study, Packer investigated the central role of departments in gender equity development in research universities. She found four stages of gender equity: closed door, in which women were not hired at all; revolving door, in which junior women faculty were hired but received no encouragement in their quest for tenure; door ajar, in which women may have earned tenure but were unlikely to win promotion to full professor; and open door, in which departments rewarded women for their involvement in women's issues, providing equitable treatment in tenure and promotion decisions (Packer, p. 53). My interviews and experience corroborate the persistence of these attitudes across a range of institutions. They also substantiate the importance of departmental stability and "open door" environments in overcoming tokenism and discriminatory practices that give the appearance of affirmative action compliance but fall short of the reality in terms of institutional goals.

Compensating Women Faculty

Salary differentials are larger for women in both percentages and actual dollars in every academic rank. More important, these differentials exist at every type of public and private institution—two-year, four-year, and graduate research universities. In fall 1994, women full-time instructional faculty on nine-month contracts (86% of all faculty) earned only 79.9 percent of men's salaries (see table 7).[3] The breakdown by academic rank was 86.2 percent for full professors, 92.6 percent for associate professors, 93.4 percent for assistant professors, and 99.1 percent for instructors. The disparity was generally greater in private (75.5%) than in public (81.7%) institutions, especially in both four-year (76.7%) and two-year private institutions (78.7%), compared to their public counterparts (80.2% and 90.2%, respectively). Disparities were also greater in 1994 than in every year since 1972, when NCES first began to disaggregate the data by gender.

By field and academic rank, disparities in both mean basic salary and mean total income were larger for women faculty in professional programs (including business, education, engineering, and health sciences) than in either arts and sciences (arts, humanities, natural and social sciences) or

3. Data are derived from two sources: Brown (1995), and *Integrated Postsecondary Education Data, Salaries, Tenure, and Fringe Benefits of Full-Time Instructional Faculty* (Washington, D.C.: U.S. Department of Education, Office of Educational Research and Improvement, 1996).

miscellaneous fields (including agriculture, communications, home economics, library science, theology, and interdisciplinary studies) (Kopka & Korb,
1996). For example, according to NCES data, women full professors in professional fields earned only 69.5 percent of the mean basic salary and 61.8
percent of the mean total income of their male colleagues, whereas women
full professors in the arts and sciences earned 87.1 percent of mean basic
salary and 81.6 percent of the mean total income of their male colleagues.

Institutional Categories

An analysis of the 1984 Carnegie survey data from three hundred universities found that sex stratification was deeply rooted in the institutional
structure, affecting hiring, promotion, and the allocation of monetary rewards across all ranks and institutional classifications and teaching fields
(Bellas, 1993, p. 74). In private universities, women have found it difficult to
obtain comparative salary data; in the public sector, the slowness to acknowledge discrepancies has led to class action lawsuits in which remedies
were sought and won only after protracted investigations and judicial decisions. In her analysis of women's economic progress in the 1980s, Goldin argues that "gender equality may be fostered by economic progress but must
be assisted by legislation and social change" (1990, p. 217). Evidence that this
is true in higher education can be seen in data analyses conducted by the
AAUP, the Commission on Professionals in Science and Technology, and
various professional associations.

The AAUP's annual report on the economic status of faculty shows the
extent of disparities between Carnegie classifications of institutions (research, doctoral-granting, comprehensive, baccalaureate, and two-year) and
between public, private, church-related universities and colleges, as well as
between high- and low-status fields (Committee Z on the Economic Status
of the Profession, 1993). As shown in table 8, data from these surveys show
the inverse proportion of women in research universities, where salaries
are higher, and public two-year colleges, where salaries tend to be lower
(id., 1996).

Although some of this disparity may be attributed to the relative increase
in numbers of women faculty at the assistant professor level and the greater
number of reporting institutions, the data illustrate that even when differences in age or years of service are considered, women faculty earn less than
men, a fact that is mirrored in the general workforce. Specific to institutional
category, AAUP data reveal that women full professors in doctoral-granting
institutions (Category I) still earn 9.4 percent less than their male colleagues,

Table 7 Salaries of Full-Time Instructional Faculty on Nine-Month Contracts: Women's Salaries as a Percentage of Men's

	1972–73 (%)	1979–80 (%)	1984–85 (%)	1989–90 (%)	1994–95 (%)
All faculty	82.7	82.1	90.6	79.9	79.9
Professors	88.2	90.4	89.0	88.8	86.2
Associate professors	93.9	95.3	93.8	93.4	92.6
Assistant professors	84.4	95.8	93.1	92.0	93.4
Instructors	90.6	96.0	91.5	93.8	99.1
Public institutions	84.2	83.6	82.4	81.0	81.7
4-year	82.3	81.3	80.4	79.6	80.2
2-year	91.7	90.5	90.6	89.8	90.2
Private institutions	78.2	77.6	75.5	77.2	75.5
4-year	78.7	78.2	76.1	77.5	76.7
2-year	92.9	90.0	90.3	95.2	78.7

Source: U.S. Department of Education, National Center for Education Statistics, *Digest of Education Statistics,* and Integrated Postsecondary Education Data System "Salary" surveys.

a figure that is virtually unchanged since 1975 (table 9). This disparity is greater in private than public Category I universities, except at the rank of instructor. Women associate and assistant professors in Category I institutions fall, respectively, 6 and 7 percent below their male colleagues. In comprehensive and two-year institutions (Categories IIa and III), the gap in salaries between women and men full professors is even more pronounced and has been widening over the past twenty years, most noticeably in public baccalaureate institutions, where disparities range from 9 to nearly 24 percent.

Disciplinary Differences

The 1996–97 AAUP survey compares salaries for the twenty highest- and lowest-paying disciplines based on data collected by the National Association of State Universities and Land-Grant Colleges. In her analysis, Linda Bell shows that in the past decade, the gap has widened significantly: "For example, professors in the top-paying disciplines received a 54.5 percent premium over professors in the bottom-paying disciplines in 1996–97 and a more modest 30.3 percent premium in 1986–87. As another way of summarizing the same general trend, the data show salaries for professors in the top twenty paying disciplines increasing by over 65.6 percent over the ten-year

Table 8 Salaries of Full-Time Instructional Faculty: Women's Salaries as a Percentage of Men's

	Category I				Category IIA			
	1975–76	1980–81	1990–91	1995–96	1975–76	1980–81	1990–91	1995–96
All faculty								
Professors	90.3	90.6	89.9	90.6	96.2	97.1	96.2	94.9
Associate professors	96.2	94.3	94.0	94.1	96.8	96.3	95.1	95.2
Assistant professors	95.2	93.0	90.7	92.8	96.1	95.9	94.0	95.3
Instructors	95.3	93.5	89.2	96.7	95.3	96.2	94.1	94.2
Public institutions								
Professors	91.2	91.3	90.1	90.4	97.0	97.7	97.3	95.7
Associate professors	96.6	94.4	94.1	93.9	97.6	97.6	95.9	95.3
Assistant professors	95.3	93.7	90.8	93.2	96.7	96.8	94.6	95.3
Instructors	95.4	93.9	90.7	97.0	95.2	96.6	93.9	93.1
Private, independent								
Professors	87.9	89.2	88.4	89.8	92.9	89.3	93.4	93.0
Associate professors	96.5	91.0	92.9	84.2	95.5	91.2	92.6	95.8
Assistant professors	96.3	94.7	91.3	78.9	95.1	92.4	92.5	96.1
Instructors	96.7	92.9	89.2	103.5	95.8	95.3	94.3	99.5
Church related								
Professors	91.2	88.9	93.0	92.5	88.2	93.0	90.9	91.3
Associate professors	91.9	91.4	94.5	94.3	91.6	92.6	93.1	93.7
Assistant professors	92.5	91.4	92.5	94.3	92.0	93.3	92.6	94.1
Instructors	92.5	92.0	86.6	95.2	95.6	93.7	93.5	97.1

period since 1986–87 and by only 31.2 percent in the bottom-paying disciplines over the same period of time" (1997, p. 18).

Although these data are not broken down by gender, the top-paying disciplines are in fields dominated by male faculty, such as law, engineering, physics, and computer science. In comparison, the bottom-paying disciplines include such female-dominated specialties as elementary education, visual and performing arts, home economics, and general studies.

In looking more specifically at the median salaries of scientists and engineers, the Commission on Professionals in Science and Technology uses several indicators to compare the 1993 median salaries of scientists and engi-

Table 8 (*continued*)

	Category IIB				Category III			
	1975–76	1980–81	1990–91	1995–96	1975–76	1980–81	1990–91	1995–96
All faculty								
Professors	94.1	96.1	93.3	94.8	100.1	97.2	94.1	92.6
Associate professors	93.3	94.9	94.8	96.3	97.1	97.6	92.8	93.9
Assistant professors	95.5	95.5	95.7	97.3	98.2	97.2	94.8	94.2
Instructors	95.0	94.5	95.3	91.4	93.1	95.6	95.2	97.3
Public institutions								
Professors	91.0	95.4	95.6	76.4	100.0	97.3	94.3	92.8
Associate professors	93.8	95.5	97.3	96.8	97.6	102.8	92.9	94.1
Assistant professors	95.6	95.9	94.7	96.4	98.1	97.6	95.2	94.5
Instructors	94.4	92.3	92.7	96.0	93.5	95.8	95.5	128.0
Private, independent								
Professors	97.4	97.1	92.7	93.8	N/A	71.3	101.7	89.5
Associate professors	96.2	96.6	94.3	96.5	89.7	83.2	91.5	87.6
Assistant professors	97.0	96.2	96.8	97.7	97.9	91.1	90.1	86.0
Instructors	95.2	96.1	97.2	100.1	104.8	95.8	93.1	87.9
Church related								
Professors	91.6	94.7	92.7	94.2	N/A	88.9	101.2	94.1
Associate professors	93.6	94.1	94.2	95.6	94.8	101.2	104.2	97.3
Assistant professors	94.8	96.1	96.0	97.3	96.6	105.3	95.3	93.5
Instructors	95.7	95.8	96.1	98.7	99.1	103.3	104.7	95.0

Source: AAUP Bulletin and *Academe*'s Annual Report on the Economic Status of the Profession.

Note: Category I through III is the typology used by the AAUP in its analysis of faculty salary data. N / A means data not available.

neers which, in addition to degree attainment, include employment sector, primary work activity, geographic area, age, experience, gender and ethnicity (Babco, 1996). Its findings show that the wide disparities in the overall median salary for women bachelor's (22% less than men) and master's (21% less than men) degree holders are primarily a function of degree field (p. 31). For example, women with master's degrees in environmental life sciences earned 30 percent less than men, but only 1 percent less in computer and information sciences. In physics, biology, economics, and engineering,

Table 9 Faculty Salaries by Rank, Sex, and Institutional Type

Rank / Sex	All				Public			
	1975–76	1980–81	1990–91	1995–96	1975–76	1980–81	1990–91	1995–96
Category I (Doctorate Level)								
Professors								
Men	24,460	33,650	63,520	74,490	24,130	33,050	61,010	70,590
Women	22,090	30,500	57,130	67,490	22,000	30,160	55,000	63,780
Associate professors								
Men	17,970	24,830	45,510	52,780	17,930	24,720	44,610	51,400
Women	17,290	23,420	42,800	49,660	17,320	23,330	41,970	48,240
Assistant professors								
Men	14,770	20,260	39,140	45,050	14,790	20,230	38,280	43,750
Women	14,060	18,990	35,510	41,810	14,100	18,950	34,760	40,760
Instructors								
Men	11,790	16,220	28,650	31,690	11,780	16,010	27,440	30,530
Women	11,240	15,160	25,560	30,640	11,240	15,040	24,890	29,600
Category IIA (Comprehensive)								
Professors								
Men	21,610	29,090	52,490	59,990	22,000	29,650	52,410	58,990
Women	20,780	28,250	50,520	56,940	21,340	28,980	51,000	56,480
Associate professors								
Men	17,060	23,190	41,960	48,150	17,320	23,560	42,050	47,600
Women	16,510	22,330	39,890	45,840	16,910	23,000	40,330	45,360
Assistant professors								
Men	14,180	19,230	35,050	40,080	14,350	19,520	35,260	39,860
Women	13,620	18,440	32,940	38,200	13,880	18,900	33,340	38,000
Instructors								
Men	11,620	15,510	26,900	31,550	11,750	15,800	27,130	31,450
Women	11,070	14,920	25,310	29,730	11,190	15,260	25,480	29,280

women either matched or exceeded the salaries of men at both the bachelor's and the master's level. Engineers reported the highest salaries regardless of degree level, gender, or ethnicity, and S&E graduates working in business and industry earned more than those in government or educational institutions.

At the Ph.D. level, a direct correlation existed among median salary, years of experience, age, and primary work activity. However, teaching, the domi-

Table 9 *(continued)*

Rank/Sex	Private, Independent				Church Related			
	1975–76	1980–81	1990–91	1995–96	1975–76	1980–81	1990–91	1995–96
Category I (Doctorate Level)								
Professors								
Men	26,390	36,240	73,780	89,250	22,360	31,450	61,200	76,580
Women	23,190	32,310	65,200	80,190	20,390	27,950	56,900	70,820
Associate professors								
Men	18,450	25,530	50,310	59,420	17,450	24,150	45,570	55,320
Women	17,800	23,220	46,730	55,980	16,030	22,070	43,060	52,140
Assistant professors								
Men	14,750	20,480	42,860	59,420	14,460	19,970	39,190	45,900
Women	14,210	19,400	39,130	46,910	13,370	18,260	36,270	43,270
Instructors								
Men	11,740	17,020	34,210	37,420	12,020	16,820	32,090	35,690
Women	11,350	15,810	30,500	38,730	11,120	15,480	27,780	33,970
Category IIA (Comprehensive)								
Professors								
Men	21,040	29,030	53,390	64,300	19,520	25,080	51,860	61,990
Women	19,540	25,930	49,890	59,800	17,220	23,330	47,120	56,590
Associate professors								
Men	16,760	22,940	41,940	50,050	15,770	20,850	41,450	48,870
Women	16,010	20,920	38,840	47,960	14,450	19,310	38,580	45,810
Assistant professors								
Men	13,960	19,070	34,120	41,030	13,370	17,640	35,020	40,290
Women	13,280	17,620	31,570	39,430	12,300	16,460	32,430	37,920
Instructors								
Men	11,600	15,110	25,040	32,980	10,880	14,180	28,400	31,010
Women	11,110	14,400	23,570	32,820	10,400	13,290	26,540	30,120

(continued, next page)

nant work activity of doctoral scientists, continued to provide the lowest median salary ($48,200), or 36.6 percent less than management, sales, or administration ($76,000) (p. 30). When salary data are broken down by "employment sector, field of degree, and sex, women teaching in universities and four-year colleges earn 80.2 percent of what men earn, compared to 83.4 percent in business and industry and 84 percent in the federal government.

Table 9 (*continued*)

Rank / Sex	All				Public			
	1975–76	1980–81	1990–91	1995–96	1975–76	1980–81	1990–91	1995–96
Category IIB (General Baccalaureate)								
Professors								
Men	18,920	25,090	45,080	53,980	19,420	26,930	45,210	52,970
Women	17,810	24,100	42,060	51,160	17,680	25,680	43,120	40,490
Associate professors								
Men	15,100	20,230	36,570	43,120	16,220	22,390	37,840	43,870
Women	14,180	19,200	34,660	41,520	15,210	21,380	36,810	42,460
Assistant professors								
Men	12,790	17,040	30,550	36,000	13,540	18,990	32,080	37,000
Women	12,220	16,270	29,250	35,010	12,950	18,210	30,370	35,670
Instructors								
Men	10,820	14,310	25,430	29,200	11,380	15,660	27,200	29,820
Women	10,280	13,530	24,230	26,680	10,740	14,460	25,210	28,620
Category III (Two-Year Colleges with Ranks)								
Professors								
Men	21,010	25,990	45,400	52,530	21,180	26,260	45,820	52,850
Women	21,040	25,250	42,720	48,620	21,180	25,560	43,190	49,040
Associate professors								
Men	17,350	22,570	38,810	43,990	17,470	22,730	39,190	44,250
Women	16,840	22,030	36,000	41,310	17,050	23,370	36,400	41,660
Assistant professors								
Men	14,520	19,040	32,260	37,890	14,620	19,280	32,590	38,100
Women	14,260	18,510	30,570	35,710	14,340	18,810	31,040	36,010
Instructors								
Men	12,140	15,830	27,450	32,990	12,290	16,310	27,730	33,130
Women	11,300	15,130	26,140	32,110	11,490	15,620	26,490	42,420

Sources: Data for 1975–76 are from Committee Z on the Economic Status of the Profession (1976, August), Nearly keeping up: Report on the economic status of the profession, 1975–76, *AAUP Bulletin, 62* (2), 195–227. Data for 1980–81 are from Committee Z (1981, August), The rocky road through the 1980s: Annual report on the economic status of the profession, *Academe, 67* (4), 210–233. Data for 1990–91 are from Committee Z (1991, March–April), The future of academic salaries: Will the 1990s be

Table 9 (*continued*)

Rank/Sex	Private, Independent				Church Related			
	1975–76	1980–81	1990–91	1995–96	1975–76	1980–81	1990–91	1995–96
Category IIB (General Baccalaureate)								
Professors								
Men	20,520	27,130	50,240	60,630	17,760	22,690	40,540	48,730
Women	19,990	26,350	46,580	56,850	16,270	21,480	37,590	45,920
Associate professors								
Men	15,660	20,570	38,890	46,120	14,310	18,890	34,000	40,370
Women	15,060	19,870	36,680	44,500	13,400	17,770	32,030	38,610
Assistant professors								
Men	13,110	16,950	32,030	37,890	12,270	16,050	28,600	34,110
Women	12,720	16,310	31,020	37,000	11,630	15,420	27,450	33,180
Instructors								
Men	11,100	14,090	25,910	30,200	10,370	13,670	24,110	28,240
Women	10,570	13,540	25,180	30,230	9,920	13,100	23,180	27,870
Category III (Two-Year Colleges with Ranks)								
Professors								
Men	N/A	24,650	36,400	42,480	13,890	17,890	30,330	35,690
Women	N/A	17,580	37,020	38,010	N/A	15,910	30,700	33,570
Associate professors								
Men	12,770	20,250	31,290	38,290	12,740	16,210	25,880	31,130
Women	11,460	16,840	28,620	33,540	12,740	16,400	26,970	30,280
Assistant professors								
Men	11,550	15,490	28,970	35,650	10,780	13,790	23,890	27,440
Women	11,310	14,110	26,110	30,670	10,410	14,520	22,760	25,650
Instructors								
Men	8,148	12,010	22,470	29,560	9,750	11,380	19,940	22,500
Women	8,540	11,500	20,920	25,980	9,660	11,760	20,870	21,370

a bust like the 1970s or a boom like the 1980s?: Annual report on the economic status of the profession, *Academe, 77* (2): 9–32. Data for 1995–96 are from Committee Z (1996, March–April), Not so bad: Annual report on the economic status of the profession, *Academe, 82* (2), 23–38.

Note: N/A means data not available.

Variations in median salaries by academic field for women doctorates, compared to their male colleagues, were: 72.7 percent in physical sciences, 81 percent in life sciences, 84.8 percent in social sciences, and 88.6 percent in computer sciences. Indicating the persistence of the gender pay gap, these differences between men and women with Ph.D.s in science and engineering fields have changed little in the nine biennial surveys conducted by the National Research Council between 1973 and 1992 (Vetter, 1992, p. 8).

In its calculations comparing the salaries of men and women faculty in psychology, the APA Task Force expressed concern that since the implementation of antidiscrimination regulations, the salaries of women psychology faculty are still not commensurate with their numbers, and even women assistant professors are being paid an average salary that is 4 percent below men at the same rank (Task Force, 1995, p. 25). In 1973, the median salary for male and female psychology faculty had been $19,400 and $17,000. Sixteen years later, these figures were $56,300 and $48,000. Women faculty consistently earned 86 to 88 percent of what was customarily paid to men over this period, although the differentials by gender were somewhat narrower in departments with graduate programs. These disparities belie institutional claims of equal employment opportunity compliance and nondiscrimination as well as the feasibility of gender-neutral standards.

The arguments over supply and demand and productivity call into question the basis for determining equity. Should women teaching in feminized fields be subject to lower salaries? Does this not constitute covert gender bias? Conversely, should faculty in male-dominated fields (e.g., law, medicine, business, science, economics) enjoy higher compensation packages than faculty in feminized fields (e.g., education, social work, nursing)? Administrators tend to take for granted the existence of these disparate policies and practices within and across institutions in such macroeconomic terms as supply and demand, without addressing the underlying assumptions of differentiated professional status that is inherent in the reward system. This inequitable system manifests itself not only in disparate salaries but in such perquisites as directorships of R&D centers, minimal teaching loads, scientific laboratories, endowed chairs, or other badges of status. Men are more likely than women to earn these benefits based on perceptions of their entrepreneurial skills, their ability to attract external funding, and to bring recognition to their schools. An affirmative action officer at a large public research university gave me her views:

> I have developed what I call the multipocket theory of rewards, which
> means that the person who is being paid from the most grants is likely

to also be receiving the highest salary. Part of that may have to do with the perception that this individual is valuable because he or she is being written into all these grants and the pockets reflect their value. But that is not the whole story, because many people hustle money. They may be patching together ones for themselves but they are being paid out of three or four different pockets. It does mean that they are able to shake loose money from two or three different sources—the multipockets theory of remuneration. Sometimes men call me to complain that some woman is getting paid more or has more perks. What I find is that these are the pedestrian dudes, the workhorses who teach the service courses, get their funding from general departmental budgets, not the hotshots who get money from outside sources. The amount of angst in these reviews tends to escalate with the amount of money at stake.

The Ph.D. Glut

Nearly twenty-five years ago, ominous warnings were issued by the Carnegie Commission on Higher Education that an oversupply of doctorates was being produced for the numbers of available positions and that by 1980 a downturn in enrollments would result in a Ph.D. glut (Cartter, 1976). Efforts were made to channel humanities doctorates into business careers, to suspend doctoral programs, and to retrench graduate schools. The doctoral juggernaut was too powerful, however, and graduate schools have continued to produce record numbers of new Ph.D.s in the past two decades. In 1989, as one-third of the faculty reached retirement age, economic forecasts shifted to predictions of shortages between 1997 and 2003 in the supply of Ph.D.s in the arts and sciences (Bowen & Sosa, 1989). Concern is being expressed once again, however, that assessments actually conducted in the 1980s may have overestimated future needs, leading to an oversupply of doctorates. It is ironic that as women doctorates increase in number, the predicted shortages have not materialized. Not only is there more competition for fewer jobs, but the accompanying monetary rewards are also declining.

The two-decade drop (1975–95) in the proportion of Ph.D.s with definite postgraduate commitments, from 69.6 to 59.7 percent, emphasizes the frailties of the academic labor market and the lack of incentives to rectify gender inequities (Henderson et al., 1996). As the cost-benefit ratio lowers the market value of the doctorate, graduate schools risk losing the most competent and promising candidates to professional schools. This is not an idle supposition given the sizable debt that students assume in completing their graduate education and the high attrition rate among doctoral students at the dissertation stage. The pay gap and the lack of employment prospects become deterrents to academic careers as graduates find it difficult to balance high-interest student loans and limited prospects for full-time, tenured academic employment. This rejection of academic careers is reflected in the strong enrollments in graduate business, law, and medical schools by women seeking better monetary returns for their educational investment. It is also implicit in the lower proportion of 1995 doctorates planning academic employment (49% for men and 60% for women) and the higher proportion of men (27%) and women (13%) entering business and industry (Henderson et al., p. 19).

Women faculty dominate in fields and institutions that are lower paying, and thus their bargaining power has not improved commensurate with their numbers. When I asked a woman administrator at a private research university the current direction of salary equity on her campus, she responded: "We're seeing some movement on salary equity. In a private university, it's not easy to get the information on salaries, unlike a public university, where they are a matter of record. The deans are now doing studies by school to identify bottom outliers, those who are way below the average. A follow-up showed that some women are getting larger than usual increments to bring them up to speed. However, the percentage of women faculty hasn't changed and a new dean who wanted to do something positive to change the numbers had it backfire on him."

A woman directing a feminist research institute at a large private university also acknowledged the quandary of changing the culture on her campus:

Now that the university is downsizing, particularly in the medical school, we are trying to protect salaries and tenure but sometimes I think these are both moving targets. For example, I have a sneaking suspicion that as women become increasingly tenured, it is going to lose its value. So not having achieved gender equity as yet, we should definitely see ourselves as vulnerable. But we have to pick our battles now. I mean between the two extremes of moderation and confrontation, there are times when you need to confront the administration on salaries with specific goals and specific demands but there are also times when you can negotiate in a more relaxed collegial fashion. But normally my experience is that there has always been a punitive confrontation before you reach the negotiations. We all want to seek consensus, but how we get there is the question.

Women's lack of power in rectifying inequities at public universities was expressed by the coordinator of a women's task force, who explained how her state's economic priorities are at cross-purposes with those of women faculty:

> The economic and political climate in this state are beyond the power of the universities to resolve. In fact, our governor considers us to be part of the problem rather than the solution. In 1991 and 1992, pressure increased to make salaries more equitable after a survey showed that the existing schedule was unfair to women. About 40 million dollars was authorized by the legislature, who are now joint partners in salary initiatives for all state employees. The plan was to allocate this money over a period of three years. However, due to a downturn in the economy in 1992, this became a one-year adjustment. Since the state had originally authorized percentage raises, women's salaries are still $3,000 to $4,000 lower than their male colleagues.

From the perspective of a female provost for faculty relations, the challenge is to establish priorities and generate solutions for different issues: "I set up a gender equity committee of faculty and professional staff and students to identify the issues affecting women and what office should be dealing with them. We are also undergoing a process to identify all women faculty who earn less than 90 percent of the average salary of their male cohorts defined by rank and years of experience. Any women making less than 90 percent are being reviewed by a faculty committee to determine whether there is any justification for the disparity. If not, the deans will be instructed to try to reduce the inequities over a period of time."

Taking Legal Action

Title VII requires that when a salary analysis is undertaken to prove discriminatory practice, it must be done for at least a class of employees including both women and men so that all factors except gender can be held constant. Gray (1988), in studying possible discrimination in faculty salaries and their negative impact on women, provides an interesting analysis of the problems inherent in the court's treatment of complex statistical issues.[4] She comments at length on the reluctance of judges "to believe the evidence of a pattern and practice of discrimination presented by statistics. There must, they believe, be some other explanation" (1988, p. 147). Class actions gener-

---

4. The AAUP Higher Education Salary Evaluation Kit initiated in 1977 provides a recommended method for flagging women and minority persons for whom there is apparent salary inequity and for comparing costs of several methods.

ally require commonality of the claims of class members and typicality of the claims of named plaintiffs as representatives of the class (Gray, 1992). Defendants frequently seek to analyze separately each rank, each school and college, or even each department. Universities have been able to assert, successfully in some cases, that decentralization of academic decision making means that members of different departments fail the commonality test. This test is also applied in consideration of cases on their merits. As plaintiffs in a class action, women faculty, for example, would be required to show that their employer engaged in a "pattern and practice" of intentional discrimination or that some ostensibly neutral policy had a disparate impact on the aggrieved parties. The underlying concept is that no individual or class of persons should be treated differently because of their sex, race, religion, or national origin.

Class action suits brought in the 1970s and 1980s led to the development of more equitable salary schedules for women in public and private universities.[5] A landmark decision, *Rajender v. University of Minnesota*, began in 1971 as a tenure and compensation claim brought by Shyamala Rajender, an assistant professor in chemistry who found herself stuck in a dead-end, non-tenure-track position in a department that had granted tenure to only one woman in 102 years. By 1978, her claim was expanded into a class action involving thirteen hundred women faculty, administrators, and academic staff members who charged the university with sex discrimination based on salary and other disparities between men and women employees. The Rajender consent decree, signed in August 1980 and in effect until 1989, cost the university $3 million and covered hiring, promotion, tenure, and salary procedures. Among its provisions, the court imposed the formation of an equal employment opportunity committee for women having the full power of a university senate committee. The Minnesota Plan, as it became known, was a unique example of a women's commission emerging from landmark sex discrimination litigation. (See chapter 6 for an analysis of Minnesota Plans I and II.) In their in-depth analysis of "Rah Rah Rajender" (as they refer to it), LaNoue and Lee comment on the personal and professional price paid by the

5. See Sandler (1984). Sandler provides timely summaries of sex discrimination complaints and court rulings on Title VII of the Civil Rights Act in *On Campus with Women*, which is published by the Project on the Status and Education of Women (Washington, D.C.: Association of American Colleges and Universities), and in a successor publication, *About Women on Campus*, also edited by Sandler (Washington, D.C.: National Association of Women in Education).

original plaintiff, Dr. Rajender, who left academia, obtained a law degree, and became a patent attorney in California. The impact on Minnesota was unprecedented, requiring three overseers to monitor every institutional policy and personnel decision affecting women faculty for the next decade (LaNoue & Lee, 1987, p. 215).

Several class actions benefited from the Rajender decision. LaNoue and Lee cite *Melani v. Board of Higher Education*, a case brought in 1976 by women faculty and administrators at the City University of New York following its reorganization as a state-operated university (p. 215). Their claims of sex discrimination in hiring, promotion, salaries, and fringe benefits were upheld in a 1983 decision. After an unsuccessful appeal by the trustees, they were awarded retroactive pay increases and salary adjustments that LaNoue and Lee speculated could eventually cost the university "in excess of $60 million" (1987, p. 39). By 1985, the National Committee on Pay Equity, a coalition of advocates monitoring state actions, reported that forty-five states had taken some initiative to deal with pay equity issues either through task forces or commissions (15 states), job evaluation studies (15 states), set-aside funds for pay equity adjustments (6 states), or other methods. In 1988, a court order awarded $1.4 million in retroactive pay and salary increases to four hundred women faculty and librarians at the nine Massachusetts state colleges.

Not all class action suits were successful, however. In 1987, the Ninth Circuit Court of Appeals ruled that the Oregon Board of Higher Education was not guilty of intentional sex discrimination in a suit brought by twenty-two hundred women faculty under Title VII (*Penk v. Oregon Board of Higher Education*). The women sought $33 million in retroactive pay adjustments, and although the court agreed that there was a salary gender gap, it denied the claim based on the women's inability to show that there had been a systematic intent to discriminate or that discrimination was standard operating procedure of the board.

Under both Title VII and Title IX, salary discrimination claims now have to demonstrate either disparate (wrongfully motivated or differential) treatment or disparate impact (intent to discriminate) or (in some cases) both. As Committee W noted (1988), however, it was not until 1986, when the Supreme Court, in addressing salary discrimination, ruled on the inequity of superimposing equal percentage raises on unequal salaries that some remedial action was taken to narrow the salary gap for all academic ranks.

A class action suit, *Varner et al. v. Illinois State University*, originally brought in 1995 by three women faculty in the ISU College of Business and later joined by 350 former and current women faculty, asks for retroactive pay increases to bring women's salaries up to par with male colleagues (Wilson, 1996). Only 43 percent of the women who brought the suit are still employed at ISU, where women constitute 29 percent of the 728 ranked faculty, 17 percent of full professors, and 41 percent of assistant professors. In 1996, at the request of the plaintiffs, U.S. District Judge Mihm issued an order requiring ISU to make available to the plaintiffs most of the contents of a range of institutional files, including "all personnel files kept at the University, College and Department level." Since the suit alleges that ISU has underpaid women for the past fifteen years, the order covered files of all faculty who were tenured or on a tenure track line at any time from 1982 to 1996 and gave the attorneys for the women faculty the right to photocopy any or all documents from these personnel files.[6] This is one instance where the court has shown little reluctance in opening confidential materials to legal scrutiny.

Universities are sometimes charged with reverse discrimination when adjusting salaries for groups of women faculty. In a recent case, *Smith v. Virginia Commonwealth University* (1994), the VCU faculty senate voted to accept the recommendation of a salary equity committee that one-time salary increases to female faculty members be implemented based on statistically demonstrated disparities showing that, on average, VCU's female faculty earned $1,354 less than male faculty. Several factors were used in arriving at this settlement: discipline, rank, tenure, years of experience, and service as department chair. A total of 172 women faculty were granted $440,000 in salary increments under this agreement. In an *amicus curiae* brief in support of VCU, the AAUP noted that when it examined salaries of the 1,419 full-time faculty to determine if equity adjustments were warranted, the average difference in salaries was actually much larger—$10,287 in favor of male faculty. Six male faculty members appealed this decision based on the statistical model employed in making the salary adjustments and on the assertion that "sex-based salary disparities at VCU may arise because female faculty members on the average are not equally productive as males" (p. 12). The suit was settled shortly before the case was to be tried. Although the amount paid to the plaintiffs is confidential, the settlement required VCU to consider individual merit in future faculty pay adjustments (Sandler, 1997a, p. 3). From a feminist perspective, it can be argued that equal opportunity

6. Communication from Vice President and Provost John K. Urice to Illinois State University Faculty, September 27, 1996.

and merit pay are contradictory remedies and that reverse discrimination charges are merely another smokescreen that sustains and masks gender-based inequities.

Fringe Benefits

In his report to the AAUP membership at its 1975 annual meeting, Joseph Duffey observed that "economic scarcity, skepticism about the future, a faltering social commitment to higher education, and ever-increasing pressures for conformity and control, as well as new demands for accountability, [were placing] greater stress upon the profession" (1975, p. 1). Three resolutions passed at that meeting—endorsements of affirmative action, the ERA, and a uniform federal policy on pension equity—were also indicative of the changing climate for women. The pension plan proposal was vigorously opposed at the time by TIAA-CREF, the dominant university employee benefits fund, which now has $200.5 billion in assets and more than 1.8 million participants in 6,100 colleges and universities, teaching hospitals, research organizations, and private schools.

Fringe benefits, which now amount to 25–30 percent of annual compensation, contribute significantly to the economic status of the professoriate. They have not come easily or automatically to women faculty. Kaplin (1985) cites numerous Title VII cases in which plaintiffs challenged the use of sex-based mortality tables to calculate the contributions to be made or benefits received by employees in employer-sponsored retirement plans. Two of these challenged TIAA-CREF. In *Spirt v. TIAA & CREF* (1982), a suit brought by a female librarian at Long Island University, the Second Circuit ruled that the use of sex-based actuarial tables by both TIAA and CREF violated Title VII. This practice had been based on actuarial computations that women tended to outlive men and thus would receive more benefits in the course of their retirement than their male cohort. In *Peters v. Wayne State University* (1982), the Sixth Circuit ruled the opposite, that neither plan's use of sex-based tables violated Title VII. A subsequent appeal to the Supreme Court was remanded to the lower court for further consideration. The Second Circuit reaffirmed its earlier *Spirt v. TIAA & CREF* decision, determining that "retroactive relief would not impose added financial burdens on employers or on the plan" (Kaplin, 1985, p. 134). Accordingly, it ordered TIAA-CREF to use gender-neutral unisex tables in calculating benefits for all persons retiring after May 1, 1980 (a date shortly after the trial court's decision), including benefits and contributions made prior to that date. In 1984, the Supreme Court declined to hear a second appeal of the Second Circuit Court's decision, and as Kaplin points out, after Spirt "it was clear that TIAA-CREF must use unisex tables for all contributions to all annuitants retiring any time after May 1, 1980" (p. 135). At the time of this decision, 85 percent of private and 40 percent of public institutions participated in TIAA-CREF.

Parental leave has long been a major issue for many women faculty and administrators, and my interviews revealed the complexity of this recurrent problem. Between 1966 and 1977, only one in six women who attended college managed to have a career and children by the time she reached middle age. Of those who had careers, half had no children and 46 percent of them earned less than the lowest 25 percent of men of comparable age and education (Sandler, 1997b). Although the federal Pregnancy Discrimination Act (PDA) was passed in 1978, recognition of the depth of women's concerns came not from the academic establishment but from the FMLA, which was passed eight years after it was first introduced in Congress and requires employers with fifty or more employees to provide family and medical leave (Dudley & DeSimone, 1994). To be eligible for leave under the act, an employee must have worked for her or his employer for at least one year and for at least 1,250 hours during the twelve-month period immediately preceding the beginning of the leave. It entitles the employee to take up to twelve weeks of unpaid leave per year to care for a newborn child or for a child newly placed with the employee for adoption or foster care; to care for a seriously ill child, parent, or spouse; or to attend to the employee's own serious illness. Despite recent White House estimates that 18 percent of eligible workers have used FMLA in the past four years, disputes have arisen regarding gender interpretations of its provisions and its discretionary nature (Dudley & DeSimone, 1994).

Gender issues relate to work-family roles, the scarcity of affordable day care, the likelihood that tenure and childbearing years will coincide, and a particular concern of women that they will be viewed as insufficiently motivated or committed to their careers. Some universities disallow leaves for childbirths that occur outside of the regular academic year. Women who take advantage of this act may find themselves subject to more demanding teaching schedules. One young woman at a comprehensive university with a 4–4 teaching load (four courses each semester) told me, "My baby was born in May, so this fall my dean agreed to give me a two-course teaching schedule and I am also directing the women's studies program. In exchange, I will have to teach two courses without pay next summer. That will mean four nights a week for six weeks when my husband will be around to take care of the baby."

The impact of pregnancy rules under Title VII has been an important issue for women faculty, whose childbearing and tenure-track years often run simultaneously and for whom elongated tenure policies are more often granted on a discretionary basis. Feminist jurisprudence lawyers have attempted "to break down legal barriers that restrict each sex to its predefined role and create a hierarchy based on gender" and "to squeeze the male tilt out of a purportedly neutral legal structure and thus substitute genuine for merely formal gender neutrality" (Williams, 1993, p. 131). To avoid charges of overt sex discrimination and disparate impact, many institutions maintain differential tenure policies that stop the clock only for the primary caregiver, generally the mother, reinforcing expectations that women will assume responsibility for work and family roles. At a research university, an associate dean asked: "There are a few issues here: What is the responsibility of the department chair? Who will monitor fathers to see that they are using their leave to take care of a baby? What about clinical women faculty in the medical school who now have to find their own replacements? Thanks to our university senate benefits committee, who picked up the ball after the family leave act was passed, we have a stop-the-clock policy that will allow women faculty to delay tenure review for one year after the birth of a child."

The PDA applies to all employers with fifteen or more employees and makes it a violation of Title VII to discriminate on the basis of pregnancy, childbirth, and related medical conditions in either employment opportunities, health or disability insurance, or sick-leave provisions (Kaplin, 1985, p. 135). It is not entirely advantageous to women in academe, however, because of the brevity of the paid leaves (normally six weeks), quite apart from the problematic nature of women's employment and tenure status in male-dominated departments. As of 1994, eleven states and the District of Columbia had enacted laws that guarantee the jobs of working women and men in both the private and public sectors when they must be out of work temporarily for family or personal medical reasons (Lenhoff & Withers, p. 2). Only six guarantee jobs after both family and medical leaves, four guarantee jobs after family leave, two only after parental leaves, one only after leave for adoption, and thirteen during periods of pregnancy and childbirth. Women faculty with whom I spoke generally believed that work-family conflicts added complexity to their professional lives in terms of mobility, economic pressures, and their ability to establish priorities without considering spousal and child care responsibilities.

Following the enactment of nondiscrimination laws, many colleges and universities eliminated nepotism rules that had made it difficult for dual-career academic couples to find teaching jobs at the same university. In visiting campuses to talk with women faculty, I discovered that institutions often have tacit understandings to block spousal hiring policies. Women view partner-relocation programs as a benefit that may mean the difference between accepting or rejecting a job offer. At one southern state university, a senior woman faculty member remarked:

> Now they say we have no nepotism laws and that was one of the first things to go with affirmative action. But we have no partner relocation for male or female spouses either. As a result it's more difficult to get faculty and keep them. That's my issue. We've been here a year and my husband doesn't have a job. My previous university had a relocation policy for female spouses, not male spouses. It's more important for women than for men. I can probably name six or seven instances like this. Those are subtle differences; not prejudicial but they have a different impact on men and women. Sometimes it ends up in one of those long-distance relationships which is okay until you have kids and then you become a commuting family. Not a good situation.

Experience dictates that compensation is still a problem in which market forces, disciplinary differences, reputational factors, and demographic variables each play a part. The overriding issue seems to be how higher education institutions can continue to discriminate against women faculty after so many years of nondiscrimination statutes, judicial opinions, collective bargaining contracts, and significant increases in women faculty.

4

WOMEN IN THE PROFESSIONS

One of the persistent cultural myths affecting women's progress in academe arises from the erroneous assumption that as more women earn professional degrees for entry into traditionally male professions, cultural beliefs about men and women in the workplace will change and occupational sex segregation will become a vestige of another era. This myth is predicated on the supposition that the most qualified candidates earn their positions by securing the requisite credentials and thereby demonstrating their mastery of specialized knowledge and skills. Occupational sex segregation, persists, however, in the traditionally male-dominated professions of law, medicine, dentistry, business, and architecture, and in the traditionally female-dominated professions of education and library science. For that reason I examine the role of economic and political forces in sustaining the gender composition of the professions and how gender politics affects women's progress in professional schools as students, faculty, administrators, and future practitioners.

Women who, like myself, reentered the full-time workforce in the sixties and seventies were optimistic about the nature and extent of occupational shifts that resulted from antidiscrimination legislation and the growth of the academic labor market. Several reforms motivated women's entry into the professions in the 1960s and 1970s: the intervention and oversight of federal and state regulatory agencies following passage of Title VII and related legislation, the adoption of female-friendly admissions criteria, financial aid programs and scholarship support targeting women and minority candidates, and most important, an abundance of revenue-producing graduate and professional schools when occupational growth had exceeded the supply of qualified candidates. Nevertheless, sex segregation continued to mar women's progress. In their analysis of this phenomenon, Reskin and Roos (1990) use a queuing metaphor as a heuristic device to highlight "the roles of power and conflict between groups with contradictory interests in shaping

occupations' composition" and the importance of such noneconomic factors as the preferences of employers and male workers in shaping labor mar-
kets (p. 308). Noting how occupations become feminized as a result of antidiscrimination laws, changing reward systems, and occupational growth,
they draw on a series of case studies and conclude:

> Most labor queues are so overwhelmingly ordered by sex that they are
> essentially gender queues. Thus, in examining how power and conflict
> affect occupations' composition, we must bear in mind that three
> groups have a stake in which sex predominates in an occupation. These
> three groups—employers (who are overwhelmingly male), male work-
> ers, and female workers—are motivated at least partly by what members
> see to be the group interest of their own sex. Importantly, they differ
> greatly in the power to pursue those interests successfully. Nonetheless,
> the operation of the labor market necessitates that various pairs enter
> into a coalition explicitly or implicitly in opposition to the third group
> [women workers]. Occupations' sex compositions result from these
> coalitions. (1990, p. 309)

Throughout the 1970s, when job growth exceeded 20 million new positions, Reskin and Roos (1990) found that women's representation increased
in only 33 and decreased in only 3 out of a total of 397 occupational titles.
NCES data also reveal the dramatic growth of graduate and professional
education throughout the past twenty-five years and the extent to which
women are becoming the major consumers of advanced degrees. In 1993–94,
of the record number of 387,070 master's degrees awarded in 1,277 institutions of higher education, more than 54.5 percent were granted to women
(Snyder, Hoffman, & Geddes, 1996). Of the 75,418 first professional degrees
awarded, 40.7 percent were granted to women. The lines between master's
and professional degrees and between academic and vocational training have
blurred considerably in the past three decades, spurred on by university faculty, professional associations, accrediting agencies, and potential employers.

In our credential-conscious society, where degrees are viewed as legal ten-
der, the postbaccalaureate master's and first-professional degree serve vocational purposes as signifiers of professional competence in fields as disparate
as medicine, law, teaching, social work, and nursing. As a result, 82 percent
of all masters' degrees are now awarded in professional fields, whereas only
18 percent are granted in academic disciplines (Glazer, 1986). This accelerated drive toward credentialism also manifests itself in the professionalization of the doctorate. As shown in table 2 (chapter 2), women's share of doc-

torates has increased from 29.7 to 38.5 percent in the fifteen years between 1979–80 and 1993–94: 37 percent of professional doctorates and 40 percent of academic doctorates. At the same time, the proportion of doctorates conferred in professional fields surpassed academic Ph.D.s, rising to 52.4 percent by 1993–94.

Diversification of the Ph.D. has also fostered women's increased participation. The 1995 Survey of Earned Doctorates includes fifty-two specialty doctorates in addition to the Ph.D. (e.g., the Doctor of Education, Doctor of Arts, and Doctor of Business Administration). A group of doctorates not contained in the survey but recognized as terminal degrees for professional licensing purposes include the Doctor of Psychology (Psy.D.), Doctor of Pharmacy (Pharm.D.), Doctor of Optometry (O.D.), and Doctor of Chiropracty (D.Ch.). They tend to offer flexible arrangements involving part-time and evening courses, distance learning, summer residencies, clinical internships, and other alternative delivery systems. Motivated by their interest in marketing these programs to new cohorts of students following passage of student aid and nondiscrimination laws, colleges and universities have actively and successfully recruited sizable cohorts of women in addition to minorities and nontraditional adult students. Women students now constitute the majority in veterinary medicine, optometry, pharmacy, and chiropracty, for example, but women faculty and administrators are not being hired or promoted commensurate with their predominance as degree recipients.

In a world dominated by multinational corporations, free trade zones, and sophisticated forms of telecommunications, to characterize professionals as autonomous practitioners denies the realities of a free market society. And yet the professions continue to sustain a belief system rooted in masculine concepts of status, exclusivity, individualism, and power. Three parties exercise instrumental control over the professions: rank-and-file practitioners, the knowledge elites (university faculty), and administrative elites (the state), each of which has regulated, systematized, and legitimized what counts as professional knowledge and each of which serves as a gatekeeper in granting access to a chosen profession (Burrage, 1984; Freidson, 1994). In these circumstances, the professional ideal is based on the male experience and on values generally associated with masculinity, perpetuating gender segregation, subordination, and tokenism. In tracing the rise of professionalism twenty years ago, Larson (1977) questioned the ability of the professions to reform themselves when "knowledge is acquired and produced within educational and occupational hierarchies which are, by their structure, inegalitarian, antidemocratic, and alienating" (p. 243). The impact of male dominance–female subordination cannot be easily separated from issues of race and class in the feminized professions—education, nursing, social work, and librarianship—where women comprise most of the practitioners but few of the executives.

As the structural properties of the labor market have changed over the past two decades and women have gained access to male-dominated professions, universities and employers have actively recruited male students into largely feminized occupations. Men account for only 6 percent of registered nurses, 15 percent of elementary teachers, 17 percent of librarians, and 32 percent of social workers. However, as Christine Williams (1995) found in her ethnographic study of men in these four professions, despite their smaller numbers, they are less likely to experience tokenism than women in male-dominated professions and more likely to benefit from a reward system that places a higher value on their participation.

Research on gender equity in the professions as in the academic disciplines assumes that by increasing the proportion of women in positions of importance, obstacles will no longer be insurmountable. They will simply evaporate. Feminist frameworks reveal how simplistic this notion may be in camouflaging the barriers to women's advancement and the pervasive impact of discriminatory practices on their progress. Evidence abounds that preferences (the favorite target of affirmative action opponents) are more likely to be granted to men than women. It has also been shown that gender, race, ethnicity, and class have an impact that often devalues women's professional preparation and credentials, despite the large number of qualified women graduates of law, medical, and business schools. Although Title VII, Title IX, and other affirmative action laws and policies have made it possible for women to gain access to the professions, the data show they continue to be undervalued and underrepresented. As feminist scholars have noted, women and minorities are being offered professional training in growing numbers, but both the professional schools and their accrediting organizations remain oblivious to the need to engage all stakeholders in curriculum and institutional reform and to adequately consider the importance of gender, race, ethnicity, and social class in their deliberations.

Medicine and Pharmacy

Medicine and pharmacy provide an interesting juxtaposition of the role of power and prestige in maintaining occupational sex segregation. Although he fails to acknowledge the important role of gender and race in the sociology of occupations, Eliot Freidson proposes an interesting paradigm of the professions in which occupational monopoly and authority become central criteria for distinguishing among occupations (Freidson, 1994, p. 115). He uses pharmacy and medicine as a case in point, noting the variation in control and autonomy between the pharmacist and the physician, both of whom are professionals with complex skills, educational credentials, and exclusive licenses by which they monopolize their work: "But there is a critical difference between them: the pharmacist can work only at the order of the physician, and thus may be seen to be in a critically different position in the division of labor. . . . Work as such, and the skills it entails, while not irrelevant, are not the focus for discrimination so much as the organized place of an occupation [medicine and pharmacy] in the labor market and in a division of labor" (ibid.).

The medical profession, according to Freidson, determines how many physicians are trained, who are selected for training, who are to be licensed, and thus who work: "In that way it has controlled the labor market for its services." It also exercises supervisory power over an array of technical workers, who often include pharmacists. Its control has been exercised not through negotiation with clients or employers but indirectly through "licensing, registering, and certifying legislation" (1994, p. 115). What does this locus of control mean for women as students, faculty, and practitioners of medicine and of pharmacy?

Medical Students

Women constitute 42.6 percent of all applicants, 42.9 percent of all first-year students, and 42.2 percent of all medical students (Babco, 1997, p. 251). Comparative data for men and women medical students are striking and demonstrate the significance of affirmative action for changing the demography of the status professions. Between 1970 and 1975, when Title IX regulations were promulgated, the percentage of women medical students doubled from 9 to 18 percent, increasing each consecutive year since then. The female application rate has also experienced a fourfold increase in twenty-five years, from 10.9 to 42.6 percent. The Association of American Medical Colleges (AAMC) data show that women are the majority of new entrants in nineteen medical schools, the proportion varying from 24 to 63 percent (Bickel, Croft, & Marshall, 1996, p. 4). As in Ph.D. programs, they tend to be older and more dependent on personal sources of support. Three-fourths of all applicants to medical schools are in the traditional 21-to-23-year-old cohort. Women have low attrition rates, and between 1972 and 1996 the percentage receiving M.D. degrees almost quadrupled from 11 to 41 percent. Women of color accounted for 14.5 percent of all women medical school graduates by 1996 (6.8% Asian, 5.4% African American, 2% Latina, and 0.3% Native American). To some extent, women's participation was countered by a slight decline in male applicants and entrants, paralleling similar trends in doctoral education: an increase in the proportion and number of women in graduate education and a period of relative stasis for men. By 1994, an equal percentage of men and women gained acceptance to medical schools (38%), and although still in the majority, men now account for 61 percent of all graduates, a decline from 87 percent in 1974 (Bickel, Galbraith, & Quinnie, 1995).

The AAMC's annual surveys of twelve thousand incoming and graduating medical students reported that women students had less parental support, experienced greater anxiety and depression, and were less satisfied with the adequacy of medical school instruction. In comparing the experience of women medical and law students, they found that "shortage of time, deadlines, and difficulties in a relationship with a partner were particularly stressful for women" (Bickel, 1988, p. 1580). On the plus side, women medical students experienced comparable academic performance rates to men, and they expressed greater commitment to primary care and to practicing in socioeconomically deprived areas (ibid.).

Residents

The distribution of women residents after graduation provides another important indicator of women's career development as physicians. In 1988, more women chose primary care than surgery residencies. By 1995, there was a total of 32,694 women residents, a number constituting 34 percent of all residents and representing a 12 percent increase since 1980; they were concentrated in internal medicine (26%), pediatrics (16%), family practice (12%), obstetrics/gynecology (9%), and psychiatry (8%). Only 5 percent of all women residents were in general surgery, and their presence in surgical subspecialties remains below 1 percent (ibid.).

Faculty

After completing their residencies, more women enter the professoriate, the proportion increasing from 15 to 26 percent between 1975 and 1996. The relative proportion of women and men at each rank remains unchanged, however (Bickel, Galbraith, & Quinnie, 1995, p. 2). By 1995, medical schools had 20,635 women faculty, compared to 61,583 men faculty. Women also have strong terminal credentials: 28.3 percent hold both a Ph.D. and another health degree; 60 percent have an M.D. or joint M.D. / Ph.D. (Bickel, Galbraith, & Quinnie, 1995). Eighty percent of them are white (Babco, 1997, p. 256). Women of color constitute a greater proportion of minority faculty than men of color: 8.7 percent are Asian, 3 percent Latina, 2.5 percent African American, and 0.1 percent Native American.

Women medical faculty account for 9.5 percent of all full professors and 20.6 percent of associate professors, compared to 32.3 percent of assistant professors and 44 percent of instructors. Of the 20,234 tenured medical school faculty, only 14.4 percent are women (Babco, 1997, p. 255). Their sense of isolation is exacerbated, however, because the number of women full professors who are in positions of potential power and authority average only 17 per medical school, including non-tenured and basic sciences faculty, compared to 158 men at that rank (Bickel, Croft, & Marshall, 1996). The largest percentage of women faculty continues to be in pediatrics (39%), public health (38%), obstetrics (34%), family practice (33%), and dermatology (31%). The smallest percentages are in surgery and orthopedics.

Several studies done by the AAMC and by individual medical schools highlight some of the problems women medical school faculty experience. They cite one study of a 1976 cohort of faculty showing that after an average of eleven years on a medical school faculty, only 5 percent of women compared to 23 percent of men achieved the rank of full professor despite similar preparation for academic careers (Bickel, 1988, p. 1582). Another study observed that women were more likely to start their teaching careers with fewer academic resources (e.g., research assistance, laboratories, and time for research), to author fewer publications, and even when adjustments were made for productivity factors, to be promoted less frequently (Bickel & Quinnie, 1992, p. 4). A woman faculty member attributed part of the problem to a low level of awareness: "When jobs come up or committees are appointed, nobody thinks about trying to distribute things equitably for women and there is a feeling that some jobs or assignments are distributed as perks to men but not women."

The chair of a medical school task force on the status of women commented on another aspect of the problem: pay inequity between men and women medical school faculty:

When our first report came out in '93 we found big discrepancies between the salaries of women and men in the basic sciences. The department chairs were told about this and to make every effort to correct it.

However, unlike some other schools, the dean never got the resources or came up with a plan to correct these problems. Instead, women went to their chairs and said, "I'm not being adequately compensated." The chairs agreed but said, "We don't have the money to fix the problem" or "When you apply for your next grant, change your salary request." Women began to realize that if you're not getting as much money, it affects the amount you receive in your pension. If you've been under-paid for 20 years, what you get when you start drawing your pension will be less.

When I asked about the current situation, she replied: "A few men were sympathetic and would say, "My goodness, it never occurred to me. My daughter could be affected. We have to do something about this." That was in 1993; when we looked at it three years later, the salary discrepancies were worse. The percentage increase just wasn't enough, and the men who were hired in those years got higher salaries that strengthened the disparities."

The 1997 *Chronicle of Higher Education* survey of compensation at 479 private colleges and universities (Lively, 1997) reveals that the five highest-paid faculty in research universities are typically in the medical schools, where clinical income is often reported as part of faculty compensation. For example, in twenty-six of the twenty-seven medical schools in the survey, be-tween three and five of the highest-paid employees below the presidential level were male deans or male faculty of medicine (pp. 34, 35). According to a senior woman faculty member, the problem in private medical schools may be too many options rather than too few:

We need salary ranges and structures because without them how can you say you are being treated fairly? Now it's ad hoc and everybody is free to negotiate the best deal. There is no standard and department chairs have free reins. Somebody has to monitor hiring and salary nego-tiations as well as promotion and tenure. This situation has been atten-uated by massive changes in the health care system with HMOs and medical school-teaching hospital mergers. Women like myself are paid by the hospital, not the medical school, so we may have more flexibility in our employment arrangements but our commitment to the students is going to be different than women who teach and do research full-time.

A woman section chief felt that better mentoring has to be given to women residents. She cited her own experience: "When I was offered this administrative job, I still had another year on my research fellowship. A man might have negotiated a lot more than I might because I don't think that women have been taught those management skills. Now I try to let students know that if they are going to apply for a certain kind of residency, they should be aware of the discrimination they are going to face, to do their homework and know how to negotiate. Most women are just so grateful to be asked. We have to change our attitudes, to learn these skills, and then maybe the climate that created this belief system will also change."

Department Chairs

According to the AAMC's *Directory of American Medical Education,* 1996–97, about 150 women chair medical school academic departments (85 in clinical and 65 in basic science), an increase of 58 since 1992 (Bickel, Croft, & Marshall, 1996). There are 308 division chiefs, with 27 percent in pediatrics and 34 percent in internal medicine. Few women serve as chairs of surgery, public health, psychiatry, or ophthalmology and none as chairs of otolaryngology, orthopedic surgery, or neurology (ibid.). Their highest representation as department chairs is in microbiology and family practice (10% each) and pediatrics (9.5%). Of the Council of Teaching Hospitals CEOs, only 10 percent are women. A woman administrator explained:

> Department chairs sit on the Council of Department Chairs, which makes all academic policy for this medical school, controls clinical revenues, and decides who is hired and promoted, how much they are paid, and the distribution of perks or rewards. No man is going to relinquish that kind of power and influence to a woman in his department. We have one woman department chair in parasitology—that's all. When we replaced the chair of pediatrics, they never made any effort to get a woman and that was an obvious place. When we got a new chair of ob-gyn, one of the women called the dean and said, "You know. I don't think any women were considered." He replied, "Oh yes, I interviewed a woman" and he wasn't even on the search committee.

Her explanation evokes Freidson's claim that the medical profession exercises supervisory power and control, which enables it to maintain an occupational monopoly and the division of labor. The experience of women at the upper echelons of the medical school hierarchy reveal that gender as well as race are important variables in determining who exercises collegiate control within the medical profession. It also implies women's continued disenfranchisement in positions of power and authority.

A pivotal problem in this context relates to the paucity of women medical school deans. Here, their experience parallels that of women as academic leaders in other professional schools. It resonates in the myth surrounding their absence from the sources of power in medical schools and teaching hospitals, that is, as department chairs and deans. Trying to shift the power base can be risky, as deans vie with department chairs for clinical revenues to support medical school operating budgets. One consequence is to make it more difficult for women to increase their representation as either chairs or deans of medical schools. Only five women serve as medical school deans (3%), an increase of three since 1988. One, Bernadette Healy, came to her post from the directorship of the National Institutes of Health, where women are now one-third of all tenure-track appointments, 10 percent of laboratory and branch chiefs, and 18 percent of section heads (AAMC, 1996). The reward system has channeled women into the more commonplace positions of assistant deans (118), associate deans (131), and in a few cases, senior associate deans (18).

In March 1996, a blue-ribbon committee appointed by the AAMC to review women's status in academic medicine issued a report that highlights the slow pace of change in academia (AAMC, 1996). Twenty years after affirmative action for women and the establishment of the AAMC's Women in Medicine Program, the committee found that despite women's high academic productivity, the playing field is not level. Women medical faculty continue to be "significantly less likely than men to climb the academic ladder"; to experience isolation within their departments and schools; to be the victims of cultural stereotypes and overt and covert sexism; to get minimal support in trying to juggle professional demands and family responsibilities, including maternity leaves, child care, and elder care; and to withstand the challenges of mixed mentor relationships including different standards for men and women trainees, and the difficulty of finding a mentor in the first place (p. 1). A young woman faculty member explained some of the conflicts faced by women in her generation:

> I think for most women faculty in their thirties and forties, the issues are more related to the toll it takes on your career to be part of a married couple: the problem with balancing careers, getting paid maternity leave, tensions with marriage and families. These issues are even greater than getting hired. Being pregnant is a hindrance. If you went visibly pregnant to the AMA meeting, that's an obstacle. I think if you want a

paid maternity leave, that's a problem. We're now talking about lifestyle issues which can have a real impact on your career. If you work at a research university and you are expected to publish a great deal, they ought to make allowances. The year you have a child, they shouldn't expect you to publish that much or they should stop your tenure clock.

Part-Time and Non-Tenure-Track Appointments

The issue of part-time and non-tenure-track appointments is common in medical schools. It is part of a much larger problem involving the multiplicity of categories used to define this cohort and administrative decisions to cut costs by replacing tenure-track with term appointments. Medical schools adhere to two main categories of faculty employment: basic science faculty, many with combined M.D.-Ph.D. degrees, who teach the first two years of required courses and who are likely to be employed in full-time, tenure-track positions; and clinical faculty, whose roles combine teaching and clinical services, and who are much more likely to be off the tenure track and not to be required to conduct or publish original research in peer-reviewed journals. In its 1996 status report, the AAMC noted that almost three-fourths of the 127 medical schools have a separate track for clinical faculty, whose primary responsibilities are patient care and teaching; 81 percent adhere to non-tenure-track appointments for these faculty.

The AAMC has reported that seventy-one medical schools in the United States and Canada provide for "full professional effort" (FPE) faculty and thirty-two have specific non-tenure-track policies for such faculty. Some medical schools euphemistically refer to FPE faculty as having "limited full-time status," "full status/partial load," and "reduced period of responsibility." The AAMC also noted an increase in the use of alternative tracks with such titles as "clinical educator," "clinical scholar," and "clinical pathways." Almost half (49%) provide multiyear contracts with the title of "professor of clinical medicine" or "clinical professor of medicine." According to the AAUP's Committee A, clinical faculty members have grown tenfold in the past thirty years, almost entirely due to their role as income producers. Funding for these largely non-tenure-track clinical appointments is dependent on the faculty's ability to generate income to pay for their services and extra income for other medical school purposes. This expectation by medical schools has led critics to suggest that "by the year 2000 tenure may have become a vestige of the past, at least in clinical departments" (1996, p. 41).

The AAUP expresses its concern about the impact of medical school dependence on external funding, warning that it does not augur well for either basic science faculty, nonphysician tenured and tenure-track faculty researchers in their institutions, or for their institutions. Committee A states that this trend threatens to "divert faculty dedication and effort away from teaching and university service and toward research and patient care to maintain their income and status" (p. 42). It also detects the negative impact of supporting two classes of non-tenure-track and tenurable faculty with consequent "instances of abridgement of academic freedom and due process in medical schools" (p. 42).

Having sounded the alarm, the AAMC reported that by 1996, more than two-thirds (71%) of all medical schools were using the Carnegie Foundation model to modify faculty rewards, reconceptualizing scholarship to include publication of case reports, book chapters or reviews, software development, formal evaluations of teaching performance, speeches and professional presentations, and model clinical service programs. In 1988, Harvard Medical School issued new guidelines for scientific research productivity, including a recommendation that five papers be the maximum requirement for appointment as assistant professor, seven for associate professor, and ten for full professor. More recently, it appointed an ombudsperson to handle complaints from women and minorities.

These variations in status, while increasing flexibility, add to the confusion surrounding part-time and full-time faculty status in medical school and deter women's equal participation. The AAMC, noting that female faculty often choose non-tenure or clinical tracks, challenges medical schools to seek more creative solutions to resolve women's problems related to their parental responsibilities. It also questions whether women physicians would be able to take advantage of such options as tenure extensions if those arrangements serve to remove procedural safeguards and career ladders. Should there be more equitable stop-the-clock tenure policies, part-time alternatives for research training, protected time for research among clinical faculty, and other mechanisms to assist women in managing constraints and opportunities?

We tend to think that women in medicine are a rather select group, who, having made it through medical school, internships, and residencies, are impervious to the kind of gender bias that most ordinary women are exposed to over the course of their careers. When I asked a woman medical administrator to predict the future prospects of women in academic medicine, she commented:

> Change is very slow. Unfortunately you get worn down. You want to move onto other things. I think the whole society still has to change.

I hope for my granddaughters things will be different. I have two daughters—one left a law firm because she thought she would never make partner. They were very anti-family. If a woman became pregnant they decided she wasn't partner material. When you are in medical training, there are other issues, the tenure clock and the biological clock ticking at the same time. Women ask me, "What's a good time to have a child?" I say there is never a good time, you decide when you're going to do it and then you manage. They do worry about it, though. Some schools allow an extra year for tenure to relieve some of that pressure. Here, they've changed it from seven to ten years. I'm not sure this is so good because instead of being promoted in seven years, they delay it three more years. And then there is still the issue of non-tenure-track titles. We just lost a woman psychiatrist to another medical school because our department gave her a nothing title—research associate professor—and no possibility of tenure down the road.

Sexual Harassment

Recent studies of the medical profession have begun to address the issue of sexual harassment and its impact on women medical students as well as women faculty. An AAMC investigation of women medical school graduates identified several concerns: sexist remarks (29%), denial of opportunities (10%), lower evaluations (11%), and unwanted sexual advances by school personnel (13%) (Bickel & Quinnie, 1992, p. 19). A survey by the Association of Women Surgeons cited one-half of the respondents having experienced some type of sexual harassment or gender discrimination during or after their residencies. An American Medical Women's Association analysis of its members in Massachusetts found that in one year, 54 percent of the women physicians responding to its survey had encountered some form of sex discrimination (ibid.). Another survey to measure faculty, house staff, and student perceptions of gender fairness at the University of Virginia School of Medicine found that women faculty in particular perceived their environment as significantly more inequitable and sexist than their male counterparts (Hostler & Gressard, 1993). Actions taken by the Committee on Women at UVA motivated its administration to implement changes to improve women's status, including the recruitment of more female faculty as mentors and role models.

At the Johns Hopkins University School of Medicine, a survey of full-time faculty on gender-related issues found that one-half of the women faculty had experienced isolation, exclusion from informal networks, and systematic discrimination amounting to obstacles to their career success (Stobo, Fried, & Stokes, 1993, p. 349). Two-thirds of the women and one-fourth of the men felt that women faculty were less likely to be nominated for promotion earlier than the mandated date; only one-third of the women faculty felt welcomed as members of the Hopkins scientific community; fewer than one-third of the women faculty could identify a mentor; and the environment in the Department of Medicine was less than optimal for recruiting and retaining them as faculty. As a result of these findings, multiple interventions were designed to organize a departmental task force, disseminate survey results, hold faculty-run workshops, and establish an Office of Organizational and Faculty Development. These investigations reveal many stereotypes that haunt women in the professions, especially gender-based expectations that carry over into social and professional interactions in professional practice, defining in a sense what is and is not acceptable behavior. They also challenge gender-neutral definitions of professionalism. Women who attempt to break out of those stereotypes often become targets of criticism and enmity and thwarted in their attempts to reach the pinnacle of their careers.

When Dr. Frances Conley, the only female full professor of neurosurgery in the United States, resigned from Stanford University School of Medicine in 1991, her allegations about a pattern of sexual harassment in the medical school and the promotion of a colleague whom she accused of sexist behavior focused national attention on the problem of sexism and hostile environments in medical schools. Her complaints had been met with silence and inaction by the medical school dean, but the media response was immediate and widespread, bringing into the open the pervasive problem of sexism toward women in academic medicine and raising questions about the impact of gender discrimination on the medical profession. As a result, the Stanford Medical Center appointed the Faculty Senate Committee on Sexual Harassment and Gender Insensitivity and a Hospital Task Force on Discrimination, conducted workshops on gender issues; and demoted the acting chair of neurosurgery, Dr. Gerald Silverberg. Dr. Conley then rescinded her resignation and in 1997 she was elected chair of the faculty senate. She was recently quoted in the *Chronicle of Higher Education* to the effect that six years after her protest, the atmosphere in her department remained "fairly hostile" and the situation for women in the academy was still problematic.[1]

1. Footnotes, *Chronicle of Higher Education,* June 13, 1997, p. A12. This episode was reported in both the *New York Times* (1991) and *Chronicle of Higher Education* (1991). See also Frances Conley, *Walking Out on the Boys* (New York: Farrar, Straus, & Giroux, 1998).

One of the most influential cases in antidiscrimination law occurred at the University of Iowa Medical School. Jean Jew, a Chinese-American woman, had joined the faculty as a postgraduate associate in the Department of Anatomy after receiving her M.D. in 1973. For fourteen years, she was the subject of malicious rumors that she was having a sexual relationship with the male department chair who had recruited her and that she was receiving preferential treatment as a result. "The slander campaign was extensive, reaching students throughout the College, as well as staff and faculty in other parts of the University" (Chamallas, 1997, p. 249). When Dr. Jew applied for promotion to full professor, the vote was 5–3 against her on the grounds that she had not established her research credentials, implying that her collaboration with the male department chair was costly to her career. In response to her complaint, the university tried to discredit her. Chamallas, in her analysis of the case, argues that the university's resistance to her claims of sexual harassment was "predictable given the dominant attitudes and structural conditions at the College of Medicine and in the larger University community" (p. 255). After a decade of litigation, she won in the courts, changed public opinion in the university community, and was retroactively promoted to full professor, given back pay, and compensated for her state defamation judgment and pending civil rights claim. Chamallas suggests that tokenism, sexual and racial stereotypes about Asian women, and sexism in academic medicine were contributing factors in this case (p. 256). The university took no disciplinary action against the offending professor whose actions had brought her to file a complaint in the first place, and it refused her request to transfer her tenure line to another department.

These high-profile cases motivated the Accreditation Council for Graduate Medical Education to add a new condition for reaccreditation: "Sponsoring institutions must provide residents with policies and procedures whereby complaints of sexual harassment and exploitation may be addressed" (Bickel & Quinnie, 1992, p. 24). Women with whom I spoke declared the continuing need for assertiveness and awareness training, management skills, grievance policies, mentoring, and reviews of working conditions.

Strategies for Change

The AAMC periodically reviews the status of women and minority faculty and staff as part of its professional commitment to increase diversity in medical schools. These reviews not only focus attention on how recruitment, promotion, and tenure policies encourage or deter women's advancement. They also lead to assessments of the impact of changes in health care management, affirmative action, and age-based retirement laws, the decline in federal and state capitation aid for research fellowships, and state and trustee demands for greater accountability. An AAUP report on tenure in medical schools noted the increased dependence of faculty on income from outside sources (70% from faculty practice plans) and the increased reliance for academic tenure on "scholarly research and publications, and less on teaching and service" (Committee A, 1996, p. 40).

The most recent AAMC report on Women in Medicine (WIM) (Bickel, Croft, & Marshall, 1996) acknowledged that "as economic forces threaten to dilute the academic missions of medical centers, the challenge of building a career in academic medicine is growing for both sexes. . . . A faculty appointment might well be thought of as a 'hunting license,' it is up to the individual to make the most of it" (p. 62). Also, on the basis of several well-designed cohort studies, women continue to be disadvantaged when compared to men "in garnering resources and equitable compensation and in gaining promotion and tenure" (ibid.). The report cites a number of institutional initiatives to improve women's status in academic medicine, including resource centers, formal mentoring, faculty professional development programs, and medical leadership training. It also cites the need for greater access to research grants, partner and spousal relocation programs, and the need to prime chairs as agents of change rather than as protectors of the status quo. It refers to Johns Hopkins University's proactive and interventionist role, increasing the number of women associate professors from four to twenty-six between 1990 and 1995. Admittedly, some of the motivation for actively recruiting and promoting women medical faculty originated in response to charges of sex discrimination and sexual harassment in medical schools (p. 6).

An important feminist strategy has involved organizing women's associations, task forces, specialty organizations, electronic discussion groups, and scholarly journals. The AAMC's Division of Institutional Planning and Development publishes *Women in Medicine Update,* periodic documents, and an annual statistical report on the status of women in academic medicine. It also conducts special sessions for women medical school faculty and staff in conjunction with the AAMC annual meeting and an electronic discussion group on the Internet. Specialty organizations such as Women in Neurology (WIN), Women in Neurosurgery (WINS), and the Women's Dermatological Society increase networking possibilities. Within medical schools, task forces to study the status of women and remove existing inequities have been organized at New York University, Yale University, and other medical schools. Women's health networks, such as the *Harvard Women's Health*

Newsletter, also disseminate information on women's health issues and resources. These networks have been instrumental in focusing public attention on diseases affecting women and in gaining greater resource support for basic scientific research on women's well being.

Pharmacy

Women have made tremendous gains in the past two decades as degree recipients in pharmacy and now earn two-thirds of the professional doctorates (D. Pharm.) and half of all Ph.D.s in Pharmacy. The availability of federal capitation grants linked to full enrollments motivated colleges of pharmacy to begin to recruit women students in the 1970s. Women were attracted by the possibility of higher incomes and higher status than in such traditionally female-dominated health professions as nursing and physical therapy (Phipps, 1990, p. 122). Although all health professions received more federal funding for their training programs, Phipps observed that men lost interest in becoming pharmacists as the rewards declined, the opportunities for self-employment dwindled, and work became more routinized (p. 121). As a result, between 1960 and 1988, the percentage of women pharmacists greatly increased, from 8 to 32 percent.

Higher education has been more resistant than the marketplace to the feminization of its pharmacy schools. Only six women serve as deans compared to seventy men; women comprise 22 percent of assistant and associate deans. Also paralleling other professions, women account for less than a third of all pharmacy faculty (32%), only 15.9 percent of them with tenure. They are 7.3 percent of full professors, 25.3 percent of associate professors, 48.1 percent of assistant professors, 49.5 percent of instructors, and 36.4 percent of lecturers (Babco, 1997, p. 263). Although salaries have increased, there is still a gender pay gap. Women pharmacy faculty earn less than their male colleagues, regardless of type of school, discipline, rank, or years of experience (Babco, 1996, p. 204). They also report lower salaries at almost every stage of their career, with the exception of 6-10 years in rank at the associate professor level. Those with higher degrees earn higher salaries, but women with Ph.D. degrees in pharmaceutical science still earn only 80.4 percent of the salaries of men in academia and 77.8 percent of men in industry.

Dentistry

Equity issues comparable to the situation of women in academic medicine also pervade academic dentistry and may be more critical because of the 10 percent decline in dental school enrollments within the past twenty years and the consequent loss of research, internship, and clinical teaching opportunities. The dental profession was historically male-dominated until affirmative action laws went into effect in the 1970s. Once the traditional barriers were lowered, women's application rate soared from 1.5 percent in 1970 to 36 percent by 1994. Enrollments and graduation rates grew proportionately, and by 1995–96, women accounted for 36.7 percent of all dental students and 36 percent of the thirty-six hundred graduates from the nation's fifty-four dental schools. As in other professional schools, student growth is not reflected in either dental school faculty or administration, where sex segregation has meant that virtually no women serve as deans of dental schools and only 20 percent of the full-time, tenure-track faculty are women—15 percent of associate professors and 5 percent of full professors.

Since 1982, the American Association of Dental Schools (AADS) has been conducting a survey of dental educators, collecting and analyzing data on dental school faculty by gender, ethnicity, and academic status. These data show that for the past ten years, the percentage of full-time and part-time basic and clinical faculty in dental schools has been declining steadily. Women were by 1995–96 only 18.2 percent of all dental school faculty, with an almost equal proportion serving in part-time and non-tenure track positions (19.8%) as in full-time, tenure-track positions (20%). Men, on the other hand, account for four-fifths of both part-time and full-time tenure-track faculty. Not surprisingly, women dental school faculty are younger: 55 percent are less than 40 years old, compared to 27 percent of men; 17 percent are at least 50 years old, compared to 42 percent of men. Also, as in medicine, women are more likely to teach full-time (44% compared to 36% of men). Whereas 85 percent of the 10,680 dental school faculty are white, minority females constitute 24 percent of all women faculty, compared to 10.2 percent of men faculty (Babco, 1997, p. 261). Of eight clinical specialty areas accredited by the Commission on Dental Accreditation, women are more likely to be found in pediatric dentistry, periodontics, and dental public health. Their representation is relatively low in the most prestigious specialties of oral and maxillofacial surgery, orthodontics, and endodontics.

According to AADS data, women in academic dentistry are also more likely to be instructors than men (29% versus 14%) and assistant professors than men (37% versus 31%). They are less likely to be full professors (6%) than men (22%) and associate professors (17%) than men (26%). They are also much less likely to have been granted tenure (17%) than men (30%). A longitudinal analysis of promotion rates of junior dental faculty between 1985 and 1989 found that academic credentials had a greater influence on promotion rates than other factors (AADS, 1995). For example, three out of four faculty who were promoted in the four-year period held both a clinical doctorate and another doctorate. This would seem to indicate that women need better mentoring about the importance of advanced academic degrees. It also indicates, however, the need to assess promotion and tenure policies and how these affect women's chances to challenge the occupational monopoly held by male administrators.

Law

Although women doctors have played a major role in focusing attention on women's health care, women lawyers have influenced almost every area affecting women's rights. One strategy has been the development of statewide gender bias commissions to collect and document allegations of bias in the judiciary and lobby for judges who would interpret, apply, and enforce women's rights legislation (Soll, 1993). Not surprisingly, these commissions revealed pervasive patterns of discrimination embedded within ostensibly gender-neutral judicial practices. The New Jersey Supreme Court Task Force on Women in the Courts published the first gender bias report in 1983, spurring the formation of blue-ribbon gender bias commissions by thirty-five state judiciaries, the District of Columbia, and two circuit courts by 1993.[2]

The ABA, state, and local bar associations also established commissions on the status of women and on racial and ethnic minorities in the legal profession. Lynn Schafran, director of the National Judicial Education Program to Promote Equality for Men and Women in the Courts and adviser to gender bias commissions, succinctly sums up their findings: "Individually and collectively these reports provide overwhelming evidence that gender bias permeates the court system and that women are most often its victims" (1990, p. 28). They interpret gender bias as stereotypes or misconceptions about the nature, roles, and socioeconomic realities of women's lives, and the devaluation of women and tasks traditionally perceived as women's work. The root of these problems can be found at every level of the legal profession, beginning in the law schools, where future generations of lawyers and judges obtain their introduction to legal practice. In her analysis of these commissions, Kathleen Soll foresees an essential role for law schools as well

---

2. See Soll (1993), 634, for a listing of the thirty-five state task forces. For an analysis of New York State's task force, see also Schneider (1988).

as bar associations and the judiciary in implementing task force reform recommendations (p. 646).

Laurel Bellows, who chairs the American Bar Association's (ABA) Commission on Women in the Profession, asks: "Why, in 1996, must we debate the existence of gender bias in our courts, the merits of family friendly workplace policies and the need for gender neutral evaluations?" (Bernstein, 1996, p. A9). Why indeed? In its 1996 report, the ABA commission cited pervasive problems that negatively affected women entering the legal profession—subtle and blatant structural and attitudinal barriers in the workplace and in the professional schools, complacency among women's rights advocates, consensus that the problems have been solved, and the perpetuation of stereotypes and myths about the culture of the professions and the role of its leaders. Acknowledging that its earlier predictions had been overly optimistic, the commission called for an immediate resolution to gender inequities, sexual harassment, and rank and file disparities on every measure and at every level of experience in the legal profession. It likened women lawyers' progress to the experience of Sisyphus, the mythical Greek king whose interminable struggle rolling a rock uphill it portrayed as the embodiment of women's strenuous efforts to "take control of their own professional destiny" and reach the pinnacle of the legal profession (ABA Commission, 1995, p. 3).

Lawyers

Professional associations can be instrumental in improving women's position in law as in other fields. In that context, it is encouraging to note that in the past few years, the ABA elected its first female president and its first female chair of the House of Delegates (1995), and the New York City Bar Association elected its first woman president (1996). Nevertheless, ABA data on women lawyers in the pipeline indicated that those who had graduated from law schools between 1967 and 1990 accounted for only 18 percent of law firm partners, compared to 45 percent of their male cohort. The National Association of Law Placements subsequently reported that by 1994, women accounted for 37 percent of lawyers admitted to private practice but only 12.9 percent of partners in nine hundred law firms listed in its directory of legal employers and only 11 percent of partners in the major firms (ABA Commission, 1995, p. 11). Although the majority of firms (86%) permit part-time work schedules, the Commission on Women in the Profession speculates that women lawyers may also be reluctant to take advantage of the Family Medical Leave Act, fearing reprisals in compensation, recognition, or advancement. An analysis of the gender composition of American law schools reveals a great deal about the reasons that power continues to elude women in the legal profession.

Faculty and Deans

Women law faculty and administrators constitute a very small subgroup of the knowledge elite: only 1 percent of the aggregate of women lawyers compared to those in private practice (70%), government (12%), and public interest law (6.5%) (ABA Commission, 1995). Women are 44 percent of all law students and earn 38 percent of the thirty-nine thousand J.D. degrees awarded annually. They account for 45 percent of all new entrants to the bar and 23 percent of all lawyers, a figure that is calculated to jump to 40 percent by 2010 (ibid.).

Only 28 percent of the 8,231 professionals in the nation's 178 law schools, they are clearly—and here is the crux of the problem—in the minority of academic leaders in legal education. They do not reach the top rungs of the career ladder in proportion to their numbers as students, scholars, administrators, or practitioners. Merely fourteen women (8%) serve as deans (an increase of one since 1992), compared to one-third (33%) of all associate deans, more than two-thirds (69%) of assistant deans, and 44 percent of head librarians (p. 8). In the classroom, the situation is not much better: women are only 19.3 percent of all tenured law faculty and 17 percent of full professors, compared to 40 percent of associate professors, 52 percent of assistant professors, and 67 percent of lecturers. At the most prestigious law schools, where only 20 percent of women professors teach high-visibility first year courses, the numbers are worse: 5 percent at the University of Chicago, 11 percent at Yale University, and 18 percent at Harvard Law School (p. 7). Epstein (1993) notes that women law faculty frequently teach feminized specialties such as sex discrimination, family law, and feminist jurisprudence rather than mainstream aspects of legal practice (p. 434). She also expresses concern that these faculty constitute 40 percent of contract-status or non-tenure-track faculty, including 68.4 percent of non-tenure-track teachers of legal writing, an area that has become a "new kind of women's job" in law schools (p. 436).

Women tenure-track faculty face a similar predicament to women's studies faculty or to women in other male-dominated departments—the perception that feminist legal theory, methodology, and content ascribe to unacceptable professional norms. The dominant feminist perspective in legal education views gender bias as the adherence to stereotypes or misconceptions about the nature, roles, and socioeconomic realities of women's lives and the devaluation of women and tasks traditionally viewed as women's work. Women legal scholars point out the root cause of these problems at every level of the legal profession, beginning in law schools where future generations of lawyers and judges obtain their introduction to legal practice (Guinier, Fine, & Balin, 1994; Menkel-Meadow, 1988). Rhode argues persuasively that sex disparities are narrowly interpreted, seldom focusing on "the intersection of gender with other patterns of subordination such as class, race, ethnicity, age, and sexual orientation," reinforcing attitudes that deny their existence and fortifying the illusion that collective problems have been resolved (1991, p. 1734). She urges women lawyers to expand their definition of "the no-problem problem" in a society that views gender inequality as natural and to build support for broader social initiatives than the current standard.

The AALS Special Committee on Tenuring and the Tenure Process (1994) observed what seems to be a universal commentary on professional school policies and practices—the disproportionate weight given to teaching, research, and service in the tenure process. The centrality of scholarship was evident in the committee's analyses of law school policies, whereas teaching excellence and public service were cited by only a few. Teaching excellence addressed the same broad concepts of subject matter mastery, ability to communicate material, and capacity to inspire student learning. Public service was apt to be viewed as the preserve of tenured faculty; standards for scholarship encompassed both the quantity and the quality of publications. In one case cited by the committee, a law school required two articles for awarding tenure and promotion to associate professor and two further articles for promotion to full professor; all four articles "must have been published or accepted in "journals which are considered the equivalent or better than either the school's law review or its other journals" (p. 490).

Three areas of feminist legal scholarship are of particular interest in suggesting how curriculum decision making affects women law students in particular: feminist jurisprudence, critical legal studies, and critical race feminism. Although examples of this scholarship may be published in mainstream law journals, alternative outlets occur in women's law journals published by Harvard, Yale, Stanford, and other prestigious law schools.

Feminist jurisprudence was staked out in the 1970s as a feminist critique of law and legal institutions (Menkel-Meadow, 1988). Its influences emerged from outside critical legal theory—in feminist philosophy, sociology, psychology, literary theory, and social history. It seeks to move away from the normative model of legal education in which Socratic pedagogy in the analysis of relevant facts and issues in legal cases has traditionally been the sole resource materials for developing students' understanding of various areas of the law and the skills of legal reasoning. Feminist jurisprudence examines law and society from women's point of view, seeking to redefine both teaching and learning as a more critical, problem-based process in which students are encouraged to study and analyze legal issues affecting women, such as pornography, abortion, violence against women, and sexual harassment, and to develop more reflective skills in addressing these problems (Epstein, 1993).

Critical legal studies (CLS) also originated in the 1970s as a radical movement of predominantly white male law faculty influenced by French postmodernism and focusing on critiques of individualism, deconstruction of legal doctrine, and Western cultural values. CLS scholars used deconstruction to reveal the extent and impact of power relations embedded in supposedly neutral legal concepts. In an excellent review of the intersections and divergences of feminist theory and critical legal studies, Menkel-Meadow (1988) also questions the efficacy of the traditional Socratic method, "a hierarchical notion that the teacher knows all but refuses to share it" (p. 77), arguing that it reinforces competition, individual achievement, alienation, passivity, and lack of self-confidence among women students. She favors feminist pedagogy as a means of teaching empowerment, fostering greater flexibility in legal analysis, and building trust, collaboration, and engagement with students.

Feminist CLS scholars focused specifically on the "hierarchy, passivity, depersonalization, and decontextualization of present-day legal education," challenging the "inherent logic of the law, the indeterminacy of doctrine, the role of law in legitimating particular social relations, the illegitimate hierarchies created by law and legal institutions, in short, 'the politics of law'" (Menkel-Meadow, p. 63). In 1985, the first feminist CLS conference was held, co-sponsored with feminist jurisprudence scholars. Resistance to CLS erupted at Harvard Law School in 1987, when Clare Dalton, a feminist law professor and one of the leading proponents of CLS, was denied tenure while five male colleagues received it. Of Harvard Law School's fifty-nine tenured professors, three were African-American men and five were women. Dalton filed sex discrimination complaints with the EEOC and the Massachusetts Commission against Discrimination, and her case became a divisive tenure confrontation involving sit-ins, press conferences, and demonstrations (Leatherman, 1993). Six years later, in 1993, Harvard settled out of court with Dalton, who allocated her $260,000 award to establish and direct a Domestic Violence Institute at Northeastern University, where she is now a faculty member. In 1997, Dalton was named Woman of the Year by the Women's Bar Association of Massachusetts, which eulogized her as an instrument of positive social change, which is one of the main tenets of critical legal studies (Cotts, 1997).

Critical race feminism emerged initially from the critical race studies (CRS) work of Harvard Law School's first African-American professor, Derrick Bell, and other minority scholars who believed that the civil rights movement had stalled and that the use of amicus briefs, marches, and litigation had become ineffective in eradicating de facto discrimination. CRS scholars adhere to the view that white elites tolerate or encourage racial progress for minorities only if this process also promotes white self-interest and that civil rights laws permit racial progress at a pace acceptable to the broader society. Harvard's failure to hire and tenure people of color had prompted a student protest in the spring of 1990. Bell announced that he would forego his salary until Harvard tenured an African-American woman. In 1994 he resigned from the Harvard faculty. In his book of reminiscences, *Faces at the Bottom of the Well*, he observes that the barriers to tenure were "complex, interwoven, and infinitely flexible [borne of] white superiority, faculty conservatism, scholarly conformity, and tokenism [in which] standards of qualification subtly play the role once overtly performed by policies of racial exclusion" (1992, p. 139). "The guardians of Harvard's scholarly reputation" replicated the status quo by selecting only those whose interests and ideology mirrored their own (p. 139). In her essay, "Ain't I a Feminist?" Celina Romany criticizes gender-essentialist analysis for not being inclusive enough and for failing to challenge the macrostructure of inequality or to support "the emancipation of all women," including women of color (1997, p. 20). Critical race feminists reject the theories of Gilligan and other white feminists, whom they perceive as failing to give space and voice to multiple accounts of the feminine experience or to emphasize the key variables of race, ethnicity, and social class.

Gender Bias

Citing gender barriers, gender bias, and gender discrimination in "the structures, practices, and attitudes of the legal profession," the ABA Commission (1995, p. 4) criticized the male-defined organizational cultures in law schools, where men are more likely to influence curriculum decisions as well as to chair promotion and tenure committees. It also found evidence that by late 1995, "blatant discriminatory and harassing behaviors by professors" had abated but not disappeared (p. 6). Women law students told commission interviewers about professors who discourage their participation, denigrate their performance, bait them, and refuse to recognize or rectify overt male student hostility toward them (p. 6). The commission cites a survey of sexual harassment in law schools estimating that 50 percent of women faculty experienced some form of sexual harassment in their academic preparation or their career, but only 22 percent reported the incident to a university authority, and of those who issued formal complaints, less than one-third were successful (1995, p. 37).

The impact of gender bias and hostile environments on women law students is vividly chronicled in a longitudinal ethnographic investigation conducted over a period of five years at the University of Pennsylvania Law School (Guinier, Fine, & Balin, 1994). At the time of this study, seven of the thirty-five faculty were women (five with tenure). In analyzing the experience of the university's women law students from 1987 to 1992, the authors reveal an institutional climate of gender hierarchy and exclusion based on perceived gender differences, exacerbated by "pedagogy, hierarchy and male-dominated faculty." By the end of the first year, this climate had a palpable impact on their academic performance, and by graduation it resulted in lower rates of achievement than their male cohort, as reflected in grade-point averages, class rank, law review editorships, and job offers. The authors attributed this dissonance to women students' difficulties in accommodating their values and learning styles to male-defined law school cultures. They also observed that within three years, the most successful women students learned how to survive and prosper in a dysfunctional learning environment by "becoming gentlemen" in the competition for grades, status, recognition, and successful legal careers (p. 65).

Their findings suggest that problems encountered by women lawyers originate in law schools, where, as Rhode points out in her essay on women and professional roles, conventional classroom hierarchies, authoritarian structures, and traditional legal education encourage extremes of passivity and aggressive competition but discourage independent thought, creativity, and individuality, with the result that these patterns of dominance are reinforced in authoritarian and paternalistic workplace relationships (1994, p. 50).

The study of women at the University of Pennsylvania Law School stirred my memories of advising women students on the criteria for graduate school admissions. Young women who had been "A" students throughout college did well on their LSATs, gaining admission into good law schools. They were intimidated and somewhat repelled by the competition between men and women students for grades, status, and recognition. The velvet ghetto that awaited these women belied the promise of successful legal careers in major corporate firms. As Guinier, Fine, and Balin observe (p. 69), preparing students to think like lawyers conditions them for hierarchical relationships in which male-female is equated with teacher-student, as preparation for the partner-associate, judge-counsel, and lawyer-client roles that women law students soon learn are basic to "effective lawyering."[3] These patterns are mirrored across the professions as graduate students become socialized to the expectations of their mentors, supervisors, and eventually their bosses.

Strategies for Change

The first and most obvious remedy for the lack of gender and race equity is to fully implement Title VII, hire more women faculty, promote more assistant and associate deans to full deanships, create more female partnerships in major law firms, and appoint more women to the judiciary and to executive positions (Harrington, 1994; West, 1995). As members of the president's cabinet at a typical research university, law school deanships carry many perks as stepping stones to academic presidencies (16% of all university CEOs are lawyers), foundation directorships, judicial appointments, legal consultancies in high-profile cases, and spokespersons for the profession. Therefore, the significance of appointing women as law school deans cannot be underestimated.

A second and related remedy is to assess law school procedures regarding promotion and tenure. In 1988, in her charge to the AALS Special Committee on Tenuring and the Tenure Process, president-elect Herma Hill Kay observed that: "The risk factor inherent in entry level appointments to law faculties may be relatively higher than in some other disciplines because potential law faculty candidates, unlike new Ph.D. graduates, typically are not trained either as teachers or as scholars" (AALS, 1994, p. 477). She also commented that challenges to academic judgments in the courts under Title VII and related state laws "signaled a need for law schools to examine their own standards and procedures to satisfy themselves and their critics that both the tenure decision and the tenuring process deserve confidence" (p. 478).

3. See Weiss and Melling (1988), for an ethnographic study of a cohort of women graduates of Yale Law School; see also Guinier, Fine, & Balin (1997).

The third remedy is to change the institutional climate by addressing issues related to sexual harassment and overt gender bias. In 1986, the Supreme Court unanimously ruled in *Meritor v. Vinson* that the definition of sexual harassment should be extended to include the concept of hostile environment: "an environment so offensive or hostile as to interfere with a person's ability to work," or in the case of the university, an environment that interferes with a student's ability to learn or otherwise participate (Sandler & Shoop, 1997, p. 9). A 1993 *National Law Journal* survey cited a high incidence of sexual harassment but a low report rate because of the potential damage to the complainant's career.

The fourth remedy is to increase the numbers of women of color in law school faculties and law firms. According to the ABA Multicultural Women's Network (cited in ABA Commission, 1995), minority women encounter "persistent, pervasive and unique barriers to career opportunity, growth, and advancement." Being a woman of color becomes a "double negative in the legal marketplace"; minority women attorneys must repeatedly establish their competence as professors, peers, and judges, finding themselves ghettoized into certain practice areas. Because of misconceptions and negative stereotypes, they also face problems in cracking the glass ceiling—in getting professorships, judgeships, and high-profile law partnerships.

A fifth remedy is to have written policies that inform employees of their rights and responsibilities, types of unacceptable behavior, and the mechanisms in place to handle complaints and adjudicate grievances under Title VII as well as state and local laws. Women in legal practice also cite a lack of client networking opportunities or assignments to high-profile cases and prestigious firm openings (ABA Commission, 1995). Media preoccupation with assistant district attorney Marcia Clark's hairdo and Armani suits during the O. J. Simpson trial or negative portrayals of women lawyers on television and in films illustrate the ways in which the media have perpetuated stereotypes—questioning women's motivation and level of commitment, and highlighting personal problems. Epstein suggests that these fictional representations reflect societal ambivalence toward women lawyers (1993, p. 425).

The ultimate remedy, however, will be to increase the number of women in positions of power and influence. Women in high-profile positions gain media attention that tends to overstate their representation. Two precedent-setting appointments, made by Presidents Reagan and Clinton when they selected Sandra Day O'Connor and Ruth Bader Ginsburg as Supreme Court justices in 1981 and 1994, have given women the promise of unprecedented access to judicial power and authority. Despite these appointments and the fact that 31 percent of President Clinton's appointments are female, including the first woman secretary of state in U.S. history (a former Georgetown University professor with a Ph.D. in economics), women are still underrepresented in proportion to their numbers within the electorate: 10 percent of the nation's judges, 10 percent of the U.S. Senate, 11 percent of the Congress, and 11 percent of partners in the largest law firms.

In 1992, when forty-seven women won seats in the U.S. House of Representatives, the winners predicted a new trend in American politics. Their conjecture proved overly optimistic, however. Although more women than ever registered and voted in November 1996 and record numbers ran high-profile campaigns for governor and the Congress—215 for House seats, 50 for Senate seats, and 7 for governorships—women made a net gain of only two seats in the House and one in the Senate. Ironically, in 1992, California voters elected two women senators but rescinded affirmative action in 1996. Maine also has two women senators and New Hampshire its first woman governor. Arizona gained its first woman governor in the summer of 1997, when Governor Fife Symington was convicted on seven counts of fraud. The secretary of state, Jane Dee Hull, was appointed to complete his term and was subsequently elected to a full term.

Business

Women's participation in business has been activated by increased job opportunities and, in the past twenty-five years, greater access to both undergraduate and master of business administration (M.B.A.) degree programs. Women's share of business degrees is growing, and in 1993–94 women earned 47.6 percent of all bachelors degrees granted by 1,310 schools, 36.5 percent of all master's degrees granted by 674 schools, and 28.2 percent of all doctorates (D.B.A. or Ph.D.) granted by 114 schools. It is worth noting that their share of doctorates has doubled since 1979–80, when they earned only 14.4 percent.

Women have made the greatest inroads in the field of accounting, where they now earn the majority of degrees. Between 1971 and 1993, their share of bachelors' degrees grew from 10 to 55 percent, at the master's level from 7.8 to 45.7 percent, and at the doctoral level from zero to 46 percent (Babco, 1997, p. 101). In contrast, men's share of accounting degrees peaked in the late 1970s and has remained relatively stable since then (Flynn, Leeth, & Levy, 1996, p. 29). As a result, the number of women accountants almost quadrupled from 190,000 to 731,000 between 1974 and 1994, whereas the percentage of men accountants grew by 17 percent, peaking in 1982 at 733,000 (ibid.). Their representation in the highest ranks continues to be relatively low, according to Flynn et al., who speculate that women are still subject to sex stereotyping and discrimination in major accounting firms. Even though they are more than half of all employed accountants, they are only 13 percent of partners and, in the largest firms, only 5 percent (p. 31). A gender-integrated accounting profession will occur only when business schools have a diverse teaching force that is more sensitive to the needs of women students and ends disparities in salaries, internships, and networking for women graduates.

Women faculty have as dismal a situation in business schools as in other professional schools. According to the American Assembly of Collegiate Schools of Business (AACSB), which has accredited 306 business schools in the United States and Canada, women account for only 4,465 (19.6%) of the 22,738 faculty in business schools: full professors, 8.6 percent; associate professors, 18 percent; assistant professors, 30.4 percent; and instructors, 41.4 percent (Babco, 1996, p. 249). Lower salaries for women parallel their lower numbers: the mean salaries for women who are full professors is 88.1 percent of men's salaries at this rank. A cover story about the Harvard Business School in *Business Week* (Byrne, 1993) points out that only 5 percent of Harvard's ninety-one tenured business faculty are women. The ratio at other top-ranked business schools does not appear to be much better, however: 12 percent at Northwestern's Graduate School of Management and 9 percent at the University of Pennsylvania's Wharton School. To make its business school more "woman friendly," Harvard has announced the formation of the Committee of 200 Fund to develop more inclusive case studies presenting women in management decision-making roles (Hays, 1997).

At an urban university that was founded as a business college but has since expanded into a comprehensive institution, a woman faculty member explained the imbalance among education, nursing, business, and law:

> The business school is the 800-pound gorilla; it has twice as many majors and gets most of the resources, even though liberal arts teaches the bulk of the core and breadth courses on this campus. Most of the business faculty only teach three courses but the regular load in liberal arts, education, and nursing is 4–4. On the other hand, there is only one tenured woman in the business school, and another one who was turned down a few years ago is suing the university. It's very controversial be-

cause a lot of people felt she was well qualified. Most of the women are in liberal arts, the school of nursing, and the school of education. But we're always worn down in relation to business, which gets most of the resources.

When I asked another woman about salary issues on her campus, she responded:

This place is extremely sexist. Women's salaries are a potentially hot issue. We get paid a lot less than business faculty. Every year they release statistics and say what is the median salary for every professor in each school, and every year we are several thousand dollars less compared to business. It might even be 10,000 dollars less. And they get more money for research. There's now a gender equity group of older women faculty who are trying to get the administration to release the statistics. I think the problem is that resources have traditionally gone to business and law, which have mostly men faculty, so now they have to give more money to liberal arts, education, and nursing because that's where most of the women are. Go look at their offices. I mean it looks like a corporate suite. It's much fancier; that is so typical.

The difficulty in achieving greater diversity in business as in other fields is evident in the comments of a woman teaching accounting at a suburban university: "The department rather than this business school is my view of the world, so I tend to see things in those terms. It's interesting how decentralized universities are—our worlds revolve around our departments."

As in other professions, more flexible management training programs attracted women candidates in the 1970s and 1980s, and the M.B.A. became the requisite credential for competing in a much larger applicant pool. This situation was reversed in the 1980s and 1990s, as mergers, downsizing, and outsourcing to subcontractors lessened the demand for highly trained candidates. In several fields, occupational sex segregation in job assignments has contributed to women's underrepresentation. Two case studies of women in banking and public relations demonstrate that women's progress on the corporate ladder has been more apparent than real (Reskin & Roos, 1990). In public relations, many women hold entry- and middle-management positions; they tend to find themselves channeled into technical jobs while their male colleagues control the management positions (Donato, 1990). In banking, "horizontal and vertical segregation [has] generated sex differences in performance, prestige and income," and as a result, women's credentials have hindered their progress out of retail branch management into the power centers of senior executive and commercial banking positions (Bird, 1990, p. 157).

The AACSB has taken two major steps toward redefining the nature of faculty work in schools of business and how this should be rewarded in modifying tenure and promotion criteria. In its 1997 accreditation statement, it calls for recognition of the "intellectual contributions" of faculty that more clearly reflect each school's mission. This new criterion broadens the notion of scholarship to encompass "a core set of responsibilities of higher education in business . . . [to] improve management theory and practice, and support the present and future quality of instruction at all institutions" (AACSB, 1991, p. 29). Basic and applied scholarship and instructional development provide three categories for organizing the faculty member's portfolio in support of the school's own mission:

> *Basic scholarship:* defined as the creation of new knowledge through publication in refereed journals, monographs, scholarly books, chapters, proceedings, and papers presented in a variety of venues;
>
> *Applied scholarship:* interpreted as "the application, transfer, and interpretation of knowledge to improve management practice and teaching," including publication in professional journals, presentations, public, trade, or in-house journals, book reviews, and papers;
>
> *Instructional development:* viewed as "enhancing the educational value of instructional efforts of the institution or discipline" and encompassing texts, publications in pedagogical journals, written cases, instructional software, and publicly available materials describing the design and implementation of new courses (p. 29).

AACSB guidelines distinguish different categories of schools of business: those with undergraduate and graduate degree programs but no doctorates, those with either one or the other, and those which emphasize graduate business but also include undergraduate majors.

The second AACSB initiative relates to post-tenure review, confirming its possible deployment in state institutions in twenty-eight states and recommending its implementation "to assess the level of teaching effectiveness, institutional development, and scholarship" (Morreale & Licata, 1997, p. 3). This in-depth analysis summarizes models now in use in nineteen business schools and outlines six strategies for their implementation. Although the guide purports to realign faculty roles and to address the "dead wood" argument, it does not comment on the paucity of women business school faculty. As a recent analysis of General Management Admissions Council (GMAC) data revealed, the decade-long decline in enrollments of women M.B.A. students may be due in part to the lack of gender diversity in business schools (Marks, Dugan, & Payn, 1997). Among the deterrents to women's participation cited in this study were a lack of mentors and role models, inequitable treatment of women in the workplace, along with concerns about recruitment, training, development and promotion, and a lack of acceptance of women's voices.

Architecture

Of the 13,079 B.F.A., M.F.A., and Ph.D. or D.F.A. degrees conferred in architecture in 1993, women earned 36.5 percent: 35.8 percent of all bachelors, 38.4 percent of all master's, and 31.1 percent of all doctorates. By 1996, however, women accounted for 27.2 percent of the 2,963 faculty in 120 schools of architecture; of these, only 42 percent were full time and 58 percent were part time.[4] Only 18 percent of women faculty are tenured, compared to 38 percent of men. Women are also underrepresented in leadership positions: of the 220 deans, associate deans, and department chairs listed in the architecture directory, only seven deans, four associate deans, and ten department chairs are women. In contrast, women account for two-thirds of all architectural librarians (McCommons, 1994).

A 1990 survey of 110 architectural departments and schools concluded that women continue to be marginalized in the architectural profession by the dominance of "the star system and the gendering of genius," academic traditions that perpetuate hierarchy and competition in the profession, and the field's "myopic vision," compared to more interdisciplinary and multidisciplinary programs and practices (Ahrentzen & Groat, 1992, p. 98). The gendered construction of architectural departments is evident in the apprenticeship approach to disciplinary mastery, which enshrines a coach-student relationship that is hierarchical and narrow in its interpretation of artistic creativity. Architectural and art history, as the authors point out, emphasize the study of great works and great monuments, "isolating and objectifying designer, group and work [and reinforcing the idea of] a male centered curriculum from a male perspective" (p. 99).

4. These data were provided by the Association of Collegiate Schools of Architecture, Washington, D.C.; telephone conversation, September 1997.

A 1995 Academy Award-winning documentary about Maya Lin, the female architect whose senior project won the Vietnam Memorial competition while she was still an undergraduate at Yale University, displays numerous ironies. An Asian-American woman whose vision of a war memorial had won a prestigious contest was then subjected to the kind of racism and sexism that is usually reserved for less visible public forums. At a public hearing in Washington, D.C., speakers who were mainly male Vietnam veterans succeeded in winning two modifications of her design, namely, the inclusion of an American flag and a statue of three male soldiers. More recently, a statue of female veterans has been added to the monument. Ms. Lin's dignified demeanor throughout the hearings and the entire controversy, her ability to withstand the criticism and the attacks on her professionalism, her youth, her race, and her gender, to maintain the integrity of her design, and to win such allies as Vincent Scully, professor emeritus of architecture at Yale, J. Carter Brown, then director of the National Gallery of Art, and other white males with impeccable credentials, did more to advance the cause of women architects than any affirmative action effort could have done. She subsequently demonstrated her ability in other architectural commissions: a civil rights monument in Montgomery, Alabama; the African Museum of Art in New York City; and a monument to twenty years of coeducation at Yale University.

Education and Library Science

In the professions, the "fragmented paradigm" of teaching, research, and service is most pronounced in the nation's twelve hundred schools, colleges, and departments of education, partly because of the number and variety of programs and partly because of the applied nature of the field. When compared to library science, the differential treatment accorded the feminized professions by institutions of higher education is highlighted and the consequences for women faculty and students more pronounced.

Education produces more female graduates than any other professional field. In 1994, of the 214,446 education degrees conferred, women earned 76 percent: 75.8 percent of all bachelor's and 76.5 percent of all master's degrees. Women's higher academic attainment in education is evident in the doctoral statistic alone: in 1970, they earned only 21 percent of all Ph.D./Ed.D. degrees; by 1980, this proportion more than doubled to 47.2 percent, and by 1994–95, it tripled to 62 percent.

By 1992, women constituted 51 percent of all education faculty. However,

NSOPF survey data show the persistence of the gender queue in professional schools. In the five years between 1987 and 1992, the percentage of full-time women education faculty in four-year institutions declined from 78 to 59 percent, and the percentage of women part-time faculty doubled from 22 to 41 percent (Kirshstein, Matheson, & Jing, 1997, p. 15). By 1993, NCES data show that women constituted 67 percent of all part-time faculty in schools of education but only 47 percent of full-time faculty (Snyder, Hoffman, & Geddes, 1996): 38.5 percent in master's level institutions, 40 percent in doctoral universities, and 45 percent in liberal arts colleges. By race and ethnicity, white women faculty in schools of education were more likely to be teaching part time (58.8%) than full time (41.9%); women of color accounted for an almost equal ratio of full-time (9.3%) and part-time (8.5%) education faculty. An AACTE survey of 1,700 member institutions reported that women were only 15.8 percent of education deans and 27.8 percent of department chairs (AACTE, 1994).

In contrast to higher education, women predominate in American schools. They account for almost three-fourths (73%) of the 2.6 million public school teachers—87 percent at the elementary and 53 percent at the secondary level—and three-fourths of the 380,000 private school teachers—92 percent at the elementary level and 63 percent at the secondary level (Henke, Choi, & Geis, 1996). They are still only 34.5 percent of all principals and 4 percent of all superintendents in the nation's 14,367 regular school districts, however. Women principals are also more likely to have first professional (educational specialist, 27.9%) and doctoral degrees (Ph.D./Ed.D., 9.8%) than their male counterparts.

For the past fifteen years, teachers and teacher education programs have been the subject of relentless scrutiny, unlike in any other profession. Beginning with the publication of *A Nation at Risk* (National Commission on Excellence in Education, 1983) and continuing with the formation of numerous commissions and task forces to restructure teacher education, this ongoing critique has had a profoundly negative impact on public perceptions of American education and on the teaching profession. Three of the most influential reports in teacher education have been *Tomorrow's Teachers*, issued by a coalition of education deans in research universities (the Holmes Group, 1986); *A Nation Prepared: Educating Teachers for the 21st Century* (Carnegie Task Force on Teaching as a Profession, 1986); and most recently, *What Matters Most: Teaching for America's Future* (National Commission on Teaching & America's Future, 1996).

Those of us who teach in schools of education are well aware of the significant cutbacks being made in full-time faculty and program development despite the demonstrated need for teachers. Many states have acted to eliminate or severely restrict teacher education programs under the pretense of raising academic standards and cutting operating budgets. Part of the budget cuts are being made through the elimination of undergraduate education degrees, as recommended in 1986 by the Holmes Group and the Carnegie Task Force on Teaching as a Profession, and echoed by several state boards of education. Pedagogical practice is being elevated to a graduate-level specialty available only to those who can meet more stringent admissions criteria and can afford the luxury of graduate school. In essence, these reports generated mainly by research universities with a limited stake in undergraduate teacher education seek to increase the status of the profession by making it a graduate specialty. This shift has attracted men as well as women for a variety of reasons: the prospect of job openings as the Vietnam generation of teachers reaches retirement age, the greater flexibility offered by the teaching lifestyle, the geographic convenience of the school as workplace, and the concept of service built into the teacher's role.

Efforts to reform teacher education do not address the growing number of part-time and non-tenure-track faculty being employed as "visiting" or "clinical" professor as well as "instructor" and "lecturer" to teach undergraduate and graduate courses and to supervise administrative interns and student teachers. These individuals may be retired teachers or principals or ABDs (all but dissertation) unable to find full-time employment. In any case, they operate outside the mainstream of departmental decision making, frequently teaching evening, weekend, or off-campus courses, with little direct guidance or supervision and no possibility of tenure.

Another contradictory approach to teacher professionalization being pursued by almost every state through alternative certification, particularly for urban schools, is to issue emergency certificates and temporary credentials to liberal arts graduates who may complete their certification requirements through school-based induction programs. This dual-track approach parallels the trend to outsourcing of teacher education underway in the United Kingdom, where 80 percent of all teacher training has been shifted to the local school authorities, who then contract with schools of education to deliver the instruction. The demise of teacher education programs runs counter to the demonstrated shortages of professionally trained and licensed teachers and the escalating administrative costs in school districts. It also conflicts with calls for higher standards, national assessment, and better-trained teachers. It further alienates the rank-and-file practitioners from administrative and knowledge elites within the universities and on state boards of education.

Efforts are now being made by those who control the teaching profession—states, professional associations, colleges of education, and governmental agencies—to raise academic standards in the education of all children. The National Commission for Accreditation of Teacher Education (NCATE) and various specialty agencies in counseling, administration, and special education are promoting national accreditation of teacher preparation and professional development programs. The national standards and assessment movement, which received a major boost from President Clinton in his 1997 State of the Union address, is endeavoring to elevate the status of the teaching profession by recognizing the central role of teachers in the education of all children, by focusing public attention on the need for better trained professionals and more resource support, and most significantly, on the adoption of voluntary curriculum and assessment standards. Better training for teachers and for the adoption of standards has elicited broad-based support among unions, parents, educators, and moderates in both political parties. Opposition has come mainly from conservative political and religious groups that advocate the privatization of education, by contracting with for-profit companies to manage public schools, providing waivers for charter schools outside the local system, and giving parents greater control over their children's education through tuition vouchers for use in private and parochial schools. These proposals send mixed messages to the public, the school systems, and in particular, to teachers and teacher educators. Alternative approaches to schooling, particularly at the elementary and middle school levels, rest on the assumption that less hierarchy and more autonomy—commodities that most teachers do not enjoy—are preferable to existing systems. They not only drain needed resources from local school districts; they also reinforce the low status of the teaching profession and the inability of teachers to resist the centralization of power and control of education.

Institutions of higher education are more likely to define their mission in relationship to their prestigious professional schools as well as their graduate schools of arts and science. Teacher education, library science, and nursing are generally not considered major players in the upper reaches of the academic hierarchy. Gender-blind discussions of the professionalization of teaching and the transformation of library science tend to ignore that these jobs are largely viewed as women's work and are often characterized by lack of autonomy, low salaries, and weak status. Those who practice medicine and law, on the other hand, enjoy greater autonomy and acknowledged expertise in their doctor-patient or lawyer-client relationships, which are generally provided on a fee-for-service basis.

Library science provides an example of a feminized field being transformed by technology into an information science. In 1994–95, women earned 77 percent of all bachelor's, master's, and doctoral degrees combined: 57.7 percent of bachelor's degrees, 78.3 percent of American Library Association-accredited master's degrees, and 59 percent of doctoral degrees. In 1995, M.L.S. programs, which account for the majority of library students, enrolled 11,746 full-time and part-time students in fifty-five accredited library schools and graduated 4,991 students. Of the 603 full-time faculty, women account for only a third of full professors but constitute the majority of associate (49.3%) and assistant (60.2%) professors, lecturers (61%), and instructors (73.3%). There has been a sharp decline among women deans and directors, from 50.8 percent in 1993 to 40.4 percent in 1995.

Institutional decisions to reduce the number of library schools in the past two decades demonstrate the importance of the political context in which feminized professions frequently operate. Fifteen prestigious library schools have been shut down in a relatively brief period of time, those at Columbia University (the oldest school of library services in the United States), the University of Chicago, Vanderbilt University, the University of Southern California, and UCLA, where library science and education were merged into the College of Education and Information Science. These closings mark the demise of this field as one dominated by the printed book and its transformation into a technologically oriented information science. They also demonstrate how downsizing priorities can be triggered by measures of institutional status and prestige. In discussing competitive characteristics of the professions, Freidson argues that "professional ideologies are intrinsically imperialistic" and that in making knowledge claims, each profession seeks more resources as a way of advancing the general good (1994, p. 69): "Much of the political activity of the professions may be characterized by appeals to the superior importance of one paradigm over another. Thus the competition between professions for jurisdiction over a particular area may be analyzed as conflicting definitions of a problem or activity each is seeking to control, and claims about the way that can best be solved or carried out. In a technocracy, the outcome of such competition establishes who is to be the technocrat and who is not" (p. 70).

The technocratic metaphor aptly describes what is occurring in librarianship. Marshall McLuhan's "Gutenberg Galaxy" has entered the electronic age, and librarianship is one of its casualties. Closing professional schools runs counter to the evident need for well-trained librarians and the strength of enrollments in remaining schools. Academic and specialty librarians typically obtain dual masters' degrees in both an academic field and library/information science. Given the bewildering array of electronic information and databases, the need for well-trained personnel is even more critical. Therefore, we may ask, why are the numbers of library schools dwindling? Many justifications are offered, primary among them the need to make fiscally responsible choices when trimming institutional budgets. Columbia claimed that its school no longer fitted the university's mission and that "Harvard, Yale and Stanford, for example, ably maintain their reputations without library schools" (Lee, 1990, p. 14). Although implicit in the choices made by presidents and trustees in determining how resources should be deployed, it would not be socially acceptable to cite the feminized nature of these schools as one reason for their demise.

Nevertheless, as Slaughter (1993) and other scholars have noted, the politics of race and gender underlies administrative decisions to close nursing, home economics, education, and library schools when health care, family life, K–12 standards, and literacy are listed as top priorities by the public, the media, and the politicians. These fields rarely enjoy the support of wealthy alumni as in the case of law, medicine, business, and engineering. An analysis of seventeen retrenchment cases reported by Committee A of the AAUP revealed gender-related patterns of retrenchment in administrative decisions to terminate degree programs between 1980 and 1990:

> Faculty who were not retrenched (science, engineering, medicine, business, law) were generally in fields that were close to major mission agencies (Department of Defense, Department of Energy, National Aeronautics and Space Administration, the National Institutes of Health), had powerful constituencies (the nuclear and defense industries, the American Medical Association), were routes to highly paid careers (business, law) that enabled graduates to donate monies to colleges and universities. Faculty who were retrenched (education, humanities, social science, fine arts, home economics) were not close to the mission agencies that provided the greatest amounts of money to higher education, did not have powerful constituencies, were not gateways to highly paid careers, and did not have graduates who donated large amounts of money to colleges and universities. (Slaughter 1993, p. 273)

Her analysis of the impact of retrenchment on women faculty showed that the seventeen programs that were terminated were "more likely to have a higher percentage of women and minorities than non-retrenched fields" in both tenure track and non-tenure-track positions (p. 273). Women students who dominated in these fields were also adversely affected by retrenchment, seriously diminishing a potential source of careers. She concluded that "postsecondary education is being restructured rather than retrenched" and that the gendered construction of these fields influences administrative decisions in strategic planning (p. 275).

Changing the lens in how we view education and library science is an important step in elevating their status. The literature suggests that from a feminist perspective, autonomy and hierarchy, both of which are equated with specialized expertise, are incompatible concepts. Liberal feminists argue that the equal treatment of men and women will lead to greater autonomy and status within the professions. Radical feminists, on the other hand, perceive the sexual division of labor as hierarchical and universal. The issues become more ambiguous as the professions rely more directly on large bureaucratic organizations for their existence. In education and library science, the incompatibility of professionalism and organizational structure has been of central importance in perpetuating the status quo. Restructuring preparation programs to elevate standards, integrate technology, and introduce new methods of teaching and learning can only have a marginal impact unless those who control the professions—practitioners, policy makers, and the professoriate—are willing to engage in a collaborative process to eliminate stratification based on gender and race.

5

WOMEN WHO LEAD

The Glass Ceiling

Phenomenon

The politics of leadership takes on a different meaning when gender becomes part of the equation. Women have no equivalent for the discredited "great man" theory of leadership. As Antonia Fraser shows in her detailed account of great women leaders in world history, the so-called Warrior Queens, "Very few outstanding women in history have achieved or been granted their place without the benefit of some kind of male-derived privilege, generally that of descent, whatever glorious destiny has ensued" (1988, p. 332). As a result, she observes, "Most Warrior Queens have underlined their claims as honorary males by emphasizing such connections," contending that only in this way could they preserve their places within the natural order. She thinks it significant that so many of these women leaders, unable to overcome the unsuitability of mothers doing battle, or their right and ability to compete on the battlefield, have turned the role of motherhood to their advantage and, in the eyes of the world, have been viewed as acting in the interests of their children (p. 332). The alternative, according to Fraser, which in some respects parallels the modern experience of radical feminists, has been to risk being perceived as descendants of the Amazons, that mythological tribe of unnaturally strong females existing outside male control. Contemporary manifestations of this issue can be seen in the sexual harassment experienced by women in the military, even though women are now one-fifth of all recruits, and in the belated recognition of this problem by male leaders in positions of power and authority. It is also evoked in discussions of women's determination to compete with men in gaining political power and influencing the policy agenda.

In reviewing management and leadership research, I am intrigued with the extent to which scholarship continues to be ghettoized. An exhaustive summary of more than seven thousand leadership studies provides but one chapter on women and leadership (and a smaller chapter on "Blacks, His-panics, and other minorities") (Bass, 1993). Although the summary draws heavily on empirical studies comparing men and women as discrete vari-ables, it contains no references to feminist research. Male political scientists, organizational theorists, and historians lament the lack of dynamic leader-ship in our nation's institutions, but most of their studies also tend to be gender neutral or male dominant.[1]

Women, on the other hand, provide most of the research on women ex-ecutives in corporate management (Davidson & Burke, 1994; Kanter, 1977; Klenke, 1996; Rosener, 1995), women in government (Bingham, 1997; Jamie-son, 1995; Kaptur, 1996), and women in academic organizations (Astin & Le-land, 1991; Johnsrud & Heck, 1994; Sagaria, 1988). Our libraries are filled with books and periodicals focusing on problems of women professionals. Such early self-help tracts as *Games Mother Never Taught You, The One-Minute Manager,* and *Dress for Success* have been superceded by a more assertive, no-nonsense advocacy of power feminism that avoids the double bind of "womb-brain" conflicts and competes more successfully with men. These nineties guides to success include *Members of the Club: The Coming of Age of Executive Women* (Driscoll & Goldberg, 1993); *Womanpower: Managing in Times of Demographic Turbulence* (Sekaran & Leong, 1992); *Fire with Fire: The New Female Power and How It Will Change the 21st Century* (Wolf, 1996); and *Beyond the Double Bind: Women and Leadership* (Jamieson, 1995).

In the 1970s and early 1980s, liberal feminists believed that the numbers of women and minorities entering the workplace would automatically make organizations more equitable and enlightened. It soon became apparent, however, that although equal opportunity employers hired and promoted more women, their actions resulted only in a thin veneer of women's equity. One of the first in-depth studies of this problem, *Men and Women of the Corporation* (Kanter, 1977), showed the masculine character of organi-zational management and business expertise and the supposition that analy-tic ability, toughness, and objectivity were viewed as "characteristics sup-posedly belonging only to men." Women experienced tokenism, being perceived as role models on the one hand and, on the other, as objectified personifications of role models, with the expectation that as managers they would live up to accepted images of womanhood. The more closely women's identities were linked to the positions they occupied, the more difficult it be-

---

1. See Bensimon, Neumann, & Birnbaum (1989) for an excellent literature review of leadership theories and their applicability to higher education.

came to extricate them. As a result, women in middle management found it easier to live with the expectations of others rather than to challenge the status quo. In effect, liberal feminism did little to change organizational cultures that impeded women's progress. In its opposition to institutional norms, radical feminism also fell short of its goals to create a woman-centered academy.

The chief concern of postmodern feminists, however, is the gendered subjectivity of career development programs and how women's work experience is constructed within the patriarchal context of the organization (Nicholson, 1996). This new generation of feminists rejects the contradictions between abstract equity doctrines and the lives and careers of professional women, viewing their experience "as one of dynamic and ongoing interaction between discourses of gender and power, and the experience and meaning of being an individual [woman] in a social context" (p. 5). It is more self-confident in moving from the margins to the center of professional activity, seeking a larger share of the economic and political rewards. Six million women now hold management positions in both the public and private sectors of the economy, and the proportion of women in these jobs has grown from 27 to 40 percent in fifteen years. Nevertheless, women managers are 11 percent of all employed women and are the minority of senior managers. After a flurry of activity in response to affirmative action and equal employment mandates throughout the 1960s and 1970s, corporations have returned to a business-as-usual outlook in promoting women and minorities into senior-level positions. By the end of the 1980s, women held only three of every one hundred executive jobs in the largest companies: 1.7 percent of corporate officers in Fortune 500 companies, and 1.3 percent of those in Fortune 50 companies. By 1995, 97 percent of senior managers of Fortune 1000 industrial and Fortune 500 companies were white, and 95 to 97 percent were male. In Fortune 2000 industrial and service companies, women—almost all of them white—accounted for only 5 percent of senior managers (Glass Ceiling Commission, 1995, pp. iii–iv). These data led the Feminist Majority Foundation to predict that at the current rate of progress, it would take women in the workplace 475 years to reach equality with men.

Part of the problem derives from the low number of women on the executive track. Only eleven of 1,216 inside directors of Fortune 500 companies are women, five of whom are related to the CEO or to the controlling family. They constitute only 10.2 percent of the 6,123 directors of Fortune 500 companies, and although 83 percent have one woman director, only twenty-three companies (0.4%) have three or more women directors (Dobrzynski, 1996,

p. D4). In 1997, when *Barrons*, a business weekly published by the Dow Jones Corporation, reviewed women's status, they found statistical and anecdotal evidence that despite a booming economy, women are still noticeably absent from executive suites: only two women serve as CEOs of Fortune 500 companies; among the next five hundred companies, there are only five (Epstein, 1997). As a result, "They lose out on the prerogative to bestow bonuses, to distribute raises, and to hire, fire, transfer, and promote. Such power remains the preserve of men" (p. 35).

Originally used in a special *Wall Street Journal* report, "The Corporate Woman" (Hymowitz & Shellhardt, 1986, p. 1D), the glass ceiling is a useful metaphor to suggest why so few women, despite their credentials and accomplishments, attain leadership positions—"why they do not appear to move up the organizational hierarchy as rapidly as men, and why they tend to be faced with more stringent promotion requirements than their male counterparts" (Klenke, 1996, p. 171). The glass ceiling graphically describes the relative scarcity of women leaders throughout the entire social structure. As one woman told me: "At the top of the pinnacle the glass ceiling is very, very high and discrimination becomes difficult to prove."

A Department of Labor inquiry initiated in 1989 by Elizabeth Dole, secretary of labor in the Bush administration, found that nine major corporations with extensive government contracts employed no women in its ranks of senior executives. Its *Report on the Glass Ceiling Initiative* (Office of Federal Contract Compliance, 1991) showed that the glass ceiling was both higher and more impenetrable than estimated and declared these nine government contractors in noncompliance with OFCC regulations.

Propelled by presidential politics and the importance of the women's vote, the Glass Ceiling Act, sponsored by Senator Bob Dole, was enacted in 1991 as Title II of the Civil Rights Restoration Act. The Glass Ceiling Commission, formed in 1992, held five hearings; commissioned eighteen research papers; surveyed twenty-five CEOs; conducted focus groups with minority executives; and analyzed demographic, social, political, and economic factors. The commission's report, *Good for Business: Making Full Use of the Nation's Human Capital* was released by Secretary of Labor Robert Reich in 1995. Although attacks on affirmative action laws and regulations in a conservative Republican-dominated Congress had further polarized public opinion and raised questions about the legitimacy of women's claims of gender bias in the workplace, the commission revealed that the EEOC had a backlog of ninety-six thousand complaints. It assigned responsibility to white male executives and middle-level supervisors for supporting a series of obstacles or multiple glass ceilings to block the access of women and minorities to the top (p. 35). Newspapers gave modest editorial coverage to the commission's findings: business periodicals such as *Fortune* magazine dismissed the glass ceiling metaphor as governmental "ceilingism" propaganda designed to primarily benefit "the diversity-training industry" (Seligman, 1995, p. 142). Ironically, critics who are the main proponents of traditional middle-class values reject the notion of change in workplace cultures to accommodate family-friendly policies. A background paper on this topic for the Glass Ceiling Commission urges employers to integrate work-family and glass ceiling initiatives, to modify unexamined and outdated merit and career-ladder structures, and to assess the impact on women of family leave and flexible work arrangement policies (Schwartz, 1994, p. 30).

As globalization has become the new mantra for universities as well as multinational corporations, it is important to note the parallels between women's situation in the United States and other Western nations. In 1989, the Hansard Society for Parliamentary Government appointed a commission to assess the professional status of women in the United Kingdom. Its report, *Women at the Top*, was severely critical of how "centres of modern academic teaching and excellence in Britain . . . remain bastions of male power and privilege" (p. 11). The Committee of Vice Chancellors and Principals, representing chief executive officers of universities in the United Kingdom, responded by issuing guidelines on equal employment opportunities for women in higher education and by establishing the Commission on University Career Opportunity. A group of forty women university managers also formed a professional network, Through the Glass Ceiling. In 1991, Opportunity 2000, launched by then prime minister John Major and a business-industry coalition, generated greater institutional participation for increasing the quality and quantity of women in the workforce. Universities that signed up for Opportunity 2000 agreed to an external audit and to developing a program for hiring and promoting women into senior-level positions (Brown, 1997, p. 113). In a discouraging assessment of these initiatives six years after the Hansard Society commission report, Nicholson, taking note of the "shadow of the glass ceiling" and the pervasive impact of conventional organizational structures on women's professional lives in the United Kingdon, found that few women hold senior influential positions in "the judiciary, the Civil Service, the legal profession, senior management, company boardroom directors, academic, media and trade unions" (1996, p. 103).

A 1987 survey of seventy-six women executives in twenty-five Fortune 100 corporations had also drawn attention to the glass ceiling problem in the

United States (Morrison, White, & Van Velsor, 1987). Its data showed that advancement from staff to line positions—not access—marked women as leaders. Such advancement enabled them to turn around a business unit, for example, start a new product line, undertake troubleshooting assignments, or challenge roles normally regarded as off limits. It concluded that in male-defined organizational cultures, "the road to the top" was bumpier than those in charge were willing to acknowledge. Women who managed to obtain senior positions came face to face with a wall of "extremely sturdy construction" that halted their progress to the executive suite. Two-thirds of the women executives surveyed thought they had plateaued or might go one level higher before reaching a dead end, aging out, or being thwarted by sex discrimination. Even though the remaining third were more optimistic, only three of the seventy-six believed they could become CEOs. The rest believed that as they approached the pinnacle of the organizational pyramid the risk-reward ratio deepened, complicated by a competitive corporate subculture that limited the pool of candidates to men and overlooked a cadre of potentially excellent women senior executives (p. 141). They wondered whether business could afford to disregard talented women administrators who had already proved their potential, why shareholders did not demand an end to this waste of talent, why top management was so resistant to the idea in practice, and why women who had given so much of their energies to employers seemed to be abandoned when the stakes reached a certain level. Five years later, follow-up interviews with twenty-five of these women revealed little change in the status quo (Morrison, White, & Van Velsor, 1992).

The existence of a glass ceiling in the nonprofit sector has been frequently observed in female-intensive occupations, where men hold most of the administrative positions while women occupy the lower ranks. For example, women teachers may dominate in K–12 classrooms, but men still occupy most of the administrative positions as principals and superintendents (Glazer, 1991). More subtle intraoccupational segregation patterns occur in higher education, where professional schools are run by male deans while women predominate at the base and in the middle, for example, in academic libraries (Irvine, 1985), teaching hospitals, and technology centers. Efforts to rescind affirmative action mandates over the past decade and attacks on advocates for women and minorities by those who argue that merit, not gender and race, should be the primary criteria for recruitment and promotion have exacerbated the situation. Making gender and race the basis for such either-or arguments invariably leads to questions about relative qualifications, commitment, and motivation; reinforces gender, race, and ethnicity stereotypes; and ultimately lulls the public into renewed acceptance of the status quo. The family values argument, which dominates much current political discussion, contributes to the widening gap between the public and the private spheres by emphasizing the bimodal character of women's lives and their marginalization in male-dominated fields. Reference to the narrow pipeline or hiring pool in this context sustains a mythology that women are not motivated, committed, or qualified enough to dismantle the barriers thwarting their progress and deterring them from undertaking their complete removal. The persistence of gender stereotypes is manifested in a series of variations on the glass ceiling theme portraying women as responsible for the shortcomings of the workplace and again illustrating the serious structural problems that permeate academic, governmental, and corporate organizations.

Both historical and social science research on women academic leaders provide a fascinating account of the pathfinders who founded women's colleges, broke new ground in the status professions, and established advocacy organizations to protect and advance women's interests (Graham, 1978; Horowitz, 1984; Hulbert & Schuster, 1993; Solomon, 1985). The history of higher education for women has often been portrayed as a bitter struggle linked to educational, social, legal, and political reforms (Clifford, 1993; Glazer & Slater, 1987). Feminist scholars in the social sciences also use a multiplicity of feminist perspectives in conducting studies of how leaders interpret their organizations and their cultures and the contextual influences that facilitate or impede their ability to lead. Bensimon indicates, in a feminist reinterpretation of leadership in higher education, the depth of androcentrism in both the epistemological origins of leadership frames—bureaucratic, symbolic, political, and collegial—and their adaptation for studying how women lead and manage organizations. In applying "the woman question" to her analysis, she shows how conventional organizational constructs "submerge the perspectives of women and other excluded groups," thus contributing to their invisibility as interpreters of organizations and administration (1993). Amey and Twombly (1993) apply discourse analysis to demonstrate how, in community colleges, male-defined ideologies have excluded or limited access to those who do not fit the leadership images of philosopher-kings and military heroes that render women invisible. They call for new formulations that "empower, facilitate, collaborate, educate" (p. 476).

Astin and Leland's study of three generations of women leaders (1991) redefines leadership based on societal outcomes that empower women and foster collective action. Their cross-generational study of women leaders and academic change identifies three distinct groups: *predecessors,* or those who laid the groundwork for the establishment of coeducation, women's studies, and gender equity; *instigators,* or those who adopted a feminist agenda and implemented it in the academy; and *inheritors,* those who reaped the benefits of the first generation of feminist leaders through the access and opportunities afforded them in their academic careers. Gillett-Karam (1994), in her study of men and women presidents in two-year colleges, employs a transformational leadership model to compare female and male leadership behaviors. Although she finds demographic differences between women and men in terms of age, experience, and parental background, she concludes that leadership skills are more apt to be situational than gendered. The perspectives of these scholars may differ, but they each ask the woman question in their reinterpretation of conventional leadership theories previously focused on traits, personality, and situational contingencies. They all share the belief that women's problems are systemic, value laden, and pervasive. Rather than portray women as victims, they suggest potential new directions that may ultimately crack the glass ceiling.

Academic Administration

Presidents and Chancellors

When Judith Rodin was appointed the first woman president of the University of Pennsylvania, this landmark event was announced on the first page of the *New York Times* Home Section (O'Neill, 1994, p. c1) with the caption "In an Ivy League of Her Own." The article began by contrasting the "gray-tweed and furrowed-brow world of academia" with Dr. Rodin's "cover-girl smile and designer clothes," and her "pert manner and bouncy determination." It saw her as a more "serious country club tennis player" than "boardroom predator." Buried in the middle of this breezy feature story was an account of her two decades at Yale University, where she served as provost and was also a contender for the presidency. Her intellectual achievements included twenty grants totaling nearly $30 million, 203 academic articles, 64 book chapters, and 10 academic books. When Ruth Simmons became president of Smith College, the news angle was her African-American heritage—"the great-great-granddaughter of slaves"—who began her journey to the presidency from a cotton farm in East Texas, where her parents were sharecroppers and she was the youngest of twelve children (Rimer, 1995, p. b8).

She was described as "elegantly dressed in a long, dark-green pleated skirt and matching jacket, with a double strand of pearls and small gold hoop earrings." Midway through this article we discovered that Dr. Simmons holds master's and doctoral degrees in romance languages from Harvard, served as dean at the University of New Orleans and as vice provost at Princeton University, and was the unanimous first choice of the fifteen-member Smith College Board of Trustees. Rather than being defined as an outstanding administrator, she was portrayed by her former colleague Henry Louis Gates as "the Jackie Robinson of college presidents," who rose above her humble origins to lead an institution symbolized by wealth and privilege.

These two examples yield both the symbolic and literal meanings noted by Bensimon and Neumann in their study of collaborative collegiate leadership (1993). The references to Dr. Rodin's physical appearance and style of dress and to Dr. Simmons' color and her modest southern origins define them through race, class, and gender rather than through their more "masculine" characteristics—superior intellect, managerial acuity, and academic and administrative expertise. Such commentary reinforces the assumption that women who compete in a man's world gain equal status by exceeding traditional standards of excellence and being pathfinders in their chosen careers while retaining their femininity and attractiveness. In contrast, in a recent announcement that an interim chancellor had been offered the permanent position as head of the State University of New York, the nation's largest multicampus public system, John Ryan was described not in terms of his attire, marital status, or family background but as a "senior statesman" with a "man-to-man approach to leadership," a troubleshooter who earned his reputation for leadership as the erstwhile "boss of Bobby Knight, the irascible Indiana University basketball coach" (Arenson, 1997, p. B1). That comment is reminiscent of Donna Shalala's response when asked why so few women become presidents of major research universities. Her one-word answer was "athletics."

The number of women presidents may be increasing, but it is considerably below pipeline proportions. Even though women have comparable credentials and have followed similar career paths, twenty years after Hanna Gray became the first woman to head the University of Chicago in 1978, only 2 percent of all women presidents head major research universities; the majority are restricted to liberal arts, two-year, and sectarian colleges. By 1995, according to ACE data, women accounted for 15 percent or 453 presidents of the nation's three thousand regionally accredited colleges and universities, a threefold increase since 1975, when 148 women served as presidents. A third of these presidents (155) headed either denominational or women's colleges; about 21 percent were members of religious orders. Women are more likely to head private than public institutions (52.3%) and to be presidents of two-year community colleges (39%). Less than a third served as vice presidents prior to assuming the presidency. Of these, 84 percent (381) are white, and 16 percent are women of color (39 blacks, 24 Hispanics, 2 Asian Americans, and 7 Native Americans) (39%). In comparing 1986 and 1992 ACE presidential databases, Touchton, Shavlik, and Davis (1993) noted demographic similarities between men and women presidents in age (51–52) and race/ethnicity (92–93% white, 5% black, 2% Hispanic, less than 1% Native American and Asian) but striking differences in marital status: among lay presidents, 48 percent of the women were married and 18 percent were widowed or divorced, compared to 93 percent of the men being married and 4 percent divorced (p. 41). Differences may also be noted in the selection process: only 5 percent of women presidents were recruited by a search firm for their current position; 50 percent were nominated; and 20 percent were serving as acting president at the time (Touchton, Shavlik, & Davis, 1993). The interaction among variables makes it difficult to draw conclusions from these data. For example, more women than men presidents have Ph.D. degrees (62% women; 53% men), but both women and men presidents come from the same three broad fields: education (40% women; 45% men), social sciences (12% women; 12% men), and humanities and the fine arts (29% women; 15% men). The same proportion also have degrees in natural sciences (5%) and law (3%). Men and women responding to another ACE survey expressed dissatisfaction with the paucity of women administrators, faculty, and trustees (Washington, 1993). Even though 55 percent thought that their institutions had an adequate number of women on search committees, only a third thought that the representation of women among senior administrators, trustees, and faculty was either excellent or very good. Forty-two percent gave their schools only fair or poor ratings.

Trustees

Boards of trustees enjoy a pivotal role in selecting presidents of colleges and universities. The relationship between the president and the board is critical to institutional harmony and financial well being, and composition is therefore central to the status of women administrators as well as women faculty. A woman president of a private liberal arts college observed that trustees have their own informal network, and her compatibility with the board members was very important to the stability of the college. In 1969, women constituted 12 percent of trustees on public and private boards. By 1987, as Taylor shows, trustees still tended to be "white, male, older, affluent, and business connected" (Taylor, 1987). Women's participation rose to 25 percent in private and 27 percent in public institutions by 1992 (Ingram, 1993). They were still clustered on the boards of community and junior colleges (26% private; 31% public), however, rather than in four-year colleges and universities (23% private; 26% public) and multicampus systems (23%). The political dimension of public sector trustee selection is demonstrable: for multicampus systems, 79 percent are either elected by popular vote or appointed by the governor or state legislature; for institutional boards, 66 percent of trustees are selected in this way. In state community college systems with either coordinating (41.5%) or governing boards (58.5%), appointments are made jointly by state and local governments, which provide the bulk of their funding (Garrett, 1993).

Because board composition is not likely to be challenged on legal grounds, women trustees often benefit informally from the support of faculty and students, and externally from the interventions of alumni, legislatures, and governors. The perfunctory attention given to board diversity is indicative of attitudes toward women in male-dominated spheres of influence and suggests the need for revising and reinterpreting conventional images of leadership. Part of the problem lies in the interaction of gender, race, and class between men and women trustees, who live in very different social worlds from their constituencies. As a consequence, their allegiances are often with their sponsors, wealthy alumni, and a small circle of senior administrators rather than with the students, faculty, and staff, who are their raisons d'être. In commenting on the difficulties of dealing with "all stars and no constellations" on boards of trustees, Chait, Holland, and Taylor (1996) note that at women's colleges, where women constitute a majority of the board members, presidents cite the refreshing lack of personal agendas and ego involvement in board deliberations.

In contrast to the political selection process used by the public sector, private higher education boards tend to be self-perpetuating (61%), encouraging the appointment of like-minded, influential, and wealthy members of the business community (Taylor, 1987, p. 21). Gendered perceptions of where power and influence reside frequently relegate women to secondary importance as the inheritors rather than producers of wealth. Minorities have fared less favorably than white women in private board appointments, with no increase in their numbers between 1977 and 1991, when only 6 percent of trustees were African American and 1 percent each were Latino, Asian, and

Native American (Ingram, 1993a, p. 369). On public boards, 13 percent of board members in 1993 were African American, 3 percent Latino, 1 percent Asian, and less than 1 percent Native American (Ingram, 1993b, p. 386).

The corporate approach to university management is a natural manifestation of the incontrovertible reality that board chairmen are often prominent in civic and business circles. The implications for presidential selection, interpersonal relationships with the president, and preoccupation with the business aspects of university operations follow as a matter of course. As Carlsen and Burdick point out in discussing community college trustees, a policy board might seek strong presidential leadership, whereas a working board would probably look to other alternatives (1994, p. 264). In the 1960s and 1970s, presidential searches were apt to be conducted within a small network of trustees and academic search committees. In the past decade, as higher education has experienced a loss of public support and a series of budget crises, particularly in the public sector, trustees have been elected and appointed with the tacit understanding that they will support policies that may include restructuring, downsizing, tuition increases, and curtailment of open admissions. The recent decision to modify tenure policies in its flagship research institution by the University of Minnesota's board of regents illustrates trustee intervention in faculty governance. The rationale given by the board cited the need for greater flexibility in terminating programs or downsizing schools. Another, more positive approach (see chapter 6) is that taken by the Arizona Board of Regents, which established a statewide commission on women.

The Association of Governing Boards estimates the need for twelve hundred new trustees each year for the community colleges alone (p. 265). The interrelationship between these boards and the political power structure are inextricably tied, however, to gender hierarchies. Until women are perceived as power brokers who can influence public policy at the local and state levels, they will continue to be underrepresented on college and university boards.

Vice Presidents

Chief academic officers (CAOs) are a smaller group than women presidents. They are the provosts, academic vice presidents, and in two-year colleges, the deans of instruction, who are second in command at colleges and universities—the academic leaders on the pathway to the presidency. McDade and Walton found that women accounted for only 208 or 15.1 percent of all chief academic officers in the nation's 1,378 four-year colleges and universities, almost half of these in liberal arts colleges (48.6%), another third in masters' level comprehensive colleges and universities, and only 17.3 percent in research and doctoral universities.[2] They were more likely to earn these positions in smaller, less prestigious institutions than in large research universities. As in the case of women presidents, almost half of the women CAOs in four-year institutions were members of religious orders: 27.6 percent in liberal arts colleges and 20.7 percent in comprehensives. The majority were in private (69.6%) rather than public institutions (29.8%). It had taken them a long time to reach this position, and having for the most part come from the faculty ranks, they had been in academia an average of 21.6 years but in the CAO position for an average of only 4.8 years. Most of them had doctorates (84% Ph.D.s; 10% Ed.D.s); more than two-thirds were full professors (68.5%), although fewer than half were tenured (48.6%); and they had published either a book (45%) or at least one article or monograph (82%).

With respect to public and private two-year colleges, I found that in 1996, three hundred or 24 percent of all deans of instruction and academic vice presidents were women. Hawthorne observed in her survey of chief academic officers of community and junior colleges that the "prototypic chief academic officer of a community, junior, or technical college in the United States today is a 50-year-old white male with a doctoral degree in education. His prior teaching experience is in the humanities, social sciences, or science/math/engineering, and his previous administrative and teaching experience is primarily in community colleges" (1994, p. 269). She concluded that community colleges had failed in their mission to recruit academic leaders no less than students of diverse race, ethnicity, and gender. Much of the problem she attributed to the inability of two-year colleges to adopt practices encouraging different cultural, gender, and racial perspectives (p. 276). The predominance of male-oriented terminal degree programs in occupational-technical education may also contribute to the lack of gender diversity among deans of instruction and students in two-year colleges.

In a study of fifteen presidential teams, Bensimon and Neumann (1993) theorized that the tendency of organizational leaders to form socially homogeneous management teams and to fill senior positions with people like them may account for their reluctance to appoint women to academic or financial vice presidencies, two areas that preoccupy the interests and attention of presidents, provosts, and trustees (p. 120). Their observation confirms

2. I am grateful to Sharon McDade for allowing me to read her work in progress.

the data showing that a gendered selection process frequently channels men and women into different career paths to the presidency. They note that women who worked in organizational cultures dominated by men were subject to different sets of expectations from trustees, faculty, students, and alumni and had different self-images from their male colleagues. In one example of male dominance, Neumann (1997, p. 112) cites the experience of a vice president—the only woman on a presidential leadership team—who felt she was being systematically silenced, invariably criticized, and frequently encouraged to "act and think more like her male colleagues." Birnbaum (1992) comments on the pivotal role of the academic vice president, who operates the institution on a day-to-day basis, in contrast to the president, who is more concerned with fund-raising and external constituencies (p. 113). He also relates the experience of women presidents who felt that trustee search committees patronized them, grilling them more extensively on financial issues and indirectly questioning their budgetary competence (p. 46). In this context, the divergent career paths of women to either the vice presidency or the presidency has implications for how women set their leadership horizons and the kinds of support they need to reach the pinnacle of the organizational hierarchy. Playing by the rules of the game remains the dominant behavioral expectation for both men and women, and as long as these rules are made by men, women will continue to find glass ceilings and other barriers obstructing their progress to the academic vice presidency.

Deans and Other Administrators

As the head of faculty within a particular school or college, with leadership responsibilities for students, staffing, budgeting, and other aspects of administration, the dean also functions as a gatekeeper in conducting faculty searches, overseeing promotion and tenure decisions, and approving the nomination of department chairs. Because the deanship affords incumbents a privileged position for gaining visibility and recognition en route to senior administrative positions, the situation of women deans is important. By 1995–96, women constituted 25.4 percent of the 5,004 deans in the CUPA sample of 1,385 colleges and universities, representing the majority in only four of the thirty-one designated fields: health-related professions (58.2%), home economics (89.5%), nursing (98.7%), and special programs (56.1%). At the other end of the spectrum, women deans are a distinct minority in the status professions: business (16.6%), law (8%), medicine (3%), engineering (3%), pharmacy (3%), veterinary medicine (0%), and dentistry (0%).

A recent survey of 113 graduate deans of arts and science, 27 percent of whom were women, revealed gender differences in career patterns similar to those of presidents and vice presidents (Kilson, 1996). More than half the women deans earned Ph.D.s a decade later than men, served fewer years in their current position, and came directly from the faculty ranks rather than through another administrative office. Although twice as many women as men aspired to the deanship (79% women; 45% men), a similar proportion encountered career obstacles en route to either a vice presidency or a presidency (48% women; 25% men). Those without informal networks of support often find themselves stymied as they near the top of the administrative hierarchy, where promotions are more likely to be based on trust than on performance. This may also account for the difficulty of crossing boundaries between public and private sector institutions and systems as well as between levels of institutions, that is, from two-year community colleges to doctoral or research universities.

An analysis of the 1995–96 CUPA administrative survey of public and private institutions (two-year, four-year, and doctoral/research universities) shows women as the minority in the five employment categories: external affairs (37.7%), student services (48.4%), executive (28.7%), administrative (34.3%), and academic affairs (34%) (Creal & Beyer, 1996). They are more likely to be in subordinate than in supervisory positions. In this sample, for example, women are 26 percent of chief academic officers, 13.8 percent of chief business officers, and 29.4 percent of chief development officers. Although they do best in external affairs and student services, they are a minority of chief student affairs (32.7%) and chief admissions officers (36.4%). The proportions are reversed in middle management: two-thirds of associate admissions directors (61.3%) are women, and more than half of all registrars (56.4%). An even lower glass ceiling impedes the progress of women of color, who constitute less than 5 percent of all administrators.

Unequal Pay for Equal Work

Although affirmative action has made it possible for women to aspire to leadership positions in higher education, two troubling trends affecting the experience of many women faculty are having a negative impact on women administrators: the increase of part-time employment and the persistence of salary disparities. The diversity of occupational job titles has had the net effect of creating alternative administrative career paths that bypass traditional seniority requirements and search procedures and offer accrued mobility outside existing organizational hierarchies (Ost & Twale, 1989). They also create parallel organizational structures characterized by the use of consultants and other contractual employees who conduct short-term projects and trade health, pension, and vacation benefits in exchange for flextime, tuition remission, and other concessions. The labor market analogy is particularly relevant in describing the propensity of public and private universities to rely increasingly on temporary staff in a number of professional and classified staff positions. In discussing a recent decision to privatize the food service workers at her institution, a woman research director commented: "People are not even addressing the political and economic consequences of these actions for the life of the university. Most of us do not take the time to look at the 'big picture' and think about what it means for gender and race equity to rely more and more on a part-time temporary workforce, not only faculty but other employees as well."

Women administrators also experience a gender pay gap (Goldin, 1990; Headlee & Elfin, 1996; Pfeffer & Davis-Blake, 1987). Because colleges and universities are labor-intensive institutions and human resource costs may range from 65 to 85 percent of operating expenditures, governing boards and administrators seek to control costs by monitoring hiring and compensation packages. CUPA salary survey data reveal the extent of disparities in women's compensation. Gender and minority breakdowns have been available only since 1993 for 171 different job titles used in 1,384 public and private institutions—doctoral (15%), comprehensive (26%), baccalaureate and two-year (23% each), and system offices and specialized institutions (13%).

By 1995–96, women constituted 19 percent of systemwide CEOs, 15.5 percent of single-unit CEOs, and 15.6 percent of executive vice presidents, but 60 percent of CEO assistants across all types of institutions. In doctoral institutions, where salaries are higher, the median salary is 23.8 percent higher for men than women CEO systemwide assistants and 20.1 percent higher for men than women presidential single-unit assistants. The pay gap for men and women assistants to the president is even higher in comprehensive institutions (27%) and four-year baccalaureate colleges (53.7%). Male executive vice presidents also earn one-third higher median salaries than their female colleagues in both two-year (34%) and four-year (37%) colleges. Fourteen administrative positions, all of which are male-dominated, now have median salaries of $100,000 or higher: university presidents and system CEOs, chief research officers, health professions officers, and deans of agriculture, architecture, dentistry, engineering, law, medicine, pharmacy, public health, and veterinary medicine. Deans of medical schools, only five of whom are women, have the highest median salaries at $201,240; admissions counselors are the lowest paid at $24,125 (Cage, 1996).

An analysis of unpublished CUPA salary data compared the effect of women's increased numbers on the administrative salaries of two cohorts of men and women in 1978 and 1984 (Pfeffer & Davis-Blake, 1987). They found that increasing the proportion of women in a specific job category within a college or university resulted in lower per capita salaries. Conversely, lower salaries led to a higher proportion of women working in those jobs. Their conclusion was, "The higher the percentage of women, the more open the organization and the less protected its administrative labor market" (p. 21). The 1996 CUPA survey shows that one decade after Pfeffer and Davis-Blake reported their findings, occupational segregation still exists and women administrators earn less than men at most levels in the five categories, even where they are in the majority (Creal & Beyer, 1996). There is an additional indicator that inequities persist in administrative categories: in 1996, although the median increase for men and women was 4.2 percent, the largest increases were in administrative (4.9%) and executive (4.5%) positions and the smallest in student services (3.9%) and external affairs (3.8%), where women administrators are proportionately higher.

The Ascent to the Summit

I spoke with women presidents, vice presidents, and deans about the routes they have taken to academic administration, the problems they encountered along the way, and the changes they recommend if women are to reach the summit in more than token numbers. Their comments illustrate the advantages as well as the limitations of statistical data in conveying the central role of gender, race, and ethnicity for women academic leaders. Their observations also suggest potential strategies for creating nonhierarchical organizations to foster women's full participation. It is important to state at the outset that even in the business world, where productivity and performance earn promotions, women rarely reach the top of the hierarchy. The academy is more credential conscious in selecting its leaders and more preoccupied with other kinds of criteria, for example, terminal degrees, scholarly achievements, and professional recognition. Undoubtedly, gender, race, ethnicity, and class also influence access and opportunity for administrative aspirants. In assessing the years of experience we have had with affirmative action, some obvious questions arise: Why are there so few women in senior administration? Where are they, and how did they get there? What are the problems they face? What solutions do they recommend? And, indeed, is women's under-representation in administration resolvable through rational argument?

As women administrators whose ideas (feminist or otherwise) have been articulated through their scholarship as well as through their personal and professional experiences, their distinctive viewpoints from within the academy provide valuable insights that go beyond statistical data analyses. Their narratives reveal the multiplicity of women's experiences and perspectives and how power and knowledge relationships often shape institutional ideologies. Therefore, a woman sociologist and president of a women's college with a multimillion-dollar endowment and a board of trustees that is largely female will have a different world view from a woman political scientist or lawyer running a coeducational research university whose trustees are wealthy corporate executives or a nun with a degree in education whose authority derives from her religious order and a board dominated by church officials.

Almost three decades have elapsed since equal employment mandates were extended to higher education, and yet women have managed to earn only a small proportion of presidencies, vice presidencies, and deanships. In order to go beyond the data and the popular media portrayals of academic leadership, I conducted interviews with women administrators on several campuses. Their accounts reveal, in the words of one president, that "the university is just one subset of society, and the same factors that prevent women from making more progress to the top of corporations or government are also at work in higher education."

Playing by the Rules

At a seminar I attended at one of the state colleges in California, a community college president told us how she had constructed her professional persona: "I bought into the system—I was decisive, a team player, flexible, didn't take myself too seriously, was aware that I was being judged by my appearance, my voice, my dress. I looked around for advocates who weren't likely to be women, to find a mentor who would single me out and work with me, show me how to administer and point out the pitfalls and landmines to me. Yes, I am encouraged about the future for women, mainly because there are so many in the middle, a critical mass, and the pool is growing. Not promoting them wouldn't make sense. There are large numbers in the community colleges right now."

For this president, the glass ceiling was a myth that could be overcome if women played by the rules of the game. The rules for her meant self-conscious declaration of her femininity rather than her more "masculine" leadership characteristics, working through the system to get where and what she wanted. This essentialist view of herself as the archetypal woman president may affirm but does little to eradicate sex role stereotypes and relationships: the importance of dressing for success and of going along to get ahead.

The antithesis of this president was the president of an elite women's college who remarked: "There is absolutely no distinction and most of us have gone from the faculty ranks to being department chair, dean, and then president or provost." Her experience is consistent with the respondents to the ACE study (Touchton, Shavlik, & Davis, 1993) who adhered, with single-minded purpose, to career paths similar to their male counterparts and credited their success to mentoring, supportive spouses, and hard work. A woman president of a four-year liberal arts college took a similar stance, asserting that after a few months in the position she realized, "I was no longer perceived as a woman to the faculty or the students. I had become 'The President' with a capital P."

From a woman serving as president of a private university comes another perspective on moving up the career ladder:

> I did not follow a typical career path but went from being a faculty member in political science at a research university to president of a women's college from which I had graduated. Being president of the college where I was also an alumna was like coming home. I was dedicated to its mission as a women's college, which was constitutive of its character, the track record of its graduates, its distinctiveness. On the other hand, I am now at an institution where the scale is much larger and I have to deal with a medical school, other professional schools, a huge physical plant, intercollegiate athletics, a much more diverse faculty and student body, many areas that my former position didn't have.

Others, however, suggested that while becoming a department chair is not a difficult transition from the faculty, the next rungs on the academic career path necessitate careful decisions. As one woman said: "I was invited to take this position as vice provost for academic affairs after serving as department chair and director of women's studies. It was a major decision, since it meant that my scholarship would have to be put on hold."

In discussing the politics of Black feminist thought, Collins (1991) places the experiences and ideas of African-American women intellectuals at the center of her analysis, capturing "the interconnections of race, gender, and social class in Black women's lives and their effect on Black feminist thought" (p. xii). She grounds her analysis in their multiple voices and experiences, encouraging white feminists, African-American men, and others to investigate the similarities and differences between their own standpoints and the unique standpoints of self and society articulated by Black women.

As I listened to African-American and Latina women administrators—presidents, vice provosts, and program directors—discuss the experience of women of color, I was mindful of Collins' assertion that by adopting an "outsider-within" stance, each of these women is seeking to overcome the contradictions between their beliefs and experiences and the dominant group's actions and ideologies, and in the process each is creating a new angle of vision about her role and her institution. An African-American woman president expressed the complexity of her situation: "I have been on this path for a long time, 15 years to be exact since I first served as dean and then provost at another college. In each position I have had to educate people about working with women and especially with black women. People are insulated from the cultural issues, and it doesn't get any easier as you go up because we bring our cultural baggage with us wherever we go. So if we go into a boardroom, it doesn't mean we necessarily become any more self-enlightened."

I asked her whether this cultural baggage made her job more difficult:

I'm constantly being challenged. It happens more frequently as an African-American woman. Once you prove yourself, okay. But I know I'm working in an environment where I'm never going to have enough money. And these are things I have no control over. The state will decide what my budget will be and how much tuition will be, and the governor will probably not raise tuition in an election year, but who knows what he will say? What he may do instead is cut the budget so much and suggest to the board that this is what they should do. Or say to the board, where are you going to get the money from? They don't have it, so where are they going to find it? Meanwhile, the lack of public confidence in higher education is a mile wide and an inch thick.

I then asked her what it was like on the other side of the glass ceiling: "The problems don't recede, and as a matter of fact you become more vulnerable in many ways because you are a woman, an African American, and an outsider. People are watching to see how you react, how you deal with faculty, with students, with the media, the trustees, the legislature. My biggest challenge, however, is trying to accomplish my objectives with dwindling resources. This makes my job very difficult and at times very frustrating."

Another African-American woman, a vice provost and the highest-ranking woman at a research university, explained that it had taken her almost thirty years to reach her current position:

When I came here I was in the school of social work, which has always been an academic culture for underrepresented groups. . . . After being promoted as a tenured associate professor, I applied for a sabbatical and fully expected to get a fellowship to a special program for women administrators. When I got my letter of rejection, I called to find out why. What I got back was—"Well you know, we gave your application a great deal of consideration and it was everybody's opinion that you were really overqualified. We were targeting women who needed some kind of push in order to have upward mobility, and you are already a tenured faculty member." I was totally dismayed because as an African-American woman, I felt they have no sense of the vulnerability, the lack of credibility, the fact that absolutely if I am going to be competitive I need even more than anybody else in the same position and they seem not to recognize that at all. So I spent that sabbatical year writing a book but kind of put administration in the back of my head.

Ultimately, she made the transition into central administration:

I was now a full professor and wasn't thinking about doing administration full time at all. But we had a woman vice provost for faculty affairs who had been a very militant activist in working for gender equity who nominated me for a national award—faculty who make a difference— and I was one of the six people they decided to honor that year. After that, I got a call from the provost asking me to take the position of acting dean of the graduate school. I was in a state of shock but didn't have a real sense of what the position entailed. When I started to talk to my friends around the university they said, "Are you out of your mind? They've never asked a woman to be graduate dean here, no less an underrepresented minority woman. They've always had men as deans and if you say no, they're off the hook for everybody else. Then they will say, we offered it to one but she turned it down so you can't say no."

So I thought I'd do it for a year, but as a matter of fact I stayed eight years as graduate dean. By then we had a new provost who said to me: "We've had all these diversity committees on campus and one of their strongest recommendations is that we have somebody in central administration with oversight for minority issues, particularly recruiting minority faculty." So I told him you give me some assistance in the graduate school and I will wear both hats for the next academic year. After one year I could see that there needed to be somebody to hold people accountable, but I still felt that this kind of position should not be marginal, peripheral, outside the mainstream. So he agreed and said I could give you the title of vice provost for faculty affairs because one of your priorities is hiring more underrepresented minority faculty, but you will also have responsibility for promotions, tenure, grievances, sexual harassment, approval of leaves, early retirement, all those kinds of issues. So I took the job on that basis, which has made it very difficult for me to complain about being overworked because in essence, I asked for it. Now we are undergoing a massive downsizing in the medical school, which has more than 1,000 faculty, and so I am up to my neck in grievances.

According to a Latina department chair, a new position of vice provost for minority affairs resulted from a committee recommendation: "We needed to have somebody who was a high-level administrator who would be in charge of coordinating all efforts regarding diversity on campus. And in the wake of civil unrest in our city, the administration decided to do some reorganization and that is how we got that position. We were an important group representing all minority groups as well as gays and lesbians and people with disabilities. The idea is to respond to any pressure point that is going on in the university, and get some sort of action through the university structure."

A female vice provost for faculty affairs, also the highest-ranking woman in her university, made this observation when asked about her chances for becoming president: "I have a feeling that if the trustees were choosing between a man and a woman presidential candidate with similar backgrounds, they would presume the man has more business sense. A woman would have to demonstrate greater accomplishments in financial background, legal experience, corporate boards, etc. I think that super-duper women rise to the top but the mediocre ones are beaten out by the mediocre men. They have to prove themselves, to have published twenty-six articles, look the part, be assertive, tough-minded."

The priority given to resolving financial and political problems reflects an important shift in the character of the presidency. In a climate where difficult decisions have to be made on resource allocation and political negotiation, it may become more rather than less difficult to elevate women into leadership positions. The change in climate has not gone unnoticed:

The attitude now is, "We took care of women in the eighties." When I was hired in 1974, about the first ten years of my career, there was a real emphasis on recruiting, promoting, and retaining women faculty and administrators, and we did see big changes. I think it gave the impression that everything is fine and the sense of urgency to do something has now dissipated. In the late eighties, the emphasis shifted to hiring and promoting minorities. One would hope it's not an either-or strategy, but I don't see searches where there is a real effort to hire women. My hunch is that if you looked at the data now, there are a lot of women on the market, but there's a kind of cap and no longer a conscious effort to monitor women's progress.

Budgetary problems also place women administrators in a Catch-22 situation as they attempt to balance advocacy for women's rights with the need to hold the line on escalating administrative costs. An African-American woman administrator compared her position to "a delicate balancing act in which I must be sensitive to the concerns of different groups and try to make things happen. It gets very difficult when our budget strings are being pulled tighter and tighter. I want to be accessible but I know I can't please everyone, so I do the best I can." She particularly noted the difficulty of women demonstrating their administrative potential while serving in assistant or associate positions: "The assumption is that these women are carrying out someone else's agenda and if they do the job really well, they either get stuck in those positions because they become too valuable to their supervisor or else they move up and out to another university."

When I asked her how this affected her attitude toward the presidency, she responded: "There are better ways to spend one's life. I mean I don't want to do another one. People are suspicious about administrators, and minorities (men and women) tend to get hired when things are worse and white men are bailing out. Women are coming into more volatile situations, exposed to problems that test their mettle. Prejudices surface in those times and we become the focal point or lightening rod because of the tumultuous times in which we lead these institutions."

The woman who takes a nontraditional career path to administration faces other problems related to her outsider status, her limited support system, and the differential standards to which she is held. One woman president commented that a major concern of the trustees was whether she would be acceptable to the male alumni and athletic team "boosters." Another president with a doctorate in educational administration and limited academic experience had come to the attention of a trustee through her leadership in a $100 million capital campaign. Women's credentials are clearly judged on the basis of criteria other than scholarship, fundraising acumen, and the nuts and bolts of organizational management.

Separate Spheres

Feminists have long argued that women's societal status has been impeded by a series of dichotomies that perpetuate separate spheres of existence for men and women—public/private, political/domestic, dominant/subordinate. An overriding theme that was echoed by the women presidents, vice provosts, and deans I interviewed was their continuing difficulty of balancing personal and professional positions. Women administrators perceive these dual roles as career inhibitors. Shirley Kenny, president of the State University of New York–Stony Brook and former president of Queens College, recently told a group of women how she waited until her five children were in school before she took a full-time administrative job from "at least nine to five" and how she relied on her husband to share family responsibilities (Humphreys, 1996, p. 2). Another woman, who was also in her second presidency, agreed: "Women have to be given a shot at doing things at every level, but very often they are written off as not capable or committed because they are women. Many of us are held back by our dedication to our families, not wanting to work seven-day weeks and fifteen-hour days and setting our priorities differently than men. This makes us seem less committed, less motivated, less interested in doing whatever needs to be done to get to the next step on the ladder. This is the problem in corporate life—men make the rules and women must play by them. Corporations make no bones about it."

A woman provost observed:

The organizational culture must change, beginning with an end to the "old boys' club attitude," which still pervades university administration in many universities. In my case, as a married woman, traditional expectations about heterosexual couples immediately placed me outside the norm. If you look at women in positions of leadership, they are single, without children, or have grown children in every case. I was the first person in senior administration with a name that was different from my husband, and while people might think this is trivial, it is representative of a place where most of the male administrators have a wife at home and only one or two have a career spouse. I know that most of the men I work with don't stop at the supermarket on the way home or drop off the dry cleaning in the morning. All the double standard issues that make it easy to say, "Everything is fine. I've got a woman vice provost, a woman vice president, and lots of women deans, so what's the big deal?"

I asked her what this had meant in her case:

They don't feel they have to make any concessions, and the bottom line expectation is that you will be available morning, noon, and night and the university is your social life. My husband and I decided at the beginning that if it feels like an extension of the workday, like a five o'clock reception for parents at the president's house, he doesn't have to go, but if it's a weekend function at someone's home, he does. Then there's a category in between where some judgment is involved. I know that men don't have to make these decisions, because they always bring their wives to every event. And I thought, this is crazy. He has his own life. He doesn't have to go to these things. But every time I come without him, I get asked: "Where's Alan?" So I've come to see how the university has been organized by men as a kind of heterosexual structure that really permeates the institution.

A woman who had been dean of humanities concurred:

Being an administrator gives a woman no personal life, impossible hours, wining and dining trustees, attending social activities. I was one of two women deans, and in addition to the impossible work schedule, I had to attend to entertaining, put my scholarship on the back burner, and do all the other things that women have to do in their daily lives. Timetables are structured around males with full-time wives, secretaries, and other adjunct staff. Women don't ask their spouses to take over their social and secretarial functions. There is no incentive for men to change the patterns of the workplace and what has been done is insufficient. The workplace has not changed to accommodate women's multiple obligations and responsibilities. It isn't women's fault, but they are blamed and held responsible.

A male dean commented sardonically: "Golf is the great equalizer, and until women are accepted into the private club environment, I'm afraid they will find it difficult to make it through the glass ceiling." Although this comment was made partly in jest, it is a chilling commentary on the social and gender stratification of American culture and gave me an Alice in Wonderland feeling about women's ability to walk through the looking glass into an essentially male refuge. As long as men believe that women's acceptance and mastery of male gamesmanship is a prerequisite for leadership positions, women will continue to find it difficult to overcome such extra-institutional barriers. What then will it take to remove the glass ceiling for all women including women of color? The potential strategies I discuss next may provide answers to that question.

6

IMPLEMENTING CHANGE

*Campus Commissions
and Feminist Pedagogy*

Three groups sought to control the higher education policy agenda following passage of Title VII and IX: the state, the universities, and the stakeholders—women and people of color. Federal guidelines for implementing nondiscriminatory practices and affirmative action plans added a new layer of bureaucracy to university-government relations, fostering animosity between the educational establishment, which viewed regulations as cumbersome and intrusive, and the federal regulatory agencies.

The Carnegie Commission on Higher Education (1973) sought to play a mediating role and to influence the direction of social justice policies and practices as part of its comprehensive blueprint for reforming postsecondary education. Its sweeping report on equal opportunity generated dozens of recommendations for increasing women's enrollments, retention, and graduation rates. These ranged from changes in admissions and financial aid to the adoption of part-time programs and accelerated degrees for reentry adult students. To increase the numbers of women and minority faculty, it also proposed three-year teaching doctorates (the Doctor of Arts) and the recruitment of faculty from the ranks of new Ph.D.s. By 1975, the Carnegie Council on Policy Studies, a reform-minded think tank funded by the Carnegie Corporation, expressed strong criticism of both the federal regulators charged with enforcing affirmative action and the newly regulated universities. It lambasted universities for their inadequate response in employing, promoting, and paying women equitably and for not doing more to eliminate discrimination. In addition to charges of foot-dragging within both the educational and political establishment, it urged university and college presidents to exercise their leadership authority in urging departments to greatly increase the number of women and minorities in all fields and ranks, creating new administrative positions, and improving employment conditions for lecturers, instructors, and part-time faculty. In issuing strong warnings to both the regulators and the regulated that federal programs were "near self-destruction," it set the stage for subsequent developments within higher education institutions throughout the 1970s.

Women's rights and minority activists initiated their own campus-based investigations, and by 1973, sixteen hundred cases had been filed with the EEOC, 45 percent of these involving sex discrimination, 38 percent race and ethnic discrimination, 12 percent multiple allegations, and 4 percent religious discrimination (Stimpson, 1993, p. 8). Presidents responded to campus activism and criticisms by appointing ad hoc and permanent commissions and setting up staff development, continuing education, and other human resource and academic programs. They appointed affirmative action and equal opportunity officers to provide them with gender and race/ethnicity data on student admissions, workforce utilization, and contract guidelines. Faculty were asked to rewrite their own personnel policies for hiring, promotion, and tenure. These actions were met with varying degrees of apathy, ambivalence, and resistance by department chairs, directors, and deans, or, alternatively, with acceptance and compliance. Affirmative action offices implemented public posting of vacancies, affirmative action advertising, new personnel hiring and grievance practices, student recruitment and scholarship programs, staff development, and various other strategies. Skeptics suggested that qualifications, merit, and other status variables were being sacrificed to preferential treatment for women and minorities based on their membership in a protected group rather than as individuals. They also disputed the role of faculty governance and academic freedom in a political environment; the conflict among goals, timetables, and quotas; and the unintended consequence of replacing enlightenment values of equality of opportunity and individual rights with a policy of group results.

At first, universities perceived affirmative action as a temporary, remedial measure that could be met through adherence to regulatory requirements and the implementation of nondiscriminatory practices. It soon became apparent, however, that a range of policies related to admissions, employment, and contracting was regarded in Washington as grossly inadequate to meet the dual tests of access and opportunity. Much greater effort would be clearly needed if sex and race bias were to be remedied. Institutions themselves complained of the high cost of complying with onerous reporting and auditing requirements and were shaken by allegations of reverse discrimination against white males and their inability to achieve consensus between advocates of equity and merit. One study conducted for the U.S. Office of Education in 1976 called affirmative action "the most controversial and volatile area relating to the employment of women and minorities in educational institutions" (Kane, 1976, p. xii). Gray and Schafer observed that by 1981, policy decisions regarding faculty status still depended on "cronyism, the old-boy network, stereotyping, hiring men on potential and women on accomplishment," practices that did not end with the passage of antidiscrimination statutes and the issuance of executive orders (p. 351). They speculated that written affirmative action plans had become pro forma exercises, unread and unacted upon by federal regulators, and warned that unless reforms were instituted, the demise of equal opportunity was entirely possible.

Four years later, Mary Gray, a former chair of the AAUP's Committee W on the Status of Women in the Academic Profession, observed that "academe has a long way to go to achieve the ideal of sex equity in faculty employment" (1985, p. 40). She cited four related concerns: adverse judicial decisions on class certification, burden of proof, comparability of work and the use of statistical data in proving discrimination; continuing judicial deference to academic decision making based on academic freedom premises; the high psychic and financial costs of pursuing an individual or class action suit, making legal redress a hollow goal for most women faculty; and the unlikelihood of legislative remedies or rigorous action from the EEOC. Women, she asserted, would be better served by initiating reforms from within (ibid.).

Affirmative action proponents based their support of this policy on three arguments: compensating disadvantaged groups for prior discrimination, correcting current inequities by increasing the proportional representation of women and minorities, and enriching the institution through cultural and gender diversity (Francis, 1993; Tierney, 1996). They argued that "racist and sexist biases pervading American culture establish a system of differential rewards that benefit certain individuals, but not on the basis of neutral criteria of talent and effort" (Hawkesworth, 1988). Opponents, on the other hand, claimed that its primary use was political, a means of legitimizing reverse discrimination, mainly against white Anglo males, encouraging preferential treatment in admissions and hiring, and perpetuating the myth of female and minority inferiority. Each side mustered support for its arguments, a factor that was not helped by piecemeal legislation, uneven media coverage, and contradictory cases that weakened the rationale for this policy.

I reviewed a range of administrative and governmental responses to affirmative action and equal employment legislation and the impact of executive, organizational, and judicial decisions on women as a protected group and as individuals. What is their role as agents of change in university policies? I explore two higher education strategies adopted by women students, faculty, and professional staff as the basis for changing institutional cultures. The first strategy, the establishment of campus commissions on the status of women, focuses on the myriad ways in which women organized to influence their institutional policy agendas. The second strategy, the application of feminist pedagogy, comprises the individual approaches that inform women's teaching and the transformation of knowledge in undergraduate and graduate classrooms.

Commissions on the Status of Women

Campus and state commissions on the status of women began as an instrumental response to federal demands that good-faith efforts be undertaken in designing affirmative action plans. I use the generic term *commission* to refer to task forces, committees, and other entities sharing similar purposes: to involve constituent groups of women in the evaluation of existing policies and the improvement of their role and status. In seeking to determine the extent of women's progress in the past twenty-five years, I have focused attention on these commissions to measure their effectiveness in advancing affirmative action goals and articulating women's concerns. Undoubtedly, other mechanisms occur through human resources and affirmative action / equal opportunity offices, and through collective bargaining units and women's studies. Conceptualized within a liberal feminist framework, the women's commission enabled university presidents to quell campus unrest in the 1960s and early 1970s, to defuse sources of potential conflict, to circumvent male-dominated power centers in the schools and colleges of their institutions, and to engage women faculty and students in a process of problem definition and agenda setting.

Although the circumstances surrounding their establishment varied, most of these commissions were driven by the demands of interest groups—students, faculty, professional staff—and were prompted by changes in the policy environment. By establishing commissions of prominent individuals with influence in the larger community, organizational leaders turned to commissions and task forces as a time-honored strategy for defusing potential sources of conflict and maintaining a democratic process of decision making. At the same time, commissions enabled them to retain control of the policy agenda and to propose changes in the status quo outside regular channels of campus governance. In this case, women's commissions operated as a useful conduit for fostering more equitable personnel policies that would encourage the admission of women students to male-dominated professional schools and the hiring of women faculty in male-only departments. From the perspective of the women's groups, their ability to influence policy was directly related to their access to such power centers as faculty senates, boards of regents, provosts and presidents. In this context, they operated within carefully defined boundaries, where their activities were closely monitored, their reporting mechanisms assured, and their recommendations vetted.

Women's commissions originated from four sources: state governing boards, presidents and provosts, faculty senates, and grass-roots campus groups. They constituted a direct response to the women's liberation movement, the passage of affirmative action and equal employment laws and regulations, and the specter of government sanctions in the form of withdrawal of federal contracts for evidence of sex discrimination. President Kennedy's Commission on the Status of Women provided an early example, and as a result, state-level women's commissions (see chapter 1) were established throughout the 1960s. Gender bias commissions have served another important purpose in focusing attention on the judiciary and on every aspect of governmental services, such as health care, social welfare, education, and criminal justice. For example, feminist lawyers have used the commission approach to attain a "fundamental restructuring of the priorities underlying judicial administration and subsidized legal services" (Rhode, 1994, p. 56). In reviewing the reports and communications of thirty women's commissions in higher education, several patterns emerge regarding their origin, development, and current status. They developed in three stages that closely parallel external events, the evolving policy environment, and the ideological beliefs of the major actors.

Early or first-stage commissions came about as the result of allegations of sex discrimination; grass-roots organizing on the part of women faculty, students, and staff; and external funding to establish continuing education programs for older women students. A high level of participation, data gathering, and consciousness raising characterized them. Second-stage commissions were generated in response to state mandates, improved monitoring and reporting systems on compensation and other terms and conditions of employment, and increased pressures for diversity. Third-stage commissions are now seeking to defend their continued operations in the light of growing conservatism concerning affirmative action, equal opportunity, resource allocation, and women's studies as the focus for feminist scholarship.

First-Stage Commissions

Gender Bias Commissions

By 1968, presidents were sanctioning campus commissions as a rejoinder to feminist activism. At the University of Michigan, for example, the president, Robben Fleming, appointed the Commission on Women in 1970 as a direct result of a class action complaint filed by women faculty and professional staff under Executive Order No. 11246. In this case, the federal government had investigated and found the university guilty of "blatant sex discrimination" and then had withheld research funds until the administration acted to redress the gender imbalance. As a result of this victory, Michigan's commission conducted a salary equity review and took other actions to advance women's interests. Two related developments directly influenced the unfolding scenario at Michigan: the operation since 1964 of a Center for the Education of Women and the establishment in 1976 of an affirmative action office. This new unit assumed statutory responsibility for developing the university's affirmative action plan, including goals and timetables and other reporting, monitoring, and oversight functions in a pattern that was repeated in other universities. Affirmative action/equal opportunity officers, who were frequently appointed as special assistants to the president, tended to have legal or human resource backgrounds and assumed quasi-legal positions as the administration's surrogate in reviewing grievances and bias complaints. Affirmative action quickly preempted women's committees, and advocates of women's empowerment gradually lost their influence.

At Michigan, when the affirmative action office was established, women faculty withdrew their support from the Commission on Women and formed the autonomous Academic Women's Caucus. Between 1976 and 1989, the Commission on Women declined in influence, losing its collective voice and, according to one observer, becoming "a vehicle for salaried staff by default rather than design despite efforts to recreate its mission in the mideighties." The Academic Women's Caucus and the Center for the Education of Women also lost their momentum in the 1980s, as a new generation of women faculty rejected campus activism and directed their energies toward their own research, teaching, and departmental committees. Michigan's administrative priorities also shifted when economic and political changes precipitated campuswide efforts to restructure the university's schools and colleges. The affirmative action office was expanded into a Division of Human Resources and Affirmative Action, and the Academic Women's Caucus became further stratified into an organization for mid-level women administrators, librarians, and office staff. According to one administrator, "It's difficult to keep up a head of steam for twenty-five years, and also faculty are stretched terribly thin and don't feel they have the time with all the pressures to publish and teach and direct dissertations."

Another early initiative occurred at the University of Minnesota, where Minnesota Plan I was instituted in 1959 with funding from the Carnegie Corporation.[1] Although two of its recommendations were adopted, for a women's center and a continuing education program, other policy proposals were not. But like many soft-money projects, the plan did little to change the status of university women.

The Grass-Roots Commission

At the University of Delaware, the women's commission originated under somewhat different circumstances. Delaware is the flagship university in a mid-Atlantic border state with only one other public university (Delaware State University), an historically black institution, and two public community colleges. As a result, the allocation of resources to facilitate integration and mission differentiation became important priorities throughout the 1960s and 1970s. Women faculty who had come to Delaware in the 1970s are now in positions of academic leadership and are united in their advocacy of women's studies. For the past twenty years, the women's studies programs, the Office of Women's Affairs, and the commission have acted as a single administrative unit charged with the responsibility of achieving gender equity throughout the institution. Its strength has emerged from three related sources: a close working relationship between the commission's first director and the university's president over a period of sixteen years (1973–89); its parallel development and symbiotic relationship with a highly developed women's studies program; and the creation of a campus culture that was inclusive of the concerns of women at all levels from the outset, giving all constituencies a place at the table—faculty, professional staff, classified staff, and students. According to one woman administrator:

> In the mid-seventies we set up the current structure with women's studies as an academic program and the commission as a kind of administrative unit that has gender equity as its primary charge. We really saw those as separate but linked phenomena, so that there have always been close ties between women's studies and women's affairs. Now the office of women's affairs and the commission are very institutionalized and

1. Miller (1996). See also LaNoue & Lee (1987), and Minnesota Plan II (1988).

part of the administrative structure, just as women's studies is a strong piece of the academic program. In the early years, there was a sense of urgency and engagement with all of the activities, and although that is not the case any more, the commitment is still there. I think that both women's studies and the commission have worked hard to ensure that women who come to campus are brought into these organizations.

Second-Stage Commissions

As the 1980s drew to a close, the confluence of internal changes and external events motivated universities to reconstitute their commitment to women's concerns. By 1989, the number of accredited higher education institutions had stabilized, and although women were 53 percent of all students, they were still only 13 percent of tenured full professors and 11 percent of college and university presidents. Some problems had been resolved, but several systemic issues resisted easy solutions: salary inequity, women's underrepresentation in scientific and professional fields, the resilience of the glass ceiling, women's predominance on the lowest rungs of the career ladder, and the differential treatment of women of color. In 1989, spurred on by the ACE Commission on Women in Higher Education (Shavlik, Touchton, & Pearson, 1989), together with a growing recognition that the pipeline was not working and pressures from minority students for a more visible commitment to campus diversity, presidents and governing boards formed committees, task forces, and commissions to conduct needs analyses, collect data and set priorities for collective action. The ACE report contained twenty recommendations "designed to mobilize and energize individuals to rethink the way campuses function relative to women" (p. 5). It called on a new group of university presidents to reaffirm or establish commissions on the status of women in the 1990s and to appoint a woman coordinator with responsibility for bringing together groups of women and preparing annual and five-year reviews on women's status. This proposal breathed new life into moribund commissions and led to the formation of two new types—state-mandated and voluntary consortia.

The State-Mandated Commission

As resource dependence shifted from institutional budgets to the state treasury, governing boards accrued greater power and influence over university governance. In assessing institutional missions in the late 1980s, diversity became a primary objective. The Arizona Board of Regents created a women's commission to assess employment conditions for women at its three research universities—Arizona State University, the University of Arizona, and Northern Arizona University—"defining a vision for women at the universities in the year 2000" and recommending board actions that would enable the universities to achieve that vision (Arizona Commission on the Status of Women, 1991). This state-level commission issued fifty recommendations and an implementation plan, Vision 2000, making each university accountable for establishing its own presidential commission, designing new equity policies and procedures, and monitoring its progress.

Arizona State's president, Lattie Coor, instituted the campuswide Commission on the Status of Women in 1991, charging it with the task of pursuing the recommendations set forth by the Regents Commission, assessing conditions for women in all employment groups and in the student body, recommending strategies and policies for implementation and compliance with the regents' plan, and advising him on emerging issues relevant to women on ASU's two campuses. Following a two-year investigation, the ASU commission reported to the president that gender equity was a goal but not yet a reality. Although the numbers of women students were growing, women faculty and professional staff had reached a plateau in their progress, and the glass ceiling was still in place. By 1992, the percentage of women faculty at ASU had increased in ten years from 19.9 percent in 1982 to only 24.3 percent, and none of the ten new hires at the rank of full professor were women. A focus group of senior women faculty expressed the view that their scholarly activities were "unappreciated," that they carried a "disproportionate burden of departmental service and struggled with excessive teaching, advising, and supervising workloads," and that in their departments, they experienced a "lack of collegiality, difficulty getting strong letters of recommendation, along with hostile colleagues and unsupportive chairs, who further undermined their progress to full rank" (Faculty & Academic Professionals Committee, 1994). They also described criteria for promotion to full rank as "moving targets" due to a "lack of clear and concise standards, poor or no communication of expectations, and gender bias."

By 1995, the task force of three university commissions issued a five-year status report to the Arizona Board of Regents, echoing the findings of the ASU commission. Women on all three campuses continued to struggle for acceptance, opportunity, and success due to gender bias, the difficulties of redefining women's traditional roles, and the persistence of assumptions regarding their special needs (Commission on the Status of Women, 1995). The task force also found evidence of occupational segregation within administrative and classified staff positions, with most women mired in the lowest entry and semiskilled pay levels in contrast to men, who commanded the majority of senior professional staff positions. This problem also permeated reports from other states with women's commissions, documenting women's prevalence in historically feminized positions and their inability to break through the glass ceiling in more than token numbers.

A major problem, and one that neither the regents nor the universities could easily resolve, was Arizona's unstable economy and legislative control of all salaries for public employees, including higher education. A succession of salary freezes had left Arizona's research universities with few resources to reduce gender inequities. This problem was exacerbated with the election of Governor Fife Symington, a critic of faculty productivity, who instituted changes in the composition of the board of regents. A three-year salary equity adjustment approved by the legislature was subsequently reduced to one year, and in its 1996 report the ASU commission called for further legislative funding to remove inequities for women faculty, classified staff, and professional employees. At Northern Arizona University, an initiative in 1993 to raise women's salaries embroiled its female president in a controversy with male faculty over charges of reverse discrimination.

By 1996, the Arizona Board of Regents had declared its intention to focus on three areas in the research universities: campus climate, professional and career development, and compensation and equity (Hoks, 1996). According to ASU's 1996 annual report, however, women complained about inconsistent messages being given to men and women faculty regarding tenure and promotion, as well as the need for legislative funding to correct salary inequities for women faculty and staff and to support management training for all employee groups. One observer noted: "Our commission has had good support from top administrators and a lot of respect from faculty, but change is a very slow process. The political climate is changing now and although this has not yet affected the regents' commitment to the women's commission, other issues now take priority—criticism of the K–12 system, the low number of African-American students, competition with the community colleges, and the state's general economic situation."

As I noted earlier, on September 5, 1997, Symington resigned as governor and power passed to a woman, Secretary of State Jane Hull. In Arizona's neighboring state, the Board of Regents of the University of California took a different approach to gender and race equity. It is ironic that the site of the nation's first federally approved affirmative action plan in 1971 also produced higher education's first resolution rescinding this policy. Opponents of the regents' action were quickly silenced by an alliance of the majority of trustees and the governor as a voting member. The UC nondiscrimination policy, issued originally in 1975 and revised in 1977 and 1990, had prohibited discrimination not only on the basis of race, color, national origin, religion, and sex, but also physical or mental disability, cancer-related medical condition, ancestry, marital status, age, sexual orientation, status as a Vietnam or special disabled veteran, and citizenship (Office of the President, 1995, p. 3).

The university's president, Jack Peltason, who resigned shortly after passage of the regents' resolution, warned that rescinding affirmative action would require major changes in admissions policies and new definitions of what constitutes merit in an academic environment, possibly jeopardizing billions of dollars received by the university for construction, research, training, public service, and federal student support.

In 1993, the UC system received $1.3 billion to support research, training and public service; $400 million in federal student support; and $1.7 billion for the purchase, design, and construction of campus facilities. By 1994, women were more than 50 percent of undergraduate students and 43 percent of graduate students. But only 22 percent of all tenure-track faculty were women, with women of color accounting for 4 percent of that total: Asian American (2%), Latina (1.2%), African American (0.8%), and American Indian (0.1%). Women administrators were also more apt to be in entry- and middle-level positions; only 21 percent were senior executives.[2]

Voluntary Consortia Commissions

The University of New Hampshire formed a commission on the status of women in 1972 to explore conditions relating to women's mobility and equality and to encourage women's full participation. It is well established, with a newsletter, bylaws delineating its policies and procedures, and a part-time paid coordinator. The coordinator recently declared that although women have made significant gains, several areas still need attention: pay equity for administrators, staff, and faculty; faculty recruitment and retention; classroom climate; sexual harassment; and safety and child care (Stapleton, 1996, p. 1). To maximize its impact on policy in the next five years, New Hampshire has joined with women's commissions in five other land-

---

2. Memorandum to the Board of Regents of the University of California from the Office of the President, *Diversity: An Introduction to the University of California's Policies and Programs* (1995), p. 9.

grant universities to organize the New England Council of Land-Grant University Women.

Mirroring Arizona's charge, the council issued its own version of Vision 2000, a major difference being that this initiative emanated from the women's commissions rather than the governing boards or chancellors (1996). The consortium called on the presidents and chancellors of the Universities of Massachusetts, New Hampshire, Vermont, Maine, Connecticut, and Rhode Island to correct hiring, promotion, tenure, compensation, and working condition inequities at all six institutions; to foster accountability, diversity, family-friendly policies, women's academic and career development; and to eliminate gender bias and sexual harassment. The preamble to its report proclaimed: "Despite some 30 years of gradual legislative change, fulfillment of the goal of gender equity has been slow, partial, and painful. The legal and ethical mandate is clear; institutions of higher education can no longer ignore the harmful effects of the inequitable allocation of resources. Our claim is not to add resources but to have our fair share of them" (New England Council of Land-Grant University Women, 1996).

A joint survey found that women in all six institutions were conspicuously underrepresented in administrative and supervisory positions and had lower status, compensation, and less job security. Women faculty also had lower salaries than male colleagues and were less likely to earn tenure or promotions to full professor; women nonexempt office staff lacked career advancement opportunities. According to the council, "Far too many women report being intimidated or silenced, when they have spoken out against these facts of university life; they also report profound distrust or dissatisfaction with available grievance and other conflict resolution mechanisms" (New England Council, p. 10).

In Pennsylvania, the Women's Consortium of the Pennsylvania State System, comprising fourteen comprehensive universities, was formed in 1980.[3] It provides one of the few examples of faculty collaboration in master's level universities that emphasize teacher education. By contrast, only one of California's twenty-three state colleges has a women's commission. Women were not recognized as an equity group in Pennsylvania until April 1988, when the

3. I thank Esther Skirball, professor of sociology, Slippery Rock University, and president, Pennsylvania State System Women's Consortium, for acquainting me with its activities. I also thank Mary Keetz, director emeritus of the Institute for Women, West Chester University, for sharing her study on the status of women faculty in the fourteen state universities. See also Keetz (1991).

state system's board of governors approved its first systemwide affirmative action and equal opportunity plan (Keetz, 1991). It bid each state university to use ACE Commission on Women guidelines (Shavlik, Touchton, & Pearson, 1989) in developing an affirmative action plan for women as well as minorities, Vietnam veterans, and the disabled. The fourteen commission plans produced in response to this order were subsequently combined into a five-year statewide affirmative action and diversity program. In contrast to the experience of the state's research universities, Keetz expressed surprise that in reviewing state system and faculty union documents, she could find "no mention of women as a separate equity group prior to the publication of the system-wide . . . affirmative action policy prospectus in 1988. . . . Nor could evidence be found that either group had analyzed or publicized information about gender equity in the State system's faculty since the publication of the Prospectus, despite the availability of the data" (Keetz, 1991, p. 1).

In essence, the state mandate empowered the women's consortium and gave it more credibility on its respective campuses. No longer existing in isolation from each other, these commissions compared their relative status on fourteen campuses and assessed their own progress in relation to women faculty in the California, New York, and New Jersey state college systems. In her analysis, Keetz had found that between 1974 and 1989, full-time female faculty had increased from 22 to 29 percent. Nevertheless, they were still only 14 percent of full professors and 24 percent of associate professors, but 46 percent of assistant professors and 59 percent of instructors. That women had little input into campus affirmative action plans suggests a top-down model of policy implementation.

In concluding her analysis, Keetz issued a call for action on behalf of the women's consortium, calling on the state system to demonstrate its commitment to educational equity: "Many of the changes in the environment on individual campuses and in the status of female faculty in the state system since the early 1970s have come about because female faculty have pressed for them collectively through the establishment and actions of such groups as the Women's Consortium of the Pennsylvania State System of Higher Education, Women's Center, Women's Studies Programs, the Institute for Women, and most recently, the Commissions on the Status of Women" (Keetz, 1991, p. 34). She later recalled that her report had been very influential, "helping us get more representation and giving us more clout. I was able to document the lack of women at all levels and in all 14 institutions."[4]

4. Telephone interview with Mary Keetz, West Chester University, October 5, 1995.

Diversity Commissions

Early criticism of affirmative action had deplored the anti-elitist approach of the federal government in singling out the nation's most prestigious research universities for discrimination complaints. Today, diversity is the number one goal of affirmative action officers and campus commissions. A 1987 minority student action at the University of Michigan that effectively shut down the campus precipitated a renewed assertion of presidential authority. The Office of Academic and Multicultural Affairs and the Commission on a Multicultural University were created as parallel structures to the Presidential Advisory Commission on Women and the Affirmative Action Advisory Council, with representatives from the university's numerous organizational units. As one official noted, "With twenty thousand employees, Michigan is a very complex organization on the far end of the spectrum in terms of decentralization. Although deans and faculty make budget and personnel decisions, the president has the power of the purse if he chooses to exercise it."

Unanimously praised as a visionary leader with a commitment to women's concerns, in 1988 University of Michigan president James Duderstadt endorsed a more inclusive women's agenda for the 1990s, representing the interests of "all women regardless of race, ethnic group, or sexual orientation, with special attention to the particular concerns of women of color" (Ad Hoc Committee on Women's Issues, December 1988). In addition to affirming the Ad Hoc Committee's recommendations, in 1989 he formed the President's Advisory Commission on Women's Issues (PACWI), revived the Center for the Education of Women, and gave his tacit recognition to the Women of Color Task Force (PACWI, 1994).

By 1987, women at Michigan constituted 48 percent of undergraduate enrollments, but only one-third of graduate students in Ph.D. and professional degree programs: 9 percent of full professors, 23 percent of associate professors, and 53 percent of non-tenure-track and part-time lecturers. They continued to be underrepresented in such male-dominated fields as business, law, medicine, and engineering, and to have lower median salaries at all ranks and all schools and larger advisement workloads. Between 1990 and 1992, they experienced an administrative decline as executive officers (from 18% to 10%), deans (22% to 16%), and associate deans (41% to 24%). The women's commission criticized status quo hiring patterns, observing that "if recent rates of change continue, by the year 2000 only 24 percent of tenured and tenure-track faculty will be women, but [they] will represent 72 percent of all lecturers" (Hollenshead, 1993). Heeding their plea, President Duderstadt launched the *Michigan Agenda for Women: Leadership for a New Century*, with the overall goal of making the University of Michigan "by the year 2000 the leader among American universities in promoting the success of women of diverse backgrounds as faculty, students, and staff, and the leading institution for the study of women and gender issues" (PACWI, 1994, p. 4).

Each academic unit was asked to develop a targeted strategy to increase women's presence and participation at all ranks, with special attention to women of color. The president and provost authorized a five-year hiring and recruitment effort (SHARE) of ten senior women faculty for any of its sixty-seven academic units where women faculty were underrepresented, that is, with only one senior woman faculty member or a lower than average percentage as calculated by Michigan's workforce utilization analysis. Incentive funding provided resources for "target-of-opportunity" hiring of women of color that bypassed the search committee process. Although measures were taken to increase the proportion of women senior administrators, by 1995 there was only one woman vice president for student affairs and four women deans of nursing, public health, social work, and letters and science. When Duderstadt resigned in September 1995 in the wake of a controversy with the board of trustees, a commission member commented that "the extent to which clearly articulated institutional commitments fight with our political reality is an important question." In an unusual turn of events, both Duderstadt and the current president, Lee Bollinger, have been named as co-defendants in the pending class action lawsuit brought by the Center for Individual Rights, which asserts that they administered preferential minority admissions policies under the Michigan Mandate that violate federal civil rights laws (Lederman, 1997b, p. A27).[5]

Fiscal concerns and diversity issues also played a key role in the Delaware experience. In its first decade, a salary equalization task force joined forces with the local AAUP chapter to obtain approval for systematic salary reviews. In 1989, however, the commission's status changed with the appoint-

---

5. Following protests by students of color demanding greater representation at the University of Michigan, President James Duderstadt adopted a strategic plan known as the Michigan Mandate. Its purpose was "to ensure that all racial and ethnic groups would be full participants in the life of the University" and that the university would become "a leader in creating a multicultural community capable of serving as a model for higher education and for society at large" (Office of the President, 1994, p. 2). The Michigan Agenda for Women was subsequently adopted in 1994 as an inclusive gender equity plan that augmented the Michigan Mandate for racial and ethnic participation (ibid.).

ment of a new president. The office of women's affairs is now part of a larger office for multicultural diversity, reporting to a vice president for faculty relations. By 1993, women were almost one-third (31.6%) of full-time faculty (a decline of 1% since 1990), constituting 19 percent of tenured faculty and 12 percent of full professors. Although they were 52 percent of professional staff, minority women accounted for only 5.7 percent of the total, leading the commission to recommend that more attention be paid to meeting affirmative action goals and timetables in hiring and promoting women, including women of color. By 1995, the commission's role had become one of raising awareness, monitoring women's status, and serving as their advocates. A former chair commented: "We address any issue that concerns women students, staff, and faculty. . . . However, we still need to address systematic gender bias in the professional staff classification system, why we have such low numbers of tenured women faculty in business, engineering, and agriculture, the low percentage of women among new faculty hires and related to that the impact of downsizing on the number of faculty slots and the high proportion of women in non-tenure track appointments."

The Rajender consent decree issued at Minnesota in 1980 had mandated that affirmative action guidelines be revised to set goals and timetables and hiring practices for each administrative unit, with special attention to the chemistry department. By 1987, the university also had a well-established women's studies department and the Center for Advanced Feminist Studies. The university was operating under a consent decree for seven years when a sex bias incident in the chemistry department in 1987 became the catalyst for renewed appeals to university officials to take concrete action and improve the campus environment. A women hired under the consent decree found feces on her desk, and although the perpetrator was never discovered, the incident prompted eleven senior women faculty to deliver a series of seven demands to the provost. These included the creation of a high-level administrative position and development of a plan to improve the climate for women, the appointment of more women to senior-level administrative positions, a reprimand to the chemistry department, meetings with department heads and administrators, and the establishment of an advisory committee to the president and the board of regents. Four policy changes occurred: women faculty received a negotiated base salary increase in 1989; the affirmative action / equal opportunity office and a university senate subcommittee on equal employment opportunity for women were invited to form a new internal monitoring system; women filed more than three hundred claims of discrimination dating back to 1973, the year of the Rajender class action suit; and a new commission on women was established to devise a plan of action that eventually became Minnesota Plan II.

The administration responded by appointing a special assistant to the vice president and director of equal opportunity and affirmative action and an associate provost with special responsibility for minority affairs. The eighty-member Commission on Women produced Minnesota Plan II in 1989, setting forth goals for the recruitment and retention of women faculty, students, and staff; greater administrative accountability; and curriculum restructuring. By the end of 1996, the Minnesota Commission was struggling with its ambiguous position as a change agent at the margins of the university, the conflict between its faculty and the board of regents regarding the continuation of tenure, the threat of faculty unionization, and the resignation of its president and appointment of a new administration.

In contrast to the experience of women in the Pennsylvania State System, the Penn State University Commission for Women was revitalized in 1992 with a much broader mandate that included racial and ethnic diversity; equal opportunity and affirmative action; and lesbian, gay, and bisexual equity. A vice provost for educational equity coordinates all diversity initiatives and supports the work of the Commission for Women and the Equal Opportunities Planning Committee, which report directly to the president. Also reporting directly to the president are the Commission on Racial and Ethnic Diversity and the Committee on Lesbian, Gay, and Bisexual Equity.

The Commission for Women was asked to review 26 recommendations and 192 implementation recommendations made in 1988 by an earlier study group of women faculty and administrators (Penn State Commission, 1994). It identified a number of problems: persistent underrepresentation of women, including women of color, among faculty and administrators. By 1992, women in executive and administrative positions had increased only slightly and remained clustered in the lower grades. Women in non-tenure-track appointments had exceeded the ratio of women in tenured or tenure-track positions. Women staff and technical service employees were concentrated in lower pay grades, and women held only six of the thirty-two executive positions and only nine of the sixty-one administrative positions (1994, p. 11). Penn State's report underscores the inadequacy of affirmative action goal-setting and the monumental task confronting rural land-grant universities in changing campus cultures, increasing diversity, and building more responsive workplaces.

At the University of Southern California, an elaborate structure of diversity committees was set up in 1991, reporting to the Coordinating Committee on Diversity. As a result of civil unrest in south-central Los Angeles following the Rodney King incident, however, a new administrative position was created with support from these committees. Since 1993, highly placed women faculty and deans have formed the Feminist Council to advise the administration on sexual harassment, pay equity, race and gender issues. According to one of its members:

> We don't operate as a sanctioned university committee but we are a group who need to be contended with. I don't know of any other institution with a group like ours. . . . We are all very busy so we concentrate on issues in which we think we can affect some change. . . . We have also taken a strong stand on affirmative action. The way in which power and privilege operate has not changed and I think a lot of young women are naïve to feel that there is a level playing field or that once they get into a structure such as a university or a corporation, they are going to make it to the top on their own. They probably are more qualified than most but quality and merit are not the system that accrues in our society. I mean that is the reality.

Third-Stage Commissions

The president or provost charges third-stage commissions with producing an action plan and recommendations on a wide range of women's issues. Two examples are the President's Commission on Women at Ohio State University and the Committee on the Recruitment and Retention of Women Faculty at Stanford University. Neither commission provides an encouraging picture of women's status in the 1990s. An ad hoc committee on the status of women conducted the first systematic analysis of the status of women at Ohio State in 1971. A second report by the Commission on Women and Minorities followed in 1977. The third-stage commission appointed by Ohio State's president in 1991 found that little had changed in fifteen years and that the campus climate was even worse for women of color: "Women still confront an environment that ignores critical gender differences, places impediments in the way of women striving to reach their full potential, and fails to recognize and respect women's professional abilities and achievements" (Ohio State University, 1992, p. 6).

Although the numbers of women across ranks and levels had improved since the 1970s, by 1991 women constituted only 15.3 percent of all full-time faculty (4.6% of full professors) and 2.9 percent of administrators, but 75 percent of part-time faculty and 34.2 percent of doctoral students. By 1993, women administrators included two deans in the twenty-one colleges, twelve department chairs, and three vice presidents. Although women in executive positions increased, staff women remained clustered in the lower-paid positions throughout the university. In strongly worded language, commission members identified a hostile campus climate and institutional barriers, both organizational and attitudinal, that impeded women's progress. Their interviews with 350 women at Ohio State disclosed "sexist attitudes and behaviors [that] continue to diminish, stereotype, and trivialize women," and evidence of sexual harassment, stress and burnout, leading them to assert that "unless the climate changes, women's experience of frustration, discrimination, and fear will not change" (Ohio State University, 1992, p. 23). They identified significant institutional barriers resulting from inequitable workloads, male-dominated departments, an overemphasis on male-female faculty competitiveness, and bias against women's research. Women were isolated in traditional female fields and excluded from the formal and informal networks in which decision-making occurred. In the context of affirmative action criticism, the commission found that "affirmative action has been ineffective; efforts are without coordination, and built-in mechanisms for accountability are few and far between. . . . [It] is not viewed as everyone's business and is not seen as relevant by many. . . . Fair and equal opportunity for women to pursue their education and careers is not the norm." The report recommended the creation of a campus climate to encourage women's full participation and productivity; policies that value their experiences in the context of academic, professional, and family roles; gender-neutral language for university policies; the encouragement of diversity in the workforce; and an organizational structure that enhances women's status, development, and quality of life (p. 27).

Another report released in 1993 by Stanford University also provided revealing data on the status of women faculty in a private research university. In 1992, in the aftermath of the Frances Conley case (discussed in chapter 4), Stanford's provost appointed the Committee on the Recruitment and Retention of Women Faculty at Stanford University. Its 1993 report showed a pattern of slow growth in the percentage of women faculty (from 7 to 16%) and of tenured women faculty (from 4 to 11%) between 1974 and 1993. By 1993, 43 percent of all departments at this university still had no tenured women, almost 40 percent of the departments hiring new faculty in the five years preceding the report had not hired a woman, and only 11 percent of the departments had one-third or more tenured women on their staffs. In framing its recommendations, the Stanford commission remarked: "The low percentage of faculty women provides us with an important warning signal. We need to change our policies and procedures and our recruitment and retention strategies" (p. 1).

The commission emphasized the need to create a culture of faculty support, increase the number and percentage of women faculty, promote salary equity and benefits to enhance recruitment and retention of women faculty, and assist women in combining work and family responsibilities. A woman provost appointed after the report's release endorsed most of its recommendations, asserting, however, that "departments make hiring decisions, not the president, provost or deans. Departments are where changes must occur" (Bartholomew, 1993, p. 11). Two years after the report was issued, little had changed: thirty departments were still without tenured women faculty, although a new position of vice president for faculty affairs had been created to monitor hiring, promotion, and tenure.

Women in positions of authority offer several reasons for the decline in influence of women's commissions in the 1990s: (1) the recognition that affirmative action and equal opportunity had become part of the institutional bureaucracy and could be ignored with impunity in a culture that delegated authority to department heads and deans; (2) the institutionalization of women's studies programs as the major focus of feminist intellectual activity; (3) the decline of campus activism paralleling the shrinking academic labor market, the diminution of career advancement options, and the unionization of faculty and staff; (4) the backlash against women in a time of diminishing resources and conflicting priorities, as evidenced in reports of the chilly climate on campuses for women students, faculty, and administrators (Sandler & Hall, 1993); (5) the multiple difficulties encountered by women of color; and (6) the influence of court decisions and consent decrees in highlighting continuing gender bias. A major focus for commissions in the nineties is to generate statistical and anecdotal data on women's status, the development of strategies for removing barriers to their participation, the implementation of diversity mandates, and the transformation of campus cultures.

Assessing the Effectiveness of Campus Commissions

Commissions have several practical functions: clarifying issues, setting priorities, collecting data, making recommendations, monitoring activities and serving as sounding boards and early warning systems for the president and his staff. In institutions with well-established commissions, fiscal support and access to the highest levels of the administrative hierarchy make it possible to influence the policy agenda. Commissions are not risk-takers, however; priorities are set within a narrow band of acceptable behavior, and much of what is seen as progressive must be perceived as compatible with mainstream male values. For example, tokenism at upper levels of university administration gives women only limited access to finance, academic administration, and other key policy-making positions. Women's ability to earn full professorships, major grants, named chairs, presidencies, and other forms of recognition and status is largely dependent on the indulgence of males in positions of power, influence, and authority.

Women's commissions on university campuses have been constrained by various factors, most particularly, the decentralization of higher education, the lack of a central coordinating structure, the limited resources with which the commissions operate, and most recently, a conservative political environment. The commission strategy illustrates the president's role as change agent and, conversely, as protector of the status quo. It also highlights the importance of different leadership styles. Commissions gained their viability from presidents who are generally male and are unlikely to step outside the mainstream in conceptualizing commissions or in giving them space within the organization. At the same time, they demonstrate the limitations that the role of university governance plays in faculty hiring, promotion, and tenure decisions. Although the president can foster a more inclusive campus environment through his or her ability to generate resources and draw public attention to policy issues, deference must also be paid to faculty, chairs, and deans in making personnel decisions. Administrative appointments and promotions tend to remain decentralized, making male dominance a self-fulfilling prophecy. As one director remarked: "The tough issues haven't been resolved. By this I mean promoting women into positions of authority, closing the salary gap, increasing the number of tenured women, recruiting and retaining women administrators, and doing more for junior faculty. There are explained differences between [disciplinary] fields but unexplained differences due to gender."

Commission staffs are small. Some are ad hoc arrangements that self-destruct after conducting their study and presenting their recommendations; others are members of statewide consortia that report to a central office rather than the campus president. Some reports are analogous to master plans: they are issued and disseminated to a select group of trusted individuals within the university community; their recommendations are evaluated for cost effectiveness and consensus purposes; some discussion is held with the concerned parties; and depending on the compatibility of the recommendations with the goals of the administration, some proposals get implemented. Although strong language permeates a few reports, for the most part women's voices are rather muted, and assertive women may find themselves being silenced by colleagues who recognize the risks in rocking the boat.

Access to institutional data varies considerably, however, and is largely dependent on the good will of the administration or on state policies governing release of this information, making it difficult to assess the extent of their effectiveness in removing gender-related pay inequities. Concern about reverse discrimination charges led the University of Wisconsin–Madison (1994) to engage in some rather interesting circumlocutions as they sought to rationalize gender-neutral and equal opportunity policies and to equate gender equity and merit. These reports are mainly descriptive, presenting the data, identifying the underlying problems, and proposing the solutions. The discourse is carefully framed within acceptable boundaries but the underlying text reveals a fair amount of frustration, discouragement, and criticism of the status quo. The costs of implementation are rarely included as part of the recommendations, which have a melancholy plaintiveness about them. The patterns of women's grievances, as catalogued in these reports, have a desensitizing effect on the reader, and one begins to wonder whether discrimination will ever end. These documents are important cultural artifacts that put into historical perspective the evolution of affirmative action policy. They show the intense optimism of the early years, when women thought that by cataloguing the problems the solutions would be self-evident. In the case of Pennsylvania State University, for example, the ambitious rendering of two hundred recommendations almost assured that only a small number of these would be achieved. The policy space cannot accommodate such a plethora of possibilities within its carefully defined parameters. Neither can such a full agenda gain the attention of leaders, whose priorities are subject to rapidly shifting forces that continuously divert their energies.

Several women chairing commissions commented on legislative rumblings for an affirmative action ban. According to one woman director: "Each institution and board of regents in this state has its own priorities. When our state system was established, we had a democratic governor. Now we have a republican governor, and the regents whom he has appointed seem more concerned with restructuring and downsizing than with diversity. We have to wait and see how much weight will be given to the women's recommendations."

In 1995, the Michigan and Delaware state legislatures considered but defeated bills that would have outlawed affirmative action policies in public higher education. The director of Delaware's Office of Women's Affairs, who also serves as a state senator, commented that the bill was defeated by a margin of only two votes in the Senate, the result of a last-minute telephone blitz by women's organizations. According to one informant: "It is being presented as a race issue because if it is also a gender issue, the tent will be broadened and more people might oppose conservative efforts to abolish it."

In the end, the institutional culture of most universities is not compatible with the needs and concerns of women in academia. Universities supporting commissions vary in size, prestige, mission, and geographic location. But recurrent themes of commission reports demonstrate strikingly similar concerns: the importance of creating a campus culture that actively supports women faculty, mid-level administrators, clerical staff, and graduate students (including teaching assistants); and the need for salary equity (still an issue on many campuses), for recruiting women into predominantly male departments and schools, for promoting them into leadership positions, and for strengthening commitments to flexible work-family roles, including mandatory stop-the-clock tenure policies and child care provisions.

The campus commission has played an important symbolic role, articulating a commitment to gender equity for women. The metaphorical significance of the millennium contributes added urgency to the message they disseminate within the university community regarding the need to affirm and respond to women's increasing participation as students and faculty by creating a transformative campus culture. Although commission members view their roles as "advocacy, monitoring, vigilance, prodding, meeting periodically with the president and the provost, sometimes together, sometimes separately, publicizing data, making recommendations," a director speculated that "the extent to which clearly articulated institutional commitments fight with our political reality is an important question." Site visits and in-person interviews document the persistence of problems in male-dominated departments and professional schools. They also substantiate women's predominance in assistant professor, part-time and non-tenure-track positions, and in feminized low-status fields. They reveal invisible barriers to women's full participation that are not evident in the national data but come to light from conversations about organizational culture and campus climate. Although the dearth of women faculty, including women of color, is often attributed to a nationwide shortage of qualified women in specialized fields, the anecdotal data raise questions about the accuracy of these beliefs. The low percentage of women faculty at the pinnacle of the profession should be an important warning signal that not enough has changed. Women continue to struggle for acceptance and success as they attempt to overcome inaccurate assumptions, diminishing resources, and conflicting priorities.

Feminist Pedagogy

Betty Friedan's *Feminine Mystique,* which came out of the humanistic tradition of the 1960s, provides an important transition from the contributions of women political activists leading campus commissions and the obstacles they face in 1998 to the intellectual work of women faculty who have pursued the path of academic feminism and whose contributions relate directly to curricular and pedagogical transformation. Friedan drew on Abraham Maslow's research for her pathfinding study of the disparity between the reality of women's lives and the biological and cultural stereotypes that thwart their ability to move from domesticity to professionalism (1963). She was not alone in shaping her arguments along traditional theoretical lines, thinking that women's lives could be reinterpreted through the use of existing ideologies. As Jane Flax (1990) aptly remarks, "By conceptualizing woman as the problem, we repeat rather than deconstruct or analyze the social relations that construct or represent us as a problem in the first place" (p. 138).[6] Maslow's influence on Friedan is an excellent example of this contradiction. While he believed that women's fulfillment is achieved through the domestic sphere and through "strong men defined culturally in terms of power, status, wealth, rank, athletic prowess rather than through self-fulfillment" (Lowry, 1979, p. 1139), Friedan argued that a greater emphasis on women's equality, rights, and human potential in the public (societal) sphere would eradicate such cultural stereotypes. She contended that sexual emancipation and self-realization came from meaningful work, that "the same range of potential ability exists for women as for men, [who] can only find their identity in work that uses their full capacities," without which they commit "a kind of suicide" (Freidan, 1963, p. 293). Recognizing the differential treatment accorded women faculty in the 1960s, she exhorted universities to desist from treating unmarried women scholars "as lepers" and to recruit married women scholars as "role models who have combined marriage and motherhood with the life of the mind" (p. 321). It is not surprising, in retro-

6. Friedan drew on two of Maslow's theories in framing her argument: Maslow (1939) and Maslow (1942).

spect, that Friedan embraced Maslow's need theory. As Jean Grimshaw points out in a critique of Maslow, his ideal society, Eupsychia, was ruled by "an elite of self-actualizers" (1989, p. 151), based on "notions of hierarchy, superiority, inferiority, dominance, and submission" (p. 153). Although his theory of self was clearly anti-egalitarian, elitist, and hierarchical, it appealed to Friedan and to other followers of the human potential movement by virtue of its "vigorous image of self-assertion, self-affirmation, and independence" (ibid.).

By 1970, the slow progress of the women's movement and their inability to make significant gains as faculty or administrators in higher education motivated feminists to reject Friedan's liberal feminist vision and to advocate a radically different agenda. Espousing the belief that masculinity and femininity are essentially conflictual, they ambitiously sought to transcend the artificiality of disciplinary boundaries and, as part of the feminist agenda, to transform the university system. This agenda was reaffirmed in an ethnographic study of women faculty in academe as recently as 1988, when Aisenberg and Harrington called for the adoption of "countervalues [that] add up to a countersystem of social order, one that opposes excessive hierarchy and exclusivity in the holding of authority, one that incorporates diversity, spreads authority through processes of cooperation, resists centrality both in the holding of political and intellectual authority and in the defining of truth and value, and protects individuality through the legitimizing of a personal component in professional life, a personal component to a professional voice" (p. 137).

Theory and Practice

Feminist pedagogy is the descriptive title most commonly given to a range of teaching approaches that seek to modify conventional models of teaching and to transform classroom cultures. It challenges women faculty "to make visible to and explore with our students the aspects of our own life histories that impact on our teaching. We must analyze relationships between our individual biographies, historical events, and the broader power relations that have shaped and constrained our possibilities and perspectives as educators" (Middleton, 1993, p. 17).

The rationale for feminist pedagogy is closely allied with Paolo Freire's theory of critical or liberatory pedagogy which asserts that teaching and learning should be "participatory, experiential, and non-hierarchical" based on such concepts as empowerment, student voice, dialogue, and critical thinking (Finke, 1993). As Weiler (1992) observes, however, in her introduction to a series of essays on the practice of critical pedagogy in schools, critical or Freirian pedagogy has tended to exclude gender or race from consideration, being concerned mainly with class reproduction and resistance in schools. She challenges her white male colleagues who teach in research universities to "address the implications of their own positions of privilege in gender, race, and class terms and to consider the ways in which they also implicitly made privileged and universal claims" in their critical theorizing (p. 4).

For two decades, feminist pedagogy has flourished largely in women's studies programs, focusing on classroom practices, curriculum choices, and evaluative strategies that emphasize empowerment and relationality among a community of women learners (Shrewsbury, 1987, p. 6). This process, in which "feminism and pedagogy converge at the point of intersection between personal experience and commitment to transformative politics" (Lewis, 1993), has fostered the growth of interdepartmental networks, sounding boards for feminist theorizing about subject matter content, scholarly research, and classroom teaching. In subjecting disciplinary knowledge to feminist analysis, the dynamics and content of classroom discourse has become more collaborative, leading to what Belenky et al. (1986) refer to as "connected teaching," in which women students are encouraged to articulate and expand their tacit knowledge, to integrate it with their personal experiences, and to develop their own authentic voices.

More recently, however, influenced by postmodern theory, feminist faculty now take a more active political stance, broadening the dialogue to question the viability of pedagogical theory within institutional contexts based on traditional power/knowledge relationships and to subject texts and theories embedded in them to closer critical scrutiny in terms of gender, race, ethnicity, sexual orientation, and class (Weedon, 1987). They argue from a constructionist perspective that "gender is not a trait of individuals at all, but simply a construct that identifies particular transactions that are understood to be appropriate to one sex" (Bohan, 1993, p. 7). No longer willing to be relegated to extradepartmental courses based on feminist concepts, they employ more active intervention strategies to extend pedagogical knowledge in their disciplines (Aaron and Walby, 1991). Teaching motivation becomes a matter of confronting the power/knowledge polarities, recognizing that women "need not take established meanings, values and power relations for granted," and that in the context of gender relations, traditional theories are relative, shifting, and often contradictory (Weedon, 1987, p. 174). As Weiler maintains, in her critique of Freire's goals of social and political transformation, the writings of feminists of color "point to the need to articulate and claim a particular historical and social identity, to locate ourselves, and to build coalitions from a recognition of the partial knowledges of our own constructed identities" (1991, p. 470).

The orchestration of class, race, and gender-related experiences in the feminist classroom provides a direct challenge to the notion of knowledge as received wisdom and the teacher as dispenser of knowledge (Lewis, 1990; Weiler, 1991). Those "pedagogical moments [that] arise in specific contexts" are described by Lewis as "the social location of the teacher and students; the geographic and historic location of the institution in which they come together; the political climate in which they work; the personalities and personal profiles of the individuals in the classroom; the readings selected for the course; and the academic background of the students" (1990, p. 487). Lewis defines feminist pedagogy as "those teaching practices aimed at creating the conditions for understanding the possibilities for and restrictions on women's autonomy and self-determination" (1993, p. 52). Viewing the feminist classroom as the site of "political struggle over meaning," she recognizes the risks inherent in challenging assumptions of male privilege and in overcoming institutional and student resistance to feminist perspectives (p. 153).

To some extent, this conflictual attitude arises from the difficulties that Lewis (1993), Middleton (1993), and other feminists encounter in implementing their pedagogies. Finke (1993) observes in her essay on the relationship among feminism, voice, and the pedagogical unconscious, when feminist pedagogues ask students to discover their own voices, in reality they seek a "particular voice that corresponds to [their] own desires as teachers, desires which have been authorized by the discursive practices of [their] disciplines and fields: English, anthropology, history, and more specifically, feminism" (p. 17). The question becomes whether empowerment can be actualized within existing institutions based on traditional teacher / student, power/knowledge relationships. She describes the acquisition of knowledge, revealed in students' diaries for a term project on feminist theorizing, as filled with "conflict and struggle, continually being renewed, recreated, and rethought in light of specific classroom practices" (p. 26).

Another view is offered by Apple and Jungck, who characterize state intervention as a form of gender politics that de-skills teachers by removing their incentives to use their formal knowledge and pedagogical skills in setting goals, establishing content, and providing instruction (1990, p. 232). Although they were referring mainly to teachers in K–12 classrooms, recent legislative actions to regulate tenure, evaluate teaching, and monitor productivity have a similar chilling effect on higher education faculty. Two recent studies show how feminist pedagogy is being employed to resist the deskilling process and to empower students and teachers. Ellsworth (1989) explores the use of critical pedagogy in teaching a course on antiracism. In recounting the difficulties that she and her students encounter in working through abstract concepts of empowerment, critical reflection, and student voice, she made a strong argument that to engage in feminist practical reasoning about issues of racism can lead teachers and students into uncharted territory about values, beliefs, and attitudes. Tetreault and Maher (1994) also adopt positionality in documenting the problems encountered by feminist faculty as they sought to implement more critical pedagogical methods in diverse classroom settings. In their study of feminist faculty, they identified a number of factors related to institutional structure, resource constraints, disciplinary differences, and student diversity, each of which facilitated or impeded the ability of feminist faculty to overcome the dualisms of teacher-student roles and to build new cultural identities.

Feminist faculty use feminist pedagogy in developing more reflective models of teaching and learning as well as in transforming their disciplines. Rosser builds on twenty-five years of scholarship in women's studies and experience with curriculum transformation to break down the gender barriers in science, mathematics, technology, and engineering (1995). In her introduction to a collection of essays on retaining women academics in the science pipeline, she proposes a useful framework for pedagogical and curriculum transformation in the sciences, culminating in a redefinition and reconstruction of the disciplines. Noting the absence of women in scientific fields and the nature and extent of the barriers to their participation, she examines the differences between scientific studies undertaken by women and men and the biases of race, class, gender, sexual orientation and religion that may pervade scientific theories and conclusions. Using both qualitative and quantitative methods in data collection, she emphasizes theories and hypotheses that are relational, interdependent, and multicausal rather than hierarchical, reductionistic, and dualistic.

A Case Study

How does feminist pedagogy work in practice? To gain first-hand knowledge of this nontraditional approach to teaching and learning, from 1992 to 1995, Betty Sichel and I studied the use of reflective journal writing as an approach to self-knowledge.[7] Our motivation derived from a fortuitous set of circumstances: we taught the course on two different campuses and in two

7. This section summarizes a collaborative project reported in Glazer and Sichel (1994).

differently constructed master's programs of the same university. On one campus, graduate students were full-time teachers who attended classes part time, with the goal of completing an accelerated master's degree in fourteen months as part of a cohort group. On the other campus, the course was available as an elective for provisionally certified teachers, a component of a traditional master's degree in which cohort enrollments were unlikely and students had little or no teaching experience. The reading list, which was modified annually, included a variety of topical texts, articles, and commentaries on current educational issues.

Our goal was to engage part-time adult students in a process of consciousness-raising and inquiry involving journal keeping, reflection, and dialogues on a range of social problems that directly or indirectly affected them and their own students, with a view to achieving closer congruence between their personal and professional lives. By encouraging a climate of feminist inquiry, we sought to recreate our role as "teacher trainers." Our goal was also to help students develop a critical voice, delve more deeply into course topics, integrate professional experience and academic knowledge, and question unexamined assumptions connected to their particular cultural, biographical, and historical circumstances. After analyzing the first group of journals and obtaining feedback from the students, we realized that by asking students to subject all perspectives to critique, including their own, we were challenging them to think about complex problems for which proposed solutions seemed elusive, inadequate, and transitory.

In ensuing semesters, we incorporated more topical articles and policy documents and initiated student-led seminars on the changing role of the state in educational policy, the disjuncture between economic equity and the rhetoric of academic excellence, the elusiveness of school reform, and the uncertain future of public education. In addition to providing us with more spontaneous avenues for two-way communication, we discovered that journal writing also strengthened their self-efficacy and self-knowledge as adults for whom student-teacher relationships were frequently construed in "self-other" rather than collegial terms. On occasion, journal comments disclosed a disjuncture between their diverse academic backgrounds, their daily work lives, and the theoretical stance of their coursework. Journal entries also revealed attitudes of powerlessness, anger, ambivalence, and confusion about the overwhelming social problems and remote policy decisions that filter into their personal and professional lives and that have an indirect impact on their work. By inviting students who are also teachers into an ongoing dialogue, we were able to move beyond mainstream theories that have little relevance to their lives, to engage in more critical analyses, and to adopt feminist pedagogies as a means of constructing more interactive, collaborative teaching models.

For various reasons, we decided to assign journal writing as an ongoing exercise. As feminists, we agreed that students often distance themselves from controversial issues rather than challenge the contents of assigned texts from their own or other perspectives. We also realized that although we were covering similar course content, the differences in student-teacher and teacher-teacher interactions could also be attributed to dissimilarities in our own scholarly commitments and intellectual interests and the contrast between our respective student demographic profiles. One of us chose to emphasize educational policy and curriculum issues; the other focused more closely on philosophical concerns underlying contemporary issues. In addition, our teaching styles and methods of scholarly inquiry also led us in different pedagogical directions.

Although we were enthusiastic and at times elated by our collaboration, working on this project for an extended period made us more aware of the complexity and difficulty of creating thematic teacher education programs that involve collective commitment to a unique focus. One of us described this problem in her journal: "Collaboration is very tenuous. It must involve trust and negotiation by all parties." The other also noted: "In my curriculum course, I teach students about the importance of collaboration and teaming and I expect them to follow through in and out of class. I now realize how difficult this process can be for those of us who are used to working on our own." Collaboration, we agreed, can be tenuous, not only because of our reluctance to relinquish our autonomy but also because our faculty roles are so ambiguous and complex. The logistics of dealing with multiple perspectives and writing styles continually challenged our resourcefulness, as did the realization that academic journal writing constituted a form of student evaluation of courses and instructors.

In reading their journals, we often saw ourselves reflected in students' writing and in the ways they sought to construct meaning of the subjects we discussed in class. We understood the challenge of journal writing, mirrored in what students wrote as we encouraged them to be more reflective, more critical, and less passive in their acceptance of other points of view. On another level, it altered the dynamics of teacher-student interactions, breaking down some of the artificial barriers between the theory and practice of curriculum and pedagogy endemic to traditional in-service programs and instilling a renewed interest in the work of women teachers.

The relative lack of progress being made by women faculty is in dramatic contrast to the shift occurring in male-female student enrollment ratios, which indicate that women are now the majority of undergraduate and graduate students. This shift in the ratio of female to male students and the lagging progress of women in the professoriate emphasize the urgency for reassessing institutional as well as pedagogical practices. It also provides further evidence that women's so-called fear of failure is a culturally constructed myth unsupported by the data on women's growing participation in graduate and professional schools. Underlying the need for reassessment is the recognition that academic institutions are gendered organizations, that gendered subtexts are embedded in academic departments and disciplines, that the epistemological development of students is not a gender-neutral process, and that, as Stewart and Chester (1982) observe in their analyses of achievement motivation theories, variations in gender motivation are due less to gender differences than to disparate social norms and expectations. In this construct, feminist pedagogies can serve as mediating frameworks to replace traditional notions of teaching motivation with more innovative and collaborative approaches.

As women faculty have entered the professoriate in increasing numbers, feminist scholarship has transformed the knowledge base in many disciplines.[8] Women humanists and scientists are now recognized in all subject areas and their works are widely published, cited, and studied. Teaching and learning have also been transformed in this process, as women have turned their attention to the development of more compatible strategies for use in feminist classrooms. These approaches have flourished mainly in women's studies programs, focusing on classroom practices, curriculum choices, and evaluative strategies within the learning community. Nevertheless, men can begin to adopt elements of these pedagogies, applying multifocal perspectives in listening to women's voices, reflecting on pedagogical practice, subjecting texts and theories to critical scrutiny, and starting a dialogue with their colleagues in women's studies programs. For example, feminists reject transmission-of-knowledge approaches and positivistic methodologies as antithetical to collaborative discourse. Therefore, the material that is taught and the methodology that is used are apt to reflect an interest in elevating women's critical voice, nurturing their potential as autonomous learners, and fostering their personal growth. Engendering pedagogical theory and practice and building on knowledge gained through two decades of feminist pedagogy provides practical strategies for changing classroom and campus cultures.

8. See Glazer (1996) for a feminist critique of theories of teaching motivation.

CONCLUSIONS

I began this research by identifying cultural myths about women's role and status in the academy and the barriers they encounter in attempting to advance in their chosen fields. Outdated assumptions sustain these myths, which embody beliefs in the inevitability of women's progress, the autonomy of their choices, and the fairness of the reward system. In basing their optimistic assessment of women's progress on evolutionary change, advocates of equal rights tend to underestimate the tenacity of obstacles deterring women's upward mobility. Women in the professions (both academic and nonacademic) are denied full participation based on their perceived differences. If they are included, it is only with the expectation that they will accommodate those differences and adapt to existing institutional norms.

The Status of Women in the 1990s

Higher education is moving toward a three-track employment system: full-time tenure track, part-time adjunct, and non-tenure-track term appointments. Women faculty by 1994 accounted for 38.7 percent of faculty, but less than two-fifths of them enjoyed full-time, tenure-track status. The more prestigious the university, the fewer the women faculty, particularly in status academic and professional fields and tenured ranks. Women remain mired in assistant professor, lecturer, and instructor slots, but men dominate in full and associate professor ranks. Policy analysts forecast that at the present rate of change, it could take women from fifty to ninety years to reach numerical parity with men. They also experience a similar gender pay gap to women college graduates in the general workforce. Both AAUP and NCES data show greater inequities in 1994 than in the past two decades, with women full-time tenure-track faculty earning 79.9 percent of their male colleagues.

Women administrators are in the minority in all five categories of university employment, reaching middle management primarily in student services and external affairs. Proof of their scarcity in the academic executive suite is evident in the data: after twenty-five years of affirmative action, only

15 percent of all chief executive officers are women, and 70 percent of these are in colleges with enrollments of fewer than three thousand students. The vertical structure of most universities and colleges compounds women's difficulties in achieving senior leadership roles. It is generally acknowledged that stepping stones include tenure, chairing departments, and serving in deanships. The image of the glass ceiling acknowledges the existence of gender hierarchies while asserting that these are transparent and surmountable within the current structure and academic reward system. Access to "fast tracks" have elements of class and social status associated with them, namely that privileged women who enjoy good mentoring, dress appropriately, secure the right credentials, and exhibit unerring judgment will be rewarded with promotions and other forms of recognition. As I found in talking with many women, these metaphors may be useful descriptors but inadequate explanations of complex and pervasive gender, race, ethnic, and other forms of bias. Unfortunately, commonly held beliefs about the glass ceiling underestimate its impermeability. Here, too, one cannot help wondering whether women are being asked to be patient Griseldas, withstanding abuses without complaint, until they are ultimately rewarded with admission to the executive suite. As we near the year 2000, it is fair to ask why it is still necessary to justify the importance of female-friendly policies.

The work of feminist legal scholars is particularly relevant in analyzing the assault on affirmative action, which is now being used as a wedge issue to divide white women and women of color. In rejecting the liberal feminist view that women can gain sex equality through their assimilation into alienating institutional structures, they adopt a more activist view of feminists as change agents. Individual and group challenges to preserve women's rights provide one avenue for seeking redress in cases of gender bias. Rhode argues persuasively that when institutions condone a "self-perpetuating cycle of experience," they support separate-but-equal world views of women's role and status (for example, the extent to which equality in formal rights masks inequality in daily life, and the fallacious assumptions that women are more likely to work part time, take extended leaves, place lower priority on advancement, and publish less than men), without looking at the root causes of employment segregation and stratification or, alternatively, when they define equality in formal rather than substantive terms, without demanding that equal access guarantee equal treatment and equal outcomes (1991, p. 1768).

Equal employment and affirmative action regulations and policies have increased women's numerical presence as students, faculty, and administrators. These gains mask gender stratification in the allocation of monetary rewards and the adjudication of legal challenges to gender bias. Judicial decisions have been contradictory and at times dismissive of women's claims, as noted in the disposition of cases regarding salary and tenure inequities. MacKinnon comments on the problems women encounter in obtaining justice in a legal system based on sex inequality: "Gender neutrality is the male standard. The special protection rule is the female standard. Masculinity or maleness is the referent for both. Approaching sex discrimination in this way, as if sex questions were difference questions and equality questions were sameness questions, merely provides new ways for the law to hold women to a male standard and to call that sex equality" (MacKinnon, 1989, p. 221).

Schafran also suggests several reasons for the judicial gender gap: "Women lack collective credibility, contextual credibility, and consequential credibility. As a group we are perceived as less competent than men; the context of the harms for which we seek redress in the courts is often completely foreign to the trier of fact; and even when harm is acknowledged, it is often minimized by a de minimis punishment for those who injure us" (Schafran, 1995, p. 42).

In sum, cultural, attitudinal, and structural constraints inhibit women's progress. National and institutional data show that gender neutrality is a fiction, sustaining rather than correcting flaws in policies affecting women's status. Women have a higher rate of employment but a lower likelihood of professional advancement. The gender pay gap condones differential salary structures for women and men in comparable positions. Throughout this book, I have presented ample documentation that dual reward systems continue to discriminate against women faculty, who lag behind men on all measures that can be termed extrinsic motivators—salary, tenure, academic rank, interpersonal relationships with male colleagues and supervisors, working conditions—with the result that job satisfaction is seriously compromised (Tack & Pattitu, 1993). Such inequities sustain male power relationships and raise questions about the validity of traditional rationales for engaging women with high achievement and power motives in gender-neutral faculty development programs. These data also show that "part-time faculty are disproportionately female" and that the disparity is even greater, "fully two to one," for women in non-tenure-track positions (Committee G, 1992, p. 42). Their cumulative impact is to call into question the liberal feminist perspective that equalizing opportunity through changes in laws and customs sufficiently motivates academic institutions to remove barriers to women's advancement.

Women are the majority of undergraduate and graduate students and, since 1982, have earned more than half of all associate, bachelor's, and master's degrees. They are rapidly approaching parity with men in both doctoral and first-professional degree programs (see tables 1 and 2). However, neither Ph.D. nor professional degree recipients (e.g., women in law, medicine, and business) are negotiating career paths commensurate with their numbers in the pipeline. The relative lack of progress being made by women faculty is in dramatic contrast to the shift occurring in male-female student enrollment ratios, which indicate that women are now the majority of undergraduate and graduate students. This shift in the ratio of female to male students and the lagging progress of women in the professoriate emphasize the urgency for reassessing institutional as well as pedagogical practices. It also provides further evidence that women's so-called fear of failure is a culturally constructed myth unsupported by the data on women's growing participation in graduate and professional schools.

In asserting that women prefer teaching to research, for example, the prophecy determines the outcome, reinforcing women's lower status. Cultural barriers encourage conformity and discourage mentoring, teamwork, and diversity. From a feminist perspective, attempts to achieve gender equity are governed by established power relations. Women, who are largely powerless within the university organization, must rely on male leadership to bring about substantive changes in their situation. It is the official discourse of that leadership, articulated by governing boards and presidents, that forms the basis for state and institutional intervention in policies affecting women's role and status as members of the academic profession.

New Barriers to Gender Equity

The changing socioeconomic, gender, and racial composition of professions challenges the notion of homogeneous professional communities with shared experiences, values, and identities. Freidson notes that "professions are divided internally by specialization and intellectual orientation into segments and by differences in interest, power, and prestige connected with the clientele being served" (1994, p. 144). He contrasts the relatively autonomous and powerful professions of law and medicine with their long traditions, distinct public images, and homogeneous systems of professional training over which they exercise significant control, and the aggregate of professions such as teaching, in which rank-and-file practitioners operate in different spheres from researchers and administrators. While he foresees the advent of greater external control of the status professions, he views governance of practice institutions and the relationship of working professionals to each other and to clients as essential to their continued strength and viability.

As women's quest for equality and justice has unfolded in the past three decades, their advance has been marred by a succession of obstacles that have been compounded by actions to make them appear less onerous. By pretending that these obstacles are both reasonable and good, those with access to power not only protect the status quo, but they also erect a new set of barriers that threatens to reverse the gains made by women over the past quarter century. These obstacles present themselves through a social backlash against access and equity policies and programs combined with external intervention in the missions and purposes of higher education. They also weaken three major tenets of professionalism: expertise, credentialism, and autonomy. Contradictory social policy initiatives further confuse the issues and undermine net gains in a postindustrial, technologically driven society that sees women's concerns as overstated and misdirected. Social justice is no longer a priority as institutions attempt to cope with more immediate problems related to restructuring, resource allocation, public negativism, and technological opportunities. In short, diverse missions, ideologies, clienteles, and delivery systems characterize the postmodern university. Resistance to this tidal wave of change comes from several constituencies motivated by different agendas.

Having entered the field of higher education in 1970, I experienced the pressures, the ambivalence, and the mixed messages emanating from the federal government, the educational establishment, and from the students, faculty, and staff. In a fuguelike manner, the tone and content of these messages have changed perceptibly throughout the past twenty-five years, responding to the orchestrations of successive presidents and their institutional counterparts. As I found in my research, the women's rights agenda has been reshaped by a legacy of judicial decisions, executive orders, bureaucratic regulations, and organizational mandates. The fiery activism of the sixties has been diverted into protection of abortion, welfare, and children's rights, and cultural pluralism has replaced ideologies that represent the perspective of one or another interest groups. Three sets of barriers must be overcome if women's progress is to continue: the assault on affirmative action, the corporatization of the university, and the loss of faculty professionalism.

Affirmative Action

Since California's Proposition 209 emerged in 1996 as the most immediate challenge to affirmative action, it has generated an ongoing national debate. As Tierney observes, the 1996 judicial ruling in the *Hopwood* case rejects the three premises on which affirmative action has been based (compensation, correction, and diversification), arguing that "specific, rather than general discrimination must be proved" (1996, p. 27). In its ruling, the Fifth Circuit said that affirmative action "treats minorities as a group rather than as individuals" and that basing admissions decisions on race "is no more rational on its own terms than would be choices based upon the physical size or blood type of applicants." In essence, it rejected the Supreme Court's 1978 decision in *Bakke v. Regents of the University of California*, asserting it can no longer be used to justify the use of race in admissions. As a potential wedge issue dividing women and people of color, gender becomes the "no-problem" problem in the Texas Law School decision, not mentioned but implicit in the court's rejection of race and ethnicity as valid criteria for admission. As Rhode observes, the intersection of gender with other patterns of subordination reinforces attitudes that deny their existence and strengthen the illusion that collective problems are resolved (1991, p. 1735). Although universities proclaim their continued commitment to affirmative action, the successful campaign to extend California's affirmative action ban to Washington and other states calls into question the rationale for commissions and other similar strategies. The implicit sanction of a retreat from goals, timetables, workforce analyses and other accoutrements of affirmative action presents universities and commissions with potentially vexatious obstacles, making their work more difficult and their future more problematic.

Underlying the controversy are contradictory and conflicting views about governmental regulation and institutional expertise, the relative merits of individual and group rights, the impact of preferential treatment and numerical goal-setting on standards of excellence, and the power of the courts in interpreting educational policies. Campus commissions on the status of women have evolved as one strategy for issue definition, agenda setting, and corrective action. Their analyses have highlighted problems relating to salaries, tenure, sexual harassment, and professional advancement, which persist despite the numbers of women in the pipeline, their years of experience, qualifications, and performance.

Equalizing opportunities occurred as a result of challenges to the established ways of conducting academic business, the formation of women's networks, and external intervention that created the illusion of progress, which was often at odds with the reality of recurring patterns of gender discrimination. As priorities have shifted from equity to excellence and from access to merit, affirmative action has been declared dysfunctional, outmoded, and most recently, unconstitutional under the equal protection clause of the Fourteenth Amendment to the Constitution. A massive backlash against the rationale for this policy has led opponents to call for dismantling and termination as the most appropriate solutions. Its proponents acknowledge that even if affirmative action survives, "it will be no more than a vestige of its former self" (Hacker, 1996, p. 28).

The Corporate University

A similar cultural view supports the corporatization of the university. A pattern of managerialism influences the adoption of policies and the utilization of facilities to attract new clienteles and resources, increase faculty accountability and productivity, and control institutional spending. This market-driven climate perpetuates gender hierarchies and challenges feminists to act as change agents. It also challenges gender-neutral assumptions that professionalism is rooted in credentialism and expertise. Male-dominated doctoral programs accentuate the hierarchical nature of the credentialing process by defining expertise and the reward system in terms of scholarly rather than pedagogical expertise. This problem is being exacerbated by a stratified system in which part-time and non-tenure-track faculty are recruited to teach, while full-time tenured faculty conduct research, publish books and articles, and advise students. The National Research Council estimates that cuts as high as 30 percent in federal and state funding of higher education research will be made in the next ten years (Kuh, 1996, p. 4). This may mean that "one third of the faculty that are currently funded by soft money can no longer be supported and the overhead that helps to subsidize less well-funded activities (say the arts and humanities) also evaporates by one-third" (ibid.).

In a market-regulated economy, occupational career changes may become more routine, particularly if teaching is subject to further state regulation and both cost of living increases and benefits lag behind other professions. Economists suggest this possibility in projecting that doctorates will enjoy higher salaries and better working conditions in private and governmental sectors than in academia. A critical perspective on the meaning of professionalism and its influences on post-baccalaureate preparation programs must also consider the implications of pervasive personnel restructuring for fulfilling diversity missions and perpetuating sex-role stereotyping and occupational hierarchies.

The Loss of Faculty Professionalism

The restructuring of the university is also manifesting itself in a loss of faculty professionalism related to proposals to modify or eliminate tenure, legislate productivity, and evaluate faculty claims to expert knowledge and academic freedom. Here, too, the conservative rhetoric is contradictory and conflicting in its co-optation of liberal arguments. Motivated by institutional goals to cut costs, freeze tuition, and rewrite strategic plans, faculty critics assert that academic freedom, job security, and tenure should be decoupled and each considered on its own merits. They couch their critique in the language of flexibility, diversity, and conservation of scarce resources on the one hand and faculty productivity and accountability on the other. To defuse the argument, they offer alternative strategies, such as the replacement of full-time retiring faculty with their part-time, non-tenure-track equivalents. Increased faculty commitment to teaching, legislated workload agreements, and alternative delivery systems become code words for the abrogation of tenure and its replacement with a system of contract employment, removing incentives and opportunities for lifetime commitment to scholarly and teaching careers. Meanwhile, legal decisions that have opened the tenure process to judicial scrutiny may have mixed implications for women by lengthening the proceedings, raising the psychic and professional costs of legal action, and resulting in more procedural safeguards by the university to protect its academic privileges.

Efforts to abrogate tenure and affirmative action policies strengthen rather than remove barriers, creating new adversarial relationships among individuals and groups. In reifying the values that guide postsecondary education, we take the risk of erecting political and cultural boundaries between K–12 and postsecondary education, between the public and private sectors of our social system, and between high- and low-status professions. Given the gatekeeping function of the universities in the admission, training, and certification of professionals, the values implicit in their policies and practices may reinforce rather than eradicate those barriers.

When viewed through a feminist lens, it is quite apparent that the general aggregate of the professions has been derived from doctrine written and practiced by men without any regard to gender, race, social class, or other differentiating characteristics. Since the 1960s, when affirmative action and antidiscrimination statutes were first adopted, women have gained access to these professions in increasing numbers. Feminists who began as women's rights enthusiasts soon found that structural barriers impeded their efforts to be full partners in their chosen professions. They turned their attention to transformation of their workplaces and the ways in which students were being trained for professional practice. Out of these efforts, a body of theoretical and methodological work informed their attempts to adopt a broader and more inclusive world view. This transformational scholarship has made greater inroads in legal education than in the other professions, partly because women lawyers are engaged in interpreting laws that are meant to protect and advance women in the first place and partly because that is the nature of legal scholarship. As more women enter medicine and dentistry, however, research and practice in these two professions are also being altered.

The problems raised by adherence to one overarching standard or set of cultural norms are manifold, particularly when affirmative action policies and programs are in such disarray. Professional institutions are not self-correcting; leadership preferences foster perpetuation of the status quo. But both the courts and the external monitoring agencies have had a greater impact on the ability of the professions to be responsive to their various constituencies. It seems essential that the accreditation agencies take a much more active role in demanding that professional schools and professional workplaces hire more women and give them more visible roles and responsibilities commensurate with their credentials rather than with their gender, race, or social class. When the gatekeepers let the institutions and their leaders know that barriers must be eliminated as a condition for reaccreditation, rankings, and other measures of legitimacy and quality, we may look forward to more equitable environments for women. Until then, glass ceilings, velvet ghettos, tokenism, and uneven playing fields will continue to be the dominant metaphors in the professional schools and in the professional workplaces.

Strategies for Change

Attacks on affirmative action, tenure, full-time employment, and other policies may be politically expedient measures to redefine the missions and purposes of higher education. In reviewing their arguments, I have been particularly concerned with the efficacy of these policies in advancing gender equity and the strategies that have been used to sustain their momentum. Proponents of equity must articulate a contrasting vision of equal rights framed more broadly in the context of economic and social justice. My analyses regarding women's progress show that after three decades of affirmative action and equal opportunity, women are still thwarted in their attempts to attain their goals at every level of the educational and professional hierarchy. In our acceptance of the boundaries that serve as political and cultural separators among our institutions, professions, specializations, ideologies, and cultures, we have emphasized what separates rather than connects us. This question needs to be considered in the context of women's lives and attempts to gain gender equity.

In building a cultural feminist theory, campus commissions have provided a perspective characterized by a search for harmony and consensus. Thus they have concentrated their energies on issues that are soluble at the highest levels of the organization. Their reports cited the need for administrations to create a campus culture of support for women faculty, women mid-level administrators, women clerical staff, and women graduate students, including teaching assistants. Some specific recommendations relate to salary equity, recruitment, and tenure-track appointments in all-male departments; the promotion and appointment of women into administrative leadership positions to counteract the ever-prevalent tokenism; and policies that facilitate women's combined family-work roles, including mandatory stop-the-clock policies and child care provisions.

When viewed from a feminist policy analysis perspective, the underlying premise—that new policies will solve old problems—fails to recognize that basic attitudinal changes are needed to create female-friendly university systems. Rather than assert that women are more likely to work part time than to earn tenure-track appointments, to teach more and publish less, to obtain their doctorates in the humanities rather than in the hard sciences, to remain single or childless, to leave rather than remain at the university, to be assistant and associate administrators rather than chief executive officers, it would be more appropriate to determine what makes institutional structures more compatible with men's lives.

Women's studies have been the academic center for achieving cultural transformation in their pedagogy and their scholarship. In the past decade, as women have begun to question the viability of consensus tactics in the context of resource constraints and attacks on faculty autonomy and academic freedom, a more combative view has emerged. Women now look to their peer groups and to grass-roots tactics rather than to institutional leaders as agents of change. Gender studies, cultural studies, and ethnic studies compete with women's studies as centers of intellectual activity. Postmodern feminists perceive the university and its policies as fraught with ambiguity, uncertainty, and multiple meanings. Within this culture, feminists perceive themselves as a loosely connected polity rather than a unified organization of activists. Academic priorities preoccupy their energies and deter their involvement in potentially intrusive policy debates. It is essential, however, that women, who are the majority of students, speak with a collective voice in this debate and assume a more central role in the policy process.

This investigation has confirmed that higher education is only one part of a much larger social canvas. It has been contextualized in many ways, in the story of education told more broadly, in public policy issues, and in university-community relationships. Our tendency to reify higher education is especially salient in understanding why it is that women have not made greater progress in the academy or in political or corporate institutions. Women cannot and do not compartmentalize their lives, which at times leaves them open to criticism that they are either too scattered and lacking in purpose or that they take themselves too seriously and try to achieve more than is appropriate for their gender. This is particularly the case for women who choose to combine motherhood and professional career, who want to "have it all."

In our commodified culture, few people question the media propensity to glorify male prominence. Men rather than women are immortalized and esteemed for their ability to achieve the emblematic status that accompanies successful careers—power, influence, fame, wealth, property, family. Higher education institutions remain predominantly white, male, and middle class. To study the women who have made progress within the academy is to engage in a self-fulfilling prophecy based on the assumption that social Darwinism has played some part, that is, the privileged status, mentoring, intellect, and publications of these women enabled them to prevail, often against considerable odds. Their legal challenges demonstrate the difficulties that confront women in a system that is not neutral in its treatment of its members. The patterns I discerned represent the rich diversity of their lives.

In analyzing efforts to rescind affirmative action, opponents are reframing the argument for its discontinuation in the language of racial and gender preferences and the denial of merit. Rather than being portrayed as enlightened liberals, affirmative action proponents find themselves accused by conservatives of advocating inequitable and unacceptable discriminatory policies and programs under the rubric of affirmative action. Women who have been its primary beneficiaries are told that preferential treatment, which meant only that gender or race counted as additional qualifications to assure diversity in employment, is no longer either necessary or legal. Powerless within higher education organizations, they must rely on male leadership to bring about substantive changes in their situation. It is the official discourse of that leadership, which presumes to be gender neutral, as articulated by governing boards and presidents that form the basis for state and institutional intervention in the policies and practices affecting women's role and status.

A critical feminist perspective rejects the dominant policy-analysis paradigm that decisions regarding specific policies and programs should be based on such neutral evaluation criteria as resource management, cost effectiveness, and organizational fit. DeLeon joins this argument in acknowledging that policy scientists have overly relied on instrumental rationality, complex problem contexts, and technocratic orientations (1994, p. 82). He suggests a neo-Deweyan approach to "participatory policy analysis" as the basis for fostering more democratic citizenship in policy making. We need to revise our models of academic leadership to reflect the gendered experience of women, to create organizational cultures and high commitment institutions that do not "add on" women but view them as transformative catalysts. Women should be encouraged to exercise their citizenship responsibility by running for election to public community college and university boards. Search firms and search committees should also be encouraged to increase the applicant pool for administrative positions. Professional preparation programs should rethink the paradigms of leadership from critical feminist and race perspectives. The potential exists for programs to reconstitute themselves by placing gender, race, and ethnicity at the center rather than the margins of their curriculum. This reconceptualization may be one way to transform higher education administration from a predominantly white male preserve.

The assault on affirmative action presents women with a major challenge. Right-wing ideologues have recognized the usefulness of the postmodern argument in their efforts to deconstruct and dismantle this policy and the laws that have sustained it in a society that is more concerned with the needs of employers than the discovery of new knowledge. Affirmative action is attacked under the guise of restoring individual rights and color-blind nondiscrimination. Feminism and multiculturalism are also attacked as anti-intellectual ideologies that threaten academic standards and family values. Ultimately, the institutional culture of most universities is not compatible with the needs and concerns of women in academia.

We need to adopt new institutional prototypes that replace hierarchical management, in-house rivalries, and ladder climbing with nonbureaucratic, responsive models. In these restructured environments, women may enjoy different roles unconstrained by adversarial and competitive relationships. There are strong feminist implications in management research that replaces the ideal bureaucratic model with more collaborative organizational forms. It may be that these collaborative models of organizational management, which analysts such as Rosabeth Kanter in *When Giants Learn to Dance* (1989) and Joanne Martin in *Cultures in Organizations* (1992) propose as alternatives to traditional organizational hierarchies, will be more compatible with women's leadership styles as troubleshooters, consensus builders, risk takers, and collaborative decision makers. Organizational cultures will have to change a great deal, however, to bring that about in complex higher education systems.

Through a feminist approach to critical policy analysis, I assessed women's progress in higher education over the past few decades. Women have exercised intellectual and moral leadership in their efforts to improve the role and status of their own and future generations. These contributions should be recognized as milestones in the history of women's lives at the close of this century. At the same time, a new mythology permeates contemporary culture, one that misrepresents the dimensions of women's continued inequality at all levels of society. Higher education will face difficult issues in the first decade of the new millennium. As educators of the next generation of women leaders, we have a responsibility to prepare students to anticipate, confront, and address them.

REFERENCES

Aaron, Jane, & Walby, Sylvia (Eds.). (1991). *Out of the margins: Women's studies in the nineties.* London: Falmer Press.

ABA Commission on the Status of Women. (1995). *Task force report to the Arizona Board of Regents.* Phoenix: Arizona State University Commission on the Status of Women.

Acosta, R. Vivian, & Carpenter, Linda J. (1992). *Women in intercollegiate sports: A longitudinal study—fifteen year update, 1977–1992.* ED352337.

Ad Hoc Committee on Women's Issues. (1988, December). *Women's agenda for the 1990s.* Ann Arbor: Ad Hoc Committee, University of Michigan.

Ahrentzen, Sherry, & Groat, Linda N. (1992, Summer). Rethinking architectural education: Patriarchal conventions and alternative visions from the perspectives of women faculty. *Journal of Architectural and Planning Research, 9*(2), 95–111.

Aisenberg, Nadya, & Harrington, Mona. (1988). *Women in academe.* Amherst: University of Massachusetts Press.

Alden, Bill. (1997, June 6). Circuit, 6–5, finds no bias by Vassar. *New York Law Journal,* 1, 3.

Alpert, Dona. (1990). Gender inequity in academia: An empirical analysis. *Initiatives, 53,* 10–12.

American Assembly of Collegiate Schools of Business. (1991). *Standards for business and accounting accreditation.* St. Louis: AACSB.

American Association of Colleges for Teacher Education. (1994). *Briefing Book 1993.* Washington, D.C.: AACTE.

American Association of Dental Schools. (1995). *Deans' briefing book, academic year 1994-1995.* Washington, D.C.: American Association of Dental Schools.

American Association of University Professors. (1993, July–August). The status of non-tenure-track faculty. *Academe, 79,* 39–51.

American Association of University Professors. (1976, October). Endorsers of the 1940 Statement of Principles on Academic Freedom and Tenure. *AAUP Bulletin, 62*(3), 301–302.

American Dental Association. (1995). *Survey of predoctoral dental institutions.* Washington, D.C.: American Dental Association.

American Federation of Teachers. (1997, February). Grad students struggle for recognition. *On Campus: News and Trends, 16*(5), 3.

Amey, Marilyn J., & Twombly, Susan B. (1993). Re-visioning leadership in community colleges. In J. S. Glazer, E. M. Bensimon, & B. K. Townsend (Eds.), *Women in higher education: A feminist perspective*, 475–492. Needham Heights, MA: Ginn Press.

Apple, Michael, & Jungck, Susan. (1990). Teach this unit: Teaching, technology, and gender in the classroom. *American Educational Research Journal, 27*, 227–251.

Arden, Eugene. (1995, January–February). Is tenure obsolete? *Academe, 81*(1), 38–39.

Arenson, Karen W. (1997, April 22). A leader for SUNY in a time of change. *New York Times*, B1, 4.

Arizona Commission on the Status of Women. (1991). *Reaching the vision: Women in Arizona's universities in the year 2000*. Phoenix: Arizona Board of Regents.

Association of American Law Schools. (1994). Report of the AALS Special Committee on Tenuring and the Tenure Process. *Journal of Legal Education, 42*(4), 477–507.

Association of American Medical Colleges. (1996). *Increasing women's leadership in academic medicine*. Washington, D.C.: AAMC.

Association of American Medical Colleges. (1996, Spring). Women moving up at NIH. *Women in Medicine Update, 10*(2), 3.

Astin, Helen S. (1969). *The woman doctorate in America: Origins, career, and family*. New York: Russell Sage.

Astin, Helen S., & Leland, Carol. (1991). *Women of influence, Women of vision: A cross-generational study of leaders and social change*. San Francisco: Jossey-Bass.

Babco, Eleanor L. (1997). *Professional women and minorities: A total human resources compendium*. 12th ed. Washington, D.C.: Commission on Professionals in Science and Technology.

Babco, Eleanor L. (1996). *Salaries of scientists, engineers, and technicians: A summary of salary surveys*. 17th ed. Washington, D.C.: Commission on Professionals in Science and Technology.

Barnard, Jessie. (1964). *Academic women*. University Park: Pennsylvania State University Press.

Baron, Tracy A. (1994). Keeping women out of the executive suite: The court's failure to apply Title VII scrutiny to upper level jobs. *University of Pennsylvania Law Review, 143*, 267–320.

Bartholomew, Karen. (1993, December 8). Senate endorses proposals to add women faculty. *Stanford University Campus Report, 26*(9), 1, 11.

Bartlett, Katherine T. (1990). Feminist legal methods. *Harvard Law Review, 103*, 829–888.

Bass, Bernard M. 1990. *Bass and Stogdill's handbook of leadership: Theory, research, and managerial applications*. 3d ed. New York: Free Press.

Belenky, Mary F., Clinchy, Blythe M., Goldberger, Nancy R., & Tarule, Jill M. (1986). *Women's ways of knowing: The development of self, voice, and mind*. New York: Basic Books.

Bell, Derrick A. (1992). *Faces at the bottom of the well: The permanence of racism*. New York: Basic Books.

Bell, Linda A. (1997, March–April). Not so good: The annual report on the economic status of the academic profession. *Academe, 83*(2), 12–23.

Bellas, Marcia L. (1993). Faculty salaries: Still a cost of being female? *Social Science Quarterly, 74*, 62–75.

Bensimon, Estela M. (1993). A feminist's reinterpretation of presidents' definitions of leadership. In J. S. Glazer, E. M. Bensimon, & B. K. Townsend (Eds.), *Women in higher education: A feminist perspective*, 465–474. ASHE Reader Series. Needham Heights, MA: Ginn Press.

Bensimon, Estela M., & Neumann, Anna. (1993). *Redesigning collegiate leadership: Teams and teamwork in higher education*. Baltimore: Johns Hopkins University Press.

Bensimon, Estela M., Neumann, Anna, & Birnbaum, Robert. (1989). *Making sense of administrative leadership: The "L" word in higher education*. ASHE-ERIC Report No. 1. Washington, D.C.: George Washington University.

Bernstein, Nina. (1996, January 8). Study says equality eludes most women in law firms. *New York Times*, A9.

Berry, Mary F. (1986). *Why ERA failed: Politics, women's rights, and the amending process of the Constitution*. Bloomington: Indiana University Press.

Bess, James L. (1997, March). Contract systems, bureaucracies and faculty motivation: The probable effects of a no-tenure policy. Paper presented at the annual meeting of the American Educational Research Association, Chicago.

Bickel, Janet. (1988, December 15). Women in medical education: A status report. *New England Journal of Medicine, 319*, 1579–1584.

Bickel, Janet, Croft, Kathy M., & Marshall, Renee. (1996). *Enhancing the environment for women in academic medicine: Resources and pathways*. Washington, D.C.: Association of American Medical Colleges.

Bickel, Janet, Galbraith, Aarolyn, & Quinnie, Renee. (1995). *Women in U.S. academic medicine, statistics 1995*. Washington, D.C.: Association of American Medical Colleges.

Bickel, Janet, & Quinnie, Renee. (1992). Addressing sexism in medicine. In *Building a stronger women's program: Enhancing the educational and professional environment*. Washington, D.C.: American Association of Medical Colleges.

Bingham, Clara. (1997). *Women on the hill: Challenging the culture of Congress*. New York: Times Books.

Bird, Chloe E. (1990). High finance, small change: Women's increased representation in bank management. In B. F. Reskin & P. A. Roos (Eds.), *Job queues, gender queues*. Philadelphia: Temple University Press, 145–166.

Birmingham, Stephen. (1967). *Our crowd: The great Jewish families of New York*. New York: Harper and Row.

Birnbaum, Robert. (1992). *How academic leadership works: Success and failure in the college presidency*. San Francisco: Jossey-Bass.

Blackburn, Robert T., & Lawrence, Janet H. (1995). *Faculty at work: Motivation, expectation, satisfaction*. Baltimore: Johns Hopkins Univeristy Press.

Bohan, Janis S. (Ed.). (1993). *Seldom seen, rarely heard: Women's place in psychology*. Boulder: Westview Press.

Bowen, William G., & Sosa, Julie A. (1989). *Prospects for faculty in the arts and sciences*. Princeton: Princeton University Press.

Boyer, Ernest L. (1990). *Scholarship reconsidered: Priorities of the professoriate.* Princeton: Carnegie Foundation for the Advancement of Teaching.

Bronner, Ethan. (1998, May 20). Fewer minorities entering U. of California. *New York Times*, A28.

Brown, Helen. (1997). Equal opportunities policy. In Heather Eggins (Ed.), *Women as leaders and managers in higher education*, 109–124. Buckingham, U.K.: SRHE and Open University Press.

Brown, Patricia. (1995, October). *Salaries, tenure, and fringe benefits, 1993–94.* Washington, D.C.: U.S. Department of Education, Office of Educational Research and Improvement.

Buechler, Steven M. (1990). *Women's movements in the United States: Women's suffrage, equal rights, and beyond.* New Brunswick, NJ: Rutgers University Press.

Burd, Stephen. (1998, May 15). House votes down proposal to bar racial preferences in admission. *Chronicle of Higher Education*, A35.

Burrage, Michael. (1984). Practitioners, professors and the state in France, the USA and England. In S. Goodlad (Ed.), *Education for the professions: Quis custodiet?* 26–38. Guilford, Surrey: SRHE and NFER-Nelson.

Byrne, John A. (1993, July 19). Harvard B-School: An American institution in need of reform. *Business Week*, 58.

Cage, Mary C. (1996, February 23). Salary increases of college administrators outpace inflation. *Chronicle of Higher Education*, A19.

Caplow, Theodore, & McGee, R. (1958). *The academic marketplace.* New York: Basic Books.

Carlsen, Charles J., & Burdick, Robert. (1994). Linked in governance: The role of the president and the board of trustees in the community college. In G. A. Baker III (Ed.), *A handbook on the community college in America: Its history, mission, and management*, 259–267. Westport, CT: Greenwood Press.

Carnegie Commission on Higher Education. (1973). *Opportunities for women in higher education.* New York: McGraw Hill.

Carnegie Council on Policy Studies in Higher Education. (1975). *Making affirmative action work in higher education: An analysis of institutional and federal policies and recommendations.* San Francisco: Jossey Bass.

Carnegie Task Force on Teaching as a Profession. (1986). *A nation prepared: Educating teachers for the twenty-first century.* Washington, D.C.: Carnegie Forum on Education and the Economy.

Cartter, Allan M. (1976). *Ph.D.s and the academic labor market.* New York: McGraw Hill.

Chait, Richard P. (1997a, January 17). Update on the tenure debate. Fifth AAHE Conference on Faculty Roles and Rewards, San Diego. Audiotape No. 97CFRR-P3.

Chait, Richard P. (1997b, July–August). Rethinking tenure: Toward new templates for academic employment. *Harvard Magazine, 99*(6), 30, 31, 90.

Chait, Richard P., Holland, Thomas P., & Taylor, Barbara E. (1996). *Improving the performance of governing boards.* Washington, D.C.: Oryx Press.

Chamallas, Martha. (1997). Anatomy of a lawsuit: *Jean Jew v. University of Iowa.* In

B. R. Sandler & R. J. Shoop (Eds.), *Sexual harassment on campus*, 248–260. Needham Heights, MA: Allyn & Bacon.

Chamberlin, Mariam K. (1988). Women as trustees. In *Women in academe: Progress and prospects*. New York: Russell Sage.

Chodorow, Nancy J. (1993). What is the relation between psychoanalytic feminism and the psychoanalytic psychology of women? In D. Rhode (Ed.), *Theoretical perspectives on sexual difference*, 114–130. New Haven: Yale University Press.

Clifford, Geraldine J. (1993). "Shaking dangerous questions from the crease": Gender and American higher education. In J. S. Glazer, E. M. Bensimon, & B. K. Townsend (Eds.), *Women in higher education: A feminist perspective*, 135–174. Needham Heights, MA: Ginn Press.

Collins, Patricia H. (1991). *Black feminist thought: Knowledge, consciousness, and the politics of empowerment*. New York: Routledge.

Commission on the Status of Women in the Legal Profession. (1996). *Unfinished business: Overcoming the Sisyphus factor*. Chicago: American Bar Association.

Commission on Women. (1993). *Guide to improving the campus climate for women*. Minneapolis: University of Minnesota.

Committee A on Academic Freedom and Tenure. (1996, January–February). Report: Tenure in the medical school. *Academe, 82*(1), 40–45.

Committee C on College and University Teaching, Research, and Publications. (1994, January–February). Report: The work of faculty: Expectations, priorities, and rewards. *Academe, 80*(1), 35–48.

Committee G on Part-Time and Non-Tenure-Track Appointments. (1992, November–December). The use and abuse of part-time faculty. *Academe, 79*(4), 33, 34.

Committee W on the Status of Women in the Academic Profession. (1988, July–August). Academic women and salary differentials. *Academe, 74*(4), 33, 34.

Committee Z on the Economic Status of the Profession. (1996, March–April). Not so bad: The annual report on the economic status of the profession, 1995–96. *Academe, 82*(2), 14–22.

Committee Z on the Economic Status of the Profession. (1993, March–April). Treading water: The annual report on the economic status of the profession, 1992–93. *Academe, 79*, 8–14.

Committee Z on the Economic Status of the Profession. (1991, March–April). The future of academic salaries: Will the 1990s be a bust like the 1970s or a boom like the 1980s? The annual report on the economic status of the profession, 1990–91. *Academe, 77*(3), 9–15.

Committee Z on the Economic Status of the Profession. (1975, August–Summer). Two steps backward: Report on the economic status of the profession, 1974–75. *AAUP Bulletin 61*(4), 118–124.

Conley, Frances. 1998. *Walking out on the boys*. New York: Farrar, Straus & Giroux.

Coppock, Vivian, Haydon, Deena, & Richter, Ingrid. (1995). *The illusions of "postfeminism": New women, old myths*. London: Routledge.

Costello, Cynthia, & Krimgold, Barbara K. (Eds.). (1996). *The American woman, 1996-97, where we stand: Women and work*. New York: W. W. Norton.

Cotts, Cynthia. (1997, December 1). Ten years after suing Harvard, Northeastern prof. wins acclaim. *National Law Journal*, 3.

Creal, Richard C., & Beyer, Kirk D. (1996). *Administration compensation survey.* Washington, D.C.: College and University Personnel Association.

Davidson, Marilyn J., & Burke, Ronald J. (Eds.). (1994). *Women in management: Current research issues.* London: Paul Chapman.

de Lauretis, Teresa. (1990). Upping the anti (sic) in feminist theory. In D. Fox & M. Keller (Eds.), *Conflicts in feminism*, 255–270. New York: Routledge.

DeLeon, Peter. (1994). Reinventing the policy sciences: Three steps back to the future. *Policy Sciences, 27*(1), 77–95.

Department of Labor. (1995, March). *Good for business: Making full use of the nation's capital: A fact-finding report of the federal Glass Ceiling Commission.* Washington, D.C.: Department of Labor.

Dobrzynski, Judith H. (1996, December 12). Women pass milestone in the boardroom. *New York Times*, D4.

Donato, Katherine M. (1990). Keepers of the corporate image: Women in public relations. In B. F. Reskin & P. A. Roos (Eds.), *Job queues, gender queues*, 129–144. Philadelphia: Temple University Press.

Driscoll, Dawn M., & Goldberg, Carol R. (1993). *Members of the club: The coming of age of executive women.* New York: Free Press.

Dudley, Adriane J., & DeSimone, Nancy E. (1994, Winter). The family medical leave act: An overview and analysis. *The Urban Lawyer, 26*(1), 83–98.

Duffey, Joseph. (1975, June). Report of the general secretary at the sixty-first annual meeting. *Academe, 61*(3), 1, 3.

Eisenstein, Zillah R. (1994). *The color of gender: Reimaging democracy.* Berkeley: University of California Press.

Ellsworth, Elizabeth. (1989, August). Why doesn't this feel empowering? Working through the repressive myths of critical pedagogy. *Harvard Educational Review, 59*(3), 297–324.

Epstein, Cynthia. (1993). Epilogue. *Women in law.* 2nd ed. New York: Basic Books.

Epstein, Gene. (1997, December 1). Low ceiling: How women are held back by sexism at work and child-rearing duties at home. *Barrons*, 35, 36, 38–40.

Faculty and Academic Professionals Committee. (1994). *Women's promotion to full rank at ASU: A report on status and recommendations.* Tempe: Arizona State University Commission on the Status of Women.

Faludi, Susan. (1991). *Backlash: The undeclared war against American women.* New York: Crown.

Finke, Laurie. (1993, January). Knowledge as bait: Feminism, voice, and the pedagogical unconscious. *College English, 55*, 7–27.

Finkelstein, Martin J., Seal, Robert K., & Schuster, Jack H. (1995). The new academic generation. Unpublished draft.

Finkin, Matthew. (Ed.). (1996). *The case for tenure.* Ithaca: ILR Press.

Firestone, Shulamith. (1970). *The dialectic of sex: The case for feminist revolution.* St. Alban's: Paladin.

Flax, Jane. (1990). *Thinking fragments: Psychoanalysis, feminism, and postmodernism in the contemporary West.* Berkeley: University of California Press.

Flynn, Patricia M., Leeth, John D., & Levy, Elliott S. (1996, Winter). The evolving gender mix in accounting: Implications for the future of the profession. *Selections, 12*(2), 28–38.

Fox-Genovese, Elizabeth. (1991). *Feminism without illusions: A critique of individualism.* Chapel Hill: University of North Carolina Press.

Francis, Leslie P. (1993). In defense of affirmative action. In S. M. Cahn (Ed.), *Affirmative action and the university: A philosophical inquiry, 9–47.* Philadelphia: Temple University Press.

Fraser, Antonia. (1988). *Boadicea's chariot: The warrior queens.* London: Weidenfeld and Nicolson.

Freidson, Eliot. (1994). *Professionalism reborn: Theory, prophecy and policy.* Cambridge: Polity Press.

Friedan, Betty. (1963). *The feminine mystique.* London: Penguin Books.

Fuhrman, Barbara S., & Grasha, Anthony F. (1994). The past, present, and future in college teaching: Where does your teaching fit? In K. A. Feldman & M. B. Paulsen (Eds.), *Teaching and learning in the college classroom, 5–20.* ASHE Reader Series. Needham Heights, MA: Ginn Press.

Galinsky, Ellen, & Bond, James T. (1996). Work and family: The experiences of mothers and fathers in the U.S. labor force. In C. Costello & B. K. Krimgold (Eds.), *The American woman, 1996-97, 79–103.* New York: W. W. Norton.

Galle Jr., William P., & Koen Jr., Clifford M. (1993, September–October). Tenure and promotion after Penn v. EEOC. *Academe, 79*(5), 19–26.

Garrett, Rick L. (1993, Spring). A profile of state community college system characteristics and their relationship to degrees of centralization. *Community College Review, 20*(5), 6–15.

Gerald, Debra, & Hussar, William J. (1995). *Projections of education statistics to 2005.* Washington, D.C.: Office of Educational Research and Improvement.

Gillett-Karam, Rosemary. (1994). Women and leadership. In G. A. Baker III (Ed.), *A handbook on the community college in America: Its history, mission, and management, 94–108.* Westport, CT: Greenwood Press.

Gilligan, Carol. (1977, November). In a different voice: Women's conceptions of self and of morality. *Harvard Educational Review, 47,* 481–517.

Ginorio, Angela B. (1995). *Warming the climate for women in academic science.* Washington, D.C.: Association of American Colleges and Universities.

Glass Ceiling Commission. (1995). *Good for business: Making full use of the nation's human capital.* Washington, D.C.: U.S. Department of Labor.

Glassick, Charles, Huber, Mary T., & Maeroff, Gene. (1997). *Scholarship assessed: Evaluation of the professoriate.* San Francisco: Jossey-Bass.

Glazer, Judith S. (1996). Beyond male theory: A feminist perspective on teaching motivation. In James L. Bess (Ed.), *Teaching well and liking it: Motivating faculty to teach effectively.* Baltimore: Johns Hopkins University Press.

Glazer, Judith S. (1993). *A teaching doctorate? The doctor of arts, then and now.* Washington, D.C.: American Association for Higher Education.

Glazer, Judith S. (1991). Feminism and professionalism in teaching and educational administration. *Educational Administration Quarterly, 27*(3), 321–342.

Glazer, Judith S. (1986). *The master's degree: Tradition, diversity, innovation.* ASHE-ERIC Report No. 6. Washington, D.C.: George Washington University.

Glazer, Judith S. (1984, Winter). Terminating entrenched policies in educational institutions: A case history of free tuition. *Educational Administration Quarterly, 7*(2), 159–173.

Glazer, Judith S. (1983). Roundtable: A retrospective on decentralization. *New York Affairs, 8*(1), 99–117.

Glazer, Judith S. (1982). Designing and managing an interuniversity consortium in a period of decline. *Journal of Higher Education, 53*(2), 178–194.

Glazer, Judith S., & Sichel, Betty. (1994, April). Patterns of journal writing in the professional development of teachers. Paper presented at the annual meeting of the American Educational Research Association, San Francisco.

Glazer, Penina M., & Slater, Miriam. (1987). *Unequal colleagues: The entrance of women into the professions, 1890–1940.* New Brunswick, NJ: Rutgers University Press.

Goldin, Claudia. (1990). *Understanding the gender gap: An economic history of American women.* New York: Oxford University Press.

Goldstein, Matthew. (1996, January 8). ABA report finds women still lag in pay, authority. *New York Law Journal, 251,* 1, 5.

Graham, Patricia A. (1978). Expansion and exclusion: A history of women in American higher education. *Signs, 3*(4), 759–773.

Grant, Christine H. B., & Curtis, Mary C. (1996). Gender equity: Judicial actions & related information. University of Iowa, Des Moines. Unpublished document.

Gray, Mary W. (1992, Spring). Commentary: Impact of the proposed civil rights and women's equity in employment act on colleges and universities. *Journal of College and University Law, 18*(4), 559–576.

Gray, Mary W. (1988). Can statistics tell us what we do not want to hear? The case of complex salary structures. *Statistical Sciences, 8*(2), 144–179.

Gray, Mary W. (1985, September–October). Resisting sex discrimination against faculty women. *Academe, 71,* 33–41.

Gray, Mary W., & Schafer, Alice T. (1981, December). Guidelines for equality: A proposal. *Academe, 67,* 351–353.

Greenhouse, Linda. (1997, August 4). A case on race puts Justice O'Connor in a familiar pivotal role. *New York Times,* A1, 12.

Grimshaw, Jean. (1989). *Feminist philosophers; Women's perspectives on philosophical traditions.* London: Harvester Wheatsheaf.

Guinier, Lani, Fine, Michelle, & Balin, Jane. (1997). *Becoming gentlemen: Women, law school, and institutional change.* Boston: Beacon Press.

Guinier, Lani, Fine, Michelle, & Balin, Jane, with Bartow, A., & Stachel, D. L. (1994, November). Becoming gentlemen: Women's experiences at one Ivy League law school. *University of Pennsylvania Law Review, 143*(1), 1–110.

Hacker, Andrew. (1996, July 11). Goodbye to affirmative action? *New York Review of Books,* 21, 24–29.

Hansard Society for Parliamentary Government. (1990). *Report of the Hansard Society Commission on women at the top.* London: Hansard Society.

Harrington, Mona. (1994). *Women lawyers: Rewriting the rules.* New York: Alfred A. Knopf.

Hawkesworth, M. E. (1988). *Theoretical issues in policy analysis.* Albany: State University of New York Press.

Haworth, Karen. (1997, April 4). Colleges, sporting groups, and lawmakers back Brown U.'s appeal in Title IX case. *Chronicle of Higher Education,* A35.

Hawthorne, Elizabeth. (1994, May–June). Leaders in teaching and learning: A profile of chief academic officers in two-year colleges. *Community College Journal of Research and Practice 18*(3), 269–278.

Hays, Constance L. (1997, November 14). Focus for M.B.A.'s turns to women. *New York Times,* 15.

Headlee, Sue, & Elfin, M. (1996). *The cost of being female.* Westport, CT: Praeger.

Healy, Patrick. (1997, November 14). Mass. leader to seek abolition of tenure. *Chronicle of Higher Education,* A36.

Heckman, Diane. (1997, Winter). On the eve of Title IX's 25th anniversary: Sex discrimination in the gym and classroom. *Nova Law Review,* 21, 545–661.

Heilbrun, Carolyn. (1988). *Writing a woman's life.* New York: Ballantine Books.

Henderson, Peter H., Clarke, Julie E., & Reynolds, Mary A. (1996). *Summary report 1995: Doctorate recipients from United States universities.* Washington, D.C.: National Academy Press.

Henke, Robin R., Choy, Susan R., & Geis, Sonya. (1996). *Schools and staffing in the United States: A statistical profile, 1993–94.* Washington, D.C.: U.S. Department of Education, Office of Educational Research and Improvement.

Herbert, Bob. (1997, November 23). Last-minute reprieve. *New York Times,* A15.

Herz, Diane E., & Wootton, Barbara H. (1996). Women in the workforce: An overview. In C. Costello & B. K. Krimgold (Eds.), *The American Woman, 1996–97,* 6th ed., 44–78. New York: W. W. Norton.

Hollenshead, Carol. (1993, December). *Women at the University of Michigan: A statistical report on the status of women students, faculty, and staff on the Ann Arbor campus.* Vol. 2. Ann Arbor: Center for the Education of Women, University of Michigan.

Holmes Group. (1986). *Tomorrow's teachers.* East Lansing, MI: Holmes Group.

Hoks, Barbara. (1996). *Commission on the Status of Women, 1995–1996 annual report.* Tempe: Arizona State University Commission on the Status of Women.

Hoks, Barbara. (1995). *Commission on the Status of Women, 1994–1995 annual report.* Tempe: Arizona State University Commission on the Status of Women.

Horowitz, Helen. (1984). *Alma mater: Design and experience in the women's colleges from their nineteenth century beginnings to the 1930s.* New York: Alfred Knopf.

Hostler, Sharon L., & Gressard, Risa P. (1993, March–April). Perceptions of the gender fairness of the medical education environment. *JAMWA, 48*(2), 51–54.

Hulbert, Kathleen D., & Schuster, Diane T. (Eds.). (1993). *Women's lives through time: Educated American women of the twentieth century.* San Francisco: Jossey-Bass.

Humphreys, Debra. (1996, Spring). Women and work: Women's working lives: The example of the college presidency. *On Campus with Women, 25*(3), 1–2.

Hymowitz, Carol, & Shellhardt, Timothy D. (1986, March 24). The corporate woman: A special report. *Wall Street Journal,* section 4, 1D–24D.

Ingram, Richard T., & Associates. (1993a). *Governing independent colleges and universities: A handbook for trustees, chief executives, and other campus leaders.* San Francisco: Jossey-Bass.

Ingram, Richard T., & Associates. (1993b). *Governing public colleges and universities: A handbook for trustees, chief executives, and other campus leaders.* San Francisco: Jossey-Bass.

Irvine, Betty Jo. (1995). *Sex segregation in librarianship: Demographic and career patterns of academic library administrators.* Westport, CT: Greenwood Press.

Jaggar, Alison M. (1983). *Feminist politics and human nature.* Totowa, NJ: Rowman & Allenheld.

Jamieson, Kathleen L. (1995). *Beyond the double bind: Women and leadership.* New York: Oxford University Press.

Johnsrud, Linda, & Heck, Ronald H. (1994, January–February). Administrative promotion within a university: The cumulative impact of gender. *Journal of Higher Education, 65*(1), 23–44.

Kane, Roslyn D. (1976). *Sex discrimination in education: A study of employment practices affecting professional personnel.* Vol. 1: *Study report.* Arlington, VA: National Center for Educational Statistics, U.S. Department of Health, Education, and Welfare.

Kanter, Rosabeth M. (1989). *When giants learn to dance: Mastering the challenges of strategy, management, and careers in the 1990s.* New York: Simon & Schuster.

Kanter, Rosabeth M. (1977). *Men and women of the corporation.* New York: Basic Books.

Kaplin, William A. (1985). *The law of higher education: A comprehensive guide to legal implications of administrative decision making.* San Francisco: Jossey-Bass.

Kaptur, Marcy. (1996). *Women of Congress: A twentieth-century odyssey.* Washington, D.C.: Congressional Quarterly.

Keetz, Mary A. (1991). *The status of female faculty in Pennsylvania's state system of higher education: An historical perspective, 1974–1989.* West Chester: Women's Consortium of the Pennsylvania State System of Higher Education.

Kilson, Marion. (1996, June). Contrast and convergence: Career paths and responsibilities of graduate deans. *CGS Communicator, 29*(6), 1, 3, 4, 10.

Kirshstein, Rita J., Matheson, Nancy, & Jing, Zhongren. (1997, September). *Instructional faculty and staff in higher education institutions: Fall 1987 and fall 1992.* Washington, D.C.: U.S. Department of Education, Office of Educational Research and Improvement.

Klein, Jeffrey S., & Pappas, Nicholas J. (1995, October 2). Discrimination in tenure decisions. *New York Law Journal, 214*(64), 3.

Klenke, Karin. (1996). *Women and leadership: A contextual perspective.* New York: Springer Publishing.

Kopka, Teresita, & Korb, Roslyn. (1996). *Women: Education and outcomes.* Washington, D.C.: Office of Educational Research and Improvement, U.S. Department of Education.

Kramarae, Cheris, & Spender, Dale. (1992). *The knowledge explosion*. New York: Routledge.

Kuh, Charlotte V. (1996, August–September). Is there a Ph.D. glut? Is that the right question? *CGS Communicator, 29*(7), 1, 3, 4.

LaNoue, George R., & Lee, Barbara A. (1987). *Academics in court: The consequences of faculty discrimination litigation*. Ann Arbor: University of Michigan Press.

Larson, Margali S. (1977). *The rise of professionalism*. Berkeley: University of California Press.

Leap, Terry L. (1993). *Tenure, discrimination, and the courts*. Ithaca: ILR Press.

Leatherman, Courtney. (1996, May 10). Fairness questions at Boston U. *Chronicle of Higher Education*, A21.

Leatherman, Courtney. (1993, October 6). Woman who took on Harvard Law School over tenure denial sees "vindication." *Chronicle of Higher Education*, A19.

Lederman, Douglas. (1997a, October 24). New briefs to high court take opposing views on key affirmative-action case. *Chronicle of Higher Education*, A27.

Lederman, Douglas. (1997b, October 24). Suit challenges affirmative action in admissions at U. of Michigan. *Chronicle of Higher Education*, A27, A28.

Lee, Jean. (1990, April 16). Library service report: School's future in limbo. *Columbia Spectator*, 1, 5, 14.

Lewin, Tamar. (1997, September 15). Women losing ground to men in widening income difference. *New York Times*, A1.

Lewin, Tamar. (1988, September 30). Feminist scholars spurring a rethinking of law. *New York Times*, B9.

Lewis, Magda. (1993). *Without a word: Teaching beyond women's silence*. New York: Routledge.

Lewis, Magda. (1990, November). Interrupting patriarchy: Politics, resistance, and transformation in the feminist classroom. *Harvard Educational Review, 60*, 467–487.

Licata, Christine. (1997). Post-tenure review: Report from the field. Fifth AAHE Conference on Faculty Roles and Rewards, San Diego. Audiotape No. 97CFRR-8.

Lively, Kit. (1997, October 24). What they earned in 1995–96: The data on private-college leaders. *Chronicle of Higher Education*, A36–57.

Livingston, Donald R. (1994). The OFCCP glass ceiling initiative. In *Pressures for change: How to successfully handle the employment law challenges of a diverse marketplace*, 1–8. Chicago: American Bar Association.

Lowry, Richard J. (Ed.) (1979). *The journals of A. H. Maslow*. Vol. 2. Monterey, CA: Brooks/Cole.

Machlup, Fritz. (1996). In defense of academic tenure. In M. W. Finkin (Ed.), *The case for tenure*, 9–25. Ithaca: ILR Press.

MacKinnon, Catherine. (1989). *Toward a feminist theory of the state*. Cambridge: Harvard University Press.

Magner, Denise K. (1997, February 14). A scholar provides an intellectual framework for plans to end or revamp tenure systems. *Chronicle of Higher Education*, A10, 11.

Magner, Denise K. (1996, September 27). Minnesota regents' proposals would effectively abolish tenure, faculty leaders say. *Chronicle of Higher Education*, A14, 15.

Marks, Janet R., Dugan, Mary Kay, & Payn, Betsy. (1997, Autumn). Why women drop out of graduate management education: Answers from GMAC data. *Selections, 14*(1), 6–10.

Martin, Joanne. (1992). Cultures in organizations: Three perspectives. New York: Oxford University Press.

Maslow, Abraham. (1942). Self-esteem (dominance-feeling) and sexuality in women. *Journal of Social Psychology, 16*, 259–294.

Maslow, Abraham. (1939). Dominance, personality and social behavior in women. *Journal of Social Psychology, 10*, 3–39.

McCommons, Richard E. (Ed.) (1994). *Guide to architecture schools*. 5th ed. Washington, D.C.: Association of Collegiate Schools of Architecture Press.

McDade, Sharon A., & Walton, Katherine D. The second in command: A profile of women academic officers. Work in progress.

Meier, Barry. (1996, November 21). Bias suits against Wall St. firms. *New York Times*, D4.

Melich, Tanya. (1995). *The Republican war against women: An insider's report from behind the lines*, 45–53. New York: Bantam Books.

Menkel-Meadow, Carrie. (1988). Feminist legal theory, critical legal studies, and legal education, or "the fem-crits go to law school." *Journal of Legal Education, 38*, 61–85.

Middleton, Sue. (1993). *Educating feminists: Life histories and pedagogy*. New York: Teachers College Press.

Miller, Jane. (1996). Transformation and reform: The Commission on Women at the University of Minnesota. Unpublished paper.

Morreale, Joseph C., & Licata, Christine M. (1997, April). *Post-tenure review: A guide book for academic administrators of colleges and schools of business*. St. Louis: American Assembly of Collegiate Schools of Business.

Morrison, Ann M., White, Randall, & Van Velsor, Ellen. (1987). Breaking the glass ceiling: Why women don't reach the top of large corporations. Rev. ed. (1992). Reading, MA: Addison-Wesley.

Myerson, Alan R. (1997, January 12). As federal bias cases drop, workers take up the fight. *New York Times*, 1, 14.

National Commission on Excellence in Education. (1983). *A nation at risk: The imperative for educational reform*. Washington, D.C.: National Commission on Excellence in Education.

National Commission on Teaching and America's Future. (1996). *What matters most: Teaching for America's future*. New York: NCTAF.

Naughton, Joseph. (1997, May 16). A new debate over disparities in coaches' salaries. *Chronicle of Higher Education*, A35.

Naughton, Joseph. (1997a, May 2). Supreme Court rejects Brown's appeal on women in sports. *Chronicle of Higher Education*, A45.

Naughton, Joseph. (1997b, April 1). Women in Division I sports programs: "The glass is half empty and half full." *Chronicle of Higher Education*, A39.

NEA Higher Education Research Center. (1996, September). Full-time non-tenure-track faculty. *Update*, 2(5), 1–3.

Neumann, Anna. (1997). Ways without words: Learning from silence and story in post-holocaust lives. In A. Neumann & P. L. Peterson (Eds.), *Learning from our lives: Women, research, and autobiography in education*, 91–123. New York: Teachers College Press.

New England Council of Land-Grant University Women. (1996). *Vision 2000*.

New York State Commission on the Quality, Cost, and Financing of Elementary and Secondary Education. (1973). *The Fleischmann report on the quality, cost, and financing of elementary and secondary education in New York State*. Vol. 3. New York: Viking Press.

Nicolson, Paula. (1996). *Gender, power, and organization: A psychological perspective*. New York: Routledge.

Office of Federal Contract Compliance. (1991). *Report on the glass ceiling initiative*. Washington, D.C.: U.S. Department of Labor.

Office of the President. (1995). Diversity: An introduction to the University of California's policies and programs. Memorandum to the Board of Regents, University of California. Unpublished document.

Office of the President. (1994, April 15). *The Michigan agenda for women: Leadership for a new century*. Ann Arbor: Office of the President, University of Michigan.

Ohio State University. (1992). *Report of the President's Commission on Women*. Columbus: President's Commission on Women, Ohio State University.

Olsen, Deborah, Maple, Sue, & Stage, Frances. (1995, May–June). Women and minority job satisfaction: Professional role interests, professional satisfactions, and institutional fit. *Journal of Higher Education*, 66(3), 267–293.

O'Neill, Molly. (1994, October 20). On campus with Dr. Judith Rodin: In an Ivy League of her own. *New York Times*, C1.

Ost, David H., & Twale, Darla J. (1989). Appointments of administrators in higher education: Reflections of administrative and organizational structures. *Initiatives*, 52(2), 23–30.

Packer, Barbara B. (1989). *Gender equity for women professors at research universities*. Harvard University, Ed.D. unpublished thesis.

Patterson, Martha P. (1996). Women's employment patterns, pension coverage, and retirement planning. In Cynthia Costello & Barbara K. Krimgold (Eds.), *The American woman, 1996-97*, 148–165. New York: W. W. Norton.

Penn State Commission for Women. (1994). *A vision for an equitable university: An assessment and update of the recommendations of the report of the strategic study group on the status of women*. State College: Pennsylvania State University.

Pfeffer, Jeffrey, & Davis-Blake, Alison. (1987). The effect of the proportion of women on salaries: The case of college administrators. *Administrative Science Quarterly*, 32, 1–24.

Phipps, Polly A. (1990). Industrial and occupational change in pharmacy: Prescription for feminization. In B. F. Reskin & P. A. Roos (Eds.), *Job queues, gender queues,* 111–129. Philadelphia: Temple University Press.

Pines, Deborah. (1996, June 1). Circuit's en banc panel wrestles with issue of employer's pretext. *New York Law Journal, 215,* 1.

Pion, G. M., Mednick, M. T., Astin, H. S., Hall, C. C. I., Kenkel, M. B., Keita, G. P., Kohout, J. L., & Kelleher, J. C. (1996, May). The shifting gender composition of psychology: Trends and implications for the discipline. *American Psychologist, 51*(5), 509–528.

President's Advisory Commission on Women's Issues (PACWI). (1994). History. Unpublished draft. Ann Arbor: PACWI, University of Michigan.

President's Advisory Commission on Women's Issues (PACWI). (1990, June 10). *1990 report and recommendations.* Ann Arbor: PACWI, University of Michigan.

Project on the Status and Education of Women. (1984, Spring). Supreme Court guts Title IX; Women students lose major portions of protection against sex discrimination. *On Campus with Women, 13*(4), 1–4.

Project on the Status and Education of Women. (1982, Fall). Interview. *On Campus with Women, 12*(2), 1–3.

Reskin, Barbara F., & Roos, Patricia A. (Eds.). (1990). *Job queues, gender queues: Explaining women's inroads into male occupations.* Philadelphia: Temple University Press.

Rhode, Deborah L. (1996, January). Career progress, yes; Equality, not quite yet. *National Law Journal,* 1.

Rhode, Deborah L. (1994). Gender and professional roles. *Fordham Law Review, 63,* 39–72.

Rhode, Deborah L. (1991). The "no-problem" problem: Feminist challenges and cultural change. *Yale Law Journal, 100,* 1731–1793.

Rich, Adrienne. (1995). *What is found there.* New York: W. W. Norton.

Rich, Adrienne. (1979). Toward a woman-centered university. In *On lies, secrets, and silence: Selected prose, 1966–1978,* 126–155. New York: Norton.

Rich, Adrienne. (1976). *Of woman born: Motherhood as experience and institution.* New York: Norton.

Richardson, Joanna. (1995, March 1). Critics target state teacher-tenure laws. *Education Week,* 1, 13.

Rimer, Sara. (1995, September 27). Smith's new president applauds her mentors. *New York Times,* B8.

Ripley, Anthony. (1972, October 5). Colleges given antibias guides. *New York Times,* 5.

Romany, Celina. (1997). Ain't I a feminist? In A. K. Wing (Ed.), *Critical race feminism: A reader.* New York: New York University Press.

Rosener, Judy B. (1995). *America's competitive secret: Utilizing women as a management strategy.* New York: Oxford University Press.

Rosser, Sue V. (1995). *Teaching the majority: Breaking the gender barrier in science, mathematics, and engineering.* New York: Teachers College Press, Athene Series.

Rowland, Robyn, & Klein, Renate. (1996). Radical feminism: History, politics, action.

In D. Bell & R. Klein (Eds.), *Radically speaking: Feminism reclaimed*. London: ZED Books.

Sagaria, Mary Ann. (1988). *Empowering women: Leadership development strategies on campus*. San Francisco: Jossey-Bass.

Sandberg, Leslie. (1997a, November 3). East Islip union says board is in contempt. *New York Teacher*, 5.

Sandberg, Leslie. (1997b, November 3). Judge tears up tenure waiver. *New York Teacher*, 3.

Sandler, Bernice R. (1997a, Winter). Women get raises despite suit filed by male profs. *About Women on Campus*, 6(1), 2, 3.

Sandler, Bernice R. (1997b, Spring). "Too strong for a woman": The five words that created Title IX. *About Women on Campus*, 6(2), 1–6.

Sandler, Bernice R. (1996, Spring). Berkeley to pay $1 million to former professor. *About Women on Campus*, 5(2), 5.

Sandler, Bernice R. (1984). Sex discrimination cases. *About Women on Campus*, 13(1), 4.

Sandler, Bernice R., & Shoop, Robert J. (Eds.). (1997). *Sexual harassment on campus: A guide for administrators, faculty, and students*. Needham Heights, MA: Allyn & Bacon.

Sandler, Bernice R., & Hall, Roberta. (1993). The campus climate revisited: Chilly climate for women faculty, administrators, and students. In J. S. Glazer, E. M. Bensimon, & B. K. Townsend (Eds.), *Women in higher education: A feminist perspective*, 175–204. Needham Heights, MA: Ginn Press.

Schafran, Lynn H. (1995, Winter). Credibility in the courts: Why is there a gender gap? *Judges' Journal*, 34(1), 5–7.

Schafran, Lynn H. (1990, February). Women and the law. Overwhelming evidence: Reports on gender bias in the courts. *Trial*, 28–34.

Schneider, Elizabeth. (1988). Task force reports on women in the courts: The challenge for legal education. *Journal of Legal Education*, 38, 87–96.

School of Library Service. (1990, April 13). A response from the faculty of the Columbia University School of Library Service to the report of the provost on the School of Library Service. Unpublished document.

Schwartz, Debra B. (1994). An examination of the impact of family-friendly policies on the glass ceiling: Final report to the Glass Ceiling Commission. New York: Families and Work Institute. Unpublished document.

Scott, Joan W. (1990). Deconstructing equality-versus-difference or, the uses of poststructuralist theory for feminism. In M. Hirsch & E. F. Keller (Eds.), *Conflicts in feminism*, 134–148. New York: Routledge.

Seals, Brenda. (1997). Faculty-to-faculty sexual harassment. In B. R. Sandler & R. J. Shoop (Eds.), *Sexual harassment on campus*, 64–84. Needham Heights, MA: Allyn & Bacon.

Sekaran, Uma, & Leong, Frederick T. L. (Eds.). (1992). *Womanpower: Managing in times of demographic turbulence*. Newbury Park: Sage.

Seligman, Daniel. (1995, May 1). Ceilingism. *Fortune*, 131, 142, 143.

Shavlik, Donna L., Touchton, Judith F., & Pearson, C. R. (Eds.). (1989). *The new agenda of women in higher education: A report of the ACE Commission on Women in Higher Education.* Washington, D.C.: American Council on Education.

Sherlock, D. (1995, Winter–Spring). A conversation with Robert Reich. *Radcliffe Quarterly, 80*(4), 6–8.

Shrewsbury, Carolyn M. (1987, Fall–Winter). What is feminist pedagogy? *Women's Studies Quarterly, 15*, 6–13.

Sineath, Timothy W. (Ed.). (1996). *Library and information science education statistical report 1996.* Raleigh: Association for Library and Information Science Education.

Skrentny, John D. (1996). *The ironies of affirmative action: Policy, culture, and justice in America.* Chicago: University of Chicago Press.

Slaughter, Sheila. (1993, May–June). Retrenchment in the 1980s: The politics of prestige and gender. *Journal of Higher Education, 64*(3), 250–282.

Smith, Dorothy E. (1987). *The everyday world as problematic: A feminist sociology.* Boston: Northeastern University Press.

Snyder, Thomas, Hoffman, Charlene, & Geddes, Claire M. (1996). *Digest of educational statistics.* Washington, D.C.: U.S. Department of Education, Office of Educational Research and Improvement.

Soll, Kathleen L. (1993). Gender bias task forces: How they have fulfilled their mandate and recommendations for change. *Southern California Review of Law and Women's Studies, 2*(2), 633–648.

Solomon, Barbara M. (1985). *In the company of educated women: A history of women and higher education in America.* New Haven: Yale University Press.

Solomon, Eric S. (1991, Fall). Women in academic dentistry: A profile. *Journal of the American College of Dentists, 58*(3), 27–32.

Sommers, Christine H. (1994). *Who stole feminism: How women have betrayed women.* New York: Simon & Schuster.

Stapleton, Jane. (1996, November). What's new in 1996? *Connections, 12*(1), 1, 2.

Stewart, Abigail J., & Chester, Nia L. (1982). Sex differences in human social motives: Achievement, affiliation, power. In A. J. Stewart (Ed.), *Motivation and society: A volume in honor of David McClelland,* 172–218. San Francisco: Jossey-Bass.

Stimpson, Catharine R. (1998, January 16). Activist trustees wield power gone awry. *Chronicle of Higher Education, 44*(19), B4, 5.

Stimpson, Catharine R. (1993). Has affirmative action gone astray? *Thought and Action, 8*(2), 5–26.

Stobo, John D., Fried, Linda P., & Stokes, Emma J. (1993, May). Commentaries: Understanding and eradicating bias against women in medicine. *Academic Medicine, 68*(5), 349.

Swedlow, Katherine R. (1994, Summer). Suing for tenure: Legal and institutional barriers. *Review of Litigation, 13*, 557–595.

Tack, Martha W., & Pattitu, Carol L. (1993). *Faculty Job Satisfaction: Women and Minorities in Peril.* ASHE-ERIC Education Report No. 4. Washington, D.C.: George Washington University.

Task Force on the Changing Gender Composition of Psychology. (1995). *Report of* the task force on changing gender composition in psychology. Washington, D.C.: American Psychological Association.

Taylor, Barbara E. (1987). *Working effectively with trustees: Building cooperative campus leadership.* ASHE-ERIC Research Report No. 2. Washington, D.C.: George Washington University.

Tetreault, Mary Kay, & Maher, Frances A. (1994). *The feminist classroom.* New York: Basic Books.

TIAA-CREF. (1997, February). Everything you always wanted to know about financial planning. *The Participant*, 6–11.

Tierney, William G. (1996). *The parameters of affirmative action: Equity and excellence in the academy.* Los Angeles: Center for Higher Education Policy Analysis.

Touchton, Judith G., Shavlik, Donna, & Davis, Lynn. (1993). *Women in presidencies: A descriptive study of women college & university presidents.* Washington, D.C.: Office of Women in Higher Education, American Council on Education.

Trautvetter, Lois C. (1995). Socialization of newly hired female faculty members: Plugging the leaking pipeline. Paper presented at annual meeting of the American Educational Research Association.

Twale, Darla J. (1992). An analysis of higher education administrative appointments: A focus on women from 1986 to 1991. Paper presented at annual meeting of the Eastern Educational Research Association. ED343515.

University of Minnesota Commission on Women. (1988). *Minnesota Plan II.* Minneapolis: University of Minnesota.

University of Wisconsin-Madison. (1994). *Gender equity efforts.* Madison: Office of Associate Vice Chancellors.

Verhovek, Sam H. (1997, March 27). Universities scramble to weigh a ruling's impact. *New York Times*, A1.

Vetter, Betty M. (1994). *Professional women and minorities: A total resource data compendium.* 11th ed. Washington, D.C.: Commission on Professionals in Science and Technology.

Vetter, Betty M. (1992). *What is holding up the glass ceiling? Barriers to women in the science and engineering workforce.* Occasional Paper 92-3. Washington, D.C.: Commission on Professionals in Science and Technology.

Washington, Charles. (1993, August 16). Administrators rate women's progress. *Higher Education & National Affairs*, 42(15), 5.

Weedon, Chris. (1987). *Feminist practice & poststructuralist theory.* Oxford: Basil Blackwell.

Weiler, Kathleen. (1992). Introduction. In K. Weiler & C. Mitchell (Eds.), *What schools can do: Critical pedagogy and practice*, 3–10. Albany: State University of New York Press.

Weiler, Kathleen. (1991, November). Freire and a feminist pedagogy of difference. *Harvard Educational Review*, 61, 449–474.

Weiss, Catherine, & Melling, Louise. The legal education of twenty women. *Stanford Law Review*, 40(1988), 1299–1369.

West, Martha S. (1995, July–August). Women faculty: Frozen in time. *Academe, 81* (4), 26–29.

West, Martha S. (1994, Spring). Gender bias in academic robes: The law's failure to protect women faculty. *Temple Law Review, 67*(1), 67–178.

Williams, Christine L. (1995). *Still a man's world: Men who do women's work.* Berkeley: University of California Press.

Williams, Wendy W. (1993). Equality's riddle: Pregnancy and the equal treatment/special treatment debate. In D. K. Weisberg (Ed.), *Feminist legal theory: Foundations,* 128–155. Philadelphia: Temple University Press.

Wilson, Robin. (1997, June 6). At Harvard, Yale, and Stanford women lose tenure bids despite backing from departments. *Chronicle of Higher Education,* A10, A11.

Wilson, Robin. (1996, November 8). 350 Female faculty members join a pay-equity dispute at Illinois State U. *Chronicle of Higher Education,* A10.

Wing, Adrien K. (Ed.). (1997). *Critical race feminism: A reader.* New York: New York University Press.

Wolf, Naomi. (1993). *Fire with fire: The new female power and how it will change the 21st century.* New York: Random House.

Zimbler, Lois J. (1994). *Faculty and instructional staff: Who are they and what do they do?* The 1993 National Study of Postsecondary Faculty. Washington, D.C.: U.S. Department of Education, Office of Educational Research and Improvement.

INDEX

abortion rights, 24, 30
academic feminism, 20–24; backlash against, 29–30, 34–35; equal rights and, x, 22, 23, 29, 30; feminist pedagogy and, 188, 192; political action and, xi, 15, 17, 25, 189, 190
academic fields: anthropology, 45, 191; art history, 132; arts, 55, 69, 70, 81–82, 91, 149; arts and sciences, 75, 153–54; biology, 67, 85; chemistry, 45, 67; communications, 82; computer science, 38, 84, 85, 90; economics, 38, 45, 66, 85, 90; English, 67, 191; environmental sciences, 67, 85; foreign languages, 45; geology, 45; history, 191; home economics, 45, 82, 84, 138, 153; information sciences, 67, 85, 137; liberal arts, 62, 129–30, 135; life sciences, 43, 44, 45, 90; mathematics, 38, 44, 67; natural sciences, 59, 81, 149; physical sciences, 38, 43, 44, 45, 49, 67, 90; physics, 45, 84, 85; political science, 45; psychology, 38, 44, 45, 48–49, 50, 90; science and engineering (S&E), 66–67, 77, 86, 90; social sciences, 43, 44, 45, 55, 67, 81, 90, 149; sociology, 45; theology, 82. *See also* humanities field; professional fields; science field
academic freedom, ix, 59, 73, 112, 166, 205; Constitution and, 74; tenure and, 67–69, 72, 74, 75, 203
academic pipeline: campus commissions and, 172, 201; degree attainment and, 39–45; faculty status and, 55, 65–66, 77, 148, 199; in psychology field, 45, 48–49
administrative positions, 78, 166; provosts, 151, 169; salaries of, 154–56; tenure decisions and, 72–73, 77, 79; women in, 109, 141, 142–43, 145–64, 178, 181–83, 196–98, 205. *See also* university presidents
admissions policies, 169; affirmative action and, 9–10, 16, 31–34, 101, 166, 167, 201; class-action suit against, 33, 179; open, 6, 61, 151

adult students, 23, 40, 103, 165, 169
affirmative action, xi, 24–34; AAUP resolution on, 97; backlash against, xi, 27–31, 38, 63–64, 143, 197–98, 200, 207; in California, 34, 56, 128, 174–75, 201; campus commissions and, 28, 165–69, 170, 177, 178, 180, 181, 184, 186; constitutionality of, 29, 32, 34; debate over, ix, 31–34, 167, 178, 183, 197, 200–202, 204; dual employment track and, 57, 59, 61, 63; feminist politics and, 12–18; implementation of, 13, 14, 15, 16, 165–68, 201; laws on, 13–14, 15, 16, 167, 170; offices of, 166, 168, 170, 178, 180, 181; in the professions, 101–4, 105, 110, 116; rescinding of, 34, 145, 186–87, 206; tenure and, 71–72, 203; tokenism and, 81; women's leadership roles and, 142, 154, 156–58
African Americans, 13, 32, 174; as academic leaders, 147–48, 149, 158–61; degree attainment by, 42–43; as faculty, 107, 123, 124; in the professions, 106, 107, 123, 124; as trustees, 150–51
age discrimination, 71, 76, 78, 116
Age Discrimination and Employment Act, 78
Allen, James E., Jr., 5, 6, 7
American Assembly of Collegiate Schools of Business (AACSB), 129–32
American Association for Higher Education Forum on Faculty Roles and Rewards, 67–68
American Association of University Professors (AAUP), 50, 97, 179; on professional status, 61, 62, 95; salary data of, 65, 66, 82–83, 93n, 96, 196; on tenure, 58–60, 67–68, 69, 79, 111–12, 116, 138
American Bar Association Commission on Women in the Professions, 120, 124
American Council on Education (ACE), 27, 34, 148–49, 158, 172, 177

American Federation of Teachers (AFT), 25, 61–62
APA Task Force on Women in Psychology, 48, 50, 90
Arizona, University of, 173
Arizona Board of Regents, 151, 172–74
Arizona State University, 173–74
Arts in Education Program, 5, 7; JDR 3rd Fund, 5
Asian Americans, 32, 42–43, 53, 106, 107, 115, 149, 150–51, 175
assimilationist ideology, x–xi, 15, 197
Association of American Medical Colleges (AAMC), 105–6, 107, 110, 111, 112, 113, 115–16
Astin, Helen S., 21–22, 146
attrition rates, 22, 91–92, 105

baccalaureate (B.A.) degrees: awarded to women, 40, 48, 128, 132, 133, 137, 199; employment and, 43, 49; salaries and, 85–86
Bakke v. University of California Board of Regents, 32–33, 201
Barnard, Jessie, 21–22
Barnard College, 74
Bell, Derrick A., 124
benefits, 38–39, 71, 95, 97–100, 144, 184; academic feminism and, 22, 23, 34; dual employment track and, 57, 60, 62; maternity leave, 99, 110–11; pensions, 39, 71, 97–98
Bennington College, 78–79
Bensimon, Estela M., 146, 148, 152
Blackmun, Harry, 74
Bloom, Catherine, 5
Boston University, 75
Boyer, Ernest L., 70
Brown University, 26–27, 63
Brown v. Board of Education, 13
business: glass ceiling in, 140–45; Ph.D. glut and, 91–92; salaries in, 81, 86–87, 90, 129, 130; sex segregation in, 101, 104; tenure in, 66, 69–70, 131; women in, 40, 49, 128–32, 153, 156, 178, 180

California, 62, 128; affirmative action in, 29, 31, 201; state university system of, 16, 80, 157
California, University of, 31–33, 56, 60, 76, 137, 201
California Civil Rights Initiative (CCRI). *See* Proposition 209

campus activism, 6, 14, 60, 123, 124, 178; campus commissions and, 166, 168–69, 170, 184
campus commissions, 113, 168–88; affirmative action and, 28, 165–69, 170, 181, 184, 186; effectiveness of, 184–88, 201; feminism and, 14, 23, 170, 205; functions of, 184–85; implementation of, xi, 94, 129, 151, 168–69; need for, 201, 205; tenure policies and, 75, 176, 187, 201, 205; voluntary consortia, 175–77
campus culture, 2, 8, 9, 185, 195; campus commissions and, 171, 174, 177, 180, 181, 183, 184, 187–88, 205
career paths, 9, 114; campus commissions and, 182, 184; of women, 20–22, 49, 65, 106, 148, 152, 153, 154, 156–64, 199
Carnegie Commission on Higher Education, 91, 165
Carnegie Corporation, 11, 62, 165, 171
Carnegie Council on Policy Studies in Higher Education, 57, 61, 165
Carnegie Foundation for the Advancement of Teaching, 112
Carnegie Task Force on Teaching as a Profession, 135
Carter, Jimmy, 25
Category I institutions. *See* doctoral-granting universities
Category IIA institutions. *See* universities: comprehensive
Category IIB institutions. *See* four-year institutions
Category III institutions. *See* two-year institutions
Center for Individual Rights, 33, 179
Chait, Richard P., 67–68, 150
Chicago, University of, 16, 121, 137, 148
child care issues, 18, 22, 23, 24, 98, 110–11, 175, 187
church-related institutions, 82, 84–85, 87, 89, 148, 149, 152
civil rights, 32, 33, 73, 115, 124, 179; legislation on, 13–14, 28, 34, 77, 143; movement for, x, 13–14, 30, 34–35, 37, 124
Civil Rights, Office of (OCR), 16, 25, 27, 28
Clark, Marcia, 127
class, 29, 104, 122, 124, 203–4; feminist pedagogy and, 190, 191, 192; leadership and, 148, 156, 192
Clinton, Bill, 19, 26, 33, 34, 127, 128, 136
coeducation, 2, 10, 26, 63, 147

doctoral programs *(cont.)*
employment track and, 57, 61, 62; post-graduate employment and, 49, 63; women in, 67, 178, 183. *See also* Ph.D. glut

Dole, Bob, 143

Dole, Elizabeth, 143

dual employment track, 57–61, 78, 135, 187; due process and, 62, 112; trends in, ix, 61–64, 202, 203

Duderstadt, James, 178–79

Duffey, Joseph, 97

education, 49, 101, 102, 104, 190, 199, 202; faculty salaries in, 81, 90; omnibus higher education act, 16, 24; public opinion of higher, 64, 151, 159, 200; salaries in, 86–87, 90; tenure debate in, 69–70; U.S. Office of, 167; women in, 44, 45, 55, 133–39, 149

Education, Department of (DOE), 25, 58

EEOC. *See* Equal Employment Opportunity Commission

Eisenstein, Zillah R., 30, 33

Elementary and Secondary Education Act (1965), 4

employment laws, 169, 184, 201–2; Executive Order 11375, 15; feminist politics and, 12–18; tenure litigation and, 71–77; women and, 37, 142, 197–98. *See also* affirmative action; labor market, academic

empowerment, 123, 146–47, 189, 190, 191, 92

engineering, 49, 192; salaries in, 38, 81, 84–86, 90; tenure in, 66–67, 77; women in, 43, 44, 55, 153, 178, 180

Epstein, Cynthia, 121, 127

Equal Employment Opportunity Act, 36, 57

Equal Employment Opportunity Commission (EEOC), 14, 15, 16, 71, 73–74, 123, 143, 166

equal opportunity offices, 94, 166, 168, 170

Equal Pay Act, 13, 16, 65

Equal Rights Amendment (ERA), 12–14, 17, 18–20, 24, 97

Equity in Athletics Disclosure Act, 26

ethnicity, 39, 124, 146, 156, 190; faculty status and, 52–53, 134; the professions and, 104, 119, 122

ethnic preferences, 31, 34

ethnic studies, 6, 45, 205

faculty: campus commissions and, 114, 169, 170, 176; of color, 50, 52–53, 74, 124, 181; data trends in, 61–64; department chairs, 109, 132, 134, 158, 183, 185, 197; dual employment track and, 57–61, 202, 203; "full professional effort," 111; governance participation of, 65, 68, 79; junior, 55–56, 58, 71, 76, 81, 185; part-time, 48, 57–60, 67–68, 196; probationary appointments to, 62, 69; professionalism of, 202–4; senior, 50, 56, 61, 63; standards for, 70–71, 73, 78; state intervention in, 191; statistical data on, 49–55; teaching assistants, 57, 60, 187, 205; unionization of, 62, 79, 181, 184; women's status in, ix, 21, 49–64, 65–67, 79, 99, 103, 198. *See also* instructor positions; lecturer positions; non-tenure-track positions; professorships; tenure; tenure-track positions

Faludi, Susan, 29

Family and Medical Leave Act (1993; FMLA), 39, 98, 120–21

family-friendly workplace policies, 39, 144, 176

family-work balance, 20–22, 30, 57, 77, 206; benefits and, 38–39, 98–99, 144; campus commissions and, 183, 184, 187, 205; glass ceiling and, 29, 144, 146; women academic leaders and, 163–64; women faculty and, 110–11, 112, 188. *See also* marital status

female-friendly policies, 29, 197, 205

Feminine Mystique (Friedan), 13, 15, 188

feminism: activism and, 14, 22–23, 30, 200, 205; backlash against, 27–31, 34; Black, 158–61; campus commissions and, 169, 170, 184, 188; collaboration and, 207–8; consciousness-raising groups and, 17–18; critical race, 122, 124; cultural theory and, 29–30, 205; education in, 1, 191; equity, 29; gender feminist academics, 29; generational differences in, x, 30–31; glass ceiling and, 146–47; higher education profession and, 12, 17; marxist, 15, 22; medical school changes and, 116–17; merit pay and, 96–97; politics of, 12–20, 34, 101, 191; postmodern, 142, 205; power, 141; progress of, ix–x; radical, 22–23, 139, 140–42; scholars and, 75, 81, 104, 146; socialist, 15, 22; women of color and, 190–91. *See also* academic feminism; liberal feminism

Illinois State University, 95–96
instructor positions, 58, 135, 166; salary disparities and, 81–89; statistical data on, 50–55; women in, 48, 117, 118, 129, 137, 177, 196
Iowa, University of, Medical School, 115

job satisfaction, ix, 55–56, 60, 198
Johns Hopkins University School of Medicine, 113–14, 116
Johnson, Lyndon, 4, 13–14, 15

Kanter, Rosabeth, 207
Kaplan, Abbott, 7–8
Kaplin, William A., 97, 98
Kennedy, John F., 12–13, 169
Kunz, Diane, 75–76

Labor, Department of, 13, 16–17, 18, 60, 143
labor market, academic, 36–39, 65–67, 184; antidiscrimination laws and, 101–4; dual employment track and, 57–61; Ph.D. glut and, 91–93; state intervention and, 101, 201. See also contract employment system; temporary employment
Labor Statistics, Bureau of, 37, 38
LaNoue, George R., 71, 72, 94–95
Latin Americans, 32, 150–51; women, 15, 42–43, 56, 106, 107, 175
law, 27, 119–28, 149, 153, 178, 204; credentialism in, 102; faculty salaries in, 84–86, 90; feminists in, 169, 204; gender bias in, 124–26; male-domination of, 125, 199; non-tenure-track faculty in, 66–67; scholarship in, 122–24; school enrollment rates in, 92; sex segregation in, 101, 104; stereotypes of women in, 119–20; tenure in, 66, 69–70, 121–22, 126
leadership positions, 140–64, 204; in academia, 147–56, 196–98; affirmative action and, 154; career paths to, 156–64; femininity and, 148, 157–58; gender issues and, 140, 148, 152, 156, 158; theories on, 140–47
Leap, Terry L., 71–74
lecturer positions, 135, 166; dual employment track and, 57, 58, 62; statistical data on, 50–55; women in, 48, 117, 121, 137, 178, 196
Lee, Barbara A., 71, 72, 94–95
legal actions, 115, 184, 206; against admissions policies, 33, 179; affirmative action and, xi, 198, 201; economic factors in,

167; against salary disparities, 82, 93–97; against sex discrimination, 16–17, 26–28, 93–97, 123–24, 166, 170, 180, 183, 198; against tenure policies, 71–77, 79, 94, 203
lesbian, gay, and bisexual equality, 181
liberal feminism, 22, 59, 139, 168, 189; organizational culture and, 141–42, 197; principles of, x, 198
library science, 101, 121, 132, 133, 136–39, 145; recruitment of males in, 104; salaries in, 82; school closings in, 137, 138; women's doctorates in, 45
Lin, Maya, 133
Long Island University, 3, 12, 62, 97
Los Angeles, Calif., 182

MacKinnon, Catherine, 17, 18, 198
Maine, University of, 176
Major, John, 144
marital status, 43, 76–77, 149, 163, 188, 205. See also family-work balance
Martin, Joanne, 208
masculine belief system, 21, 103, 104
Maslow, Abraham, 188, 189
Massachusetts, University of, 176
Massachusetts state colleges, 95
master's degrees: awarded to women, 41, 102, 128, 132, 133, 137, 199; in business administration, 41, 128, 130, 132; in fine arts, 69, 132; in library science, 137; in professional fields, 102; women's salaries with, 85–86
McGovern, George, 16
McLuhan, Marshall, 137
media influence, 127, 147–48, 157, 167
medicine: change in, strategies for, 115–17, 204; control of labor market by, 105, 199; credentialism in, 102; dual employment track in, 59, 111–13; enrollment rates for, 92; faculty salaries in, 90, 107–8, 116; hierarchy in, 109; non-tenure-track employment in, 68; sex segregation in, 101, 104–17; sexual harassment in, 112–15; tenure debate in, 69–70; women in, 105–11, 115–17, 153, 178; women's organizations in, 113, 116
mentoring support, 12, 39, 199; in business, 132; in dentistry, 119; for graduate students, 68; in medicine, 108–9, 110, 113, 114, 115, 116; in science, 44; for women academic leaders, 157, 158, 197
merit: affirmative action and, ix, 31–32, 166, 206; gender equity and, 186, 201;

glass ceiling and, 144, 145–46; salary adjustments and, 96–97

meritocracy, myth of, 73, 101

Meritor v. Vinson, 127

Mexican Americans, 43

Michigan, 62, 187

Michigan, University of, 2, 17, 33, 170–71, 178–79; *Michigan Agenda for Women: Leadership for a New Century*, 179; Michigan Mandate, 179

Minnesota, University of, 16, 79, 94–95, 151, 171, 180–81; Minnesota Plans, 94–95, 171, 181

minorities, 6, 23, 61, 139, 172; admissions policies and, 179; affirmative action and, 16, 28, 29, 32, 34, 166; entry into professions by, 101, 103, 104; faculty status of, 55, 56, 78, 107, 112, 115, 118; glass ceiling and, 142, 144, 145; hiring of, 162; inferiority myth of, 167; service demands of, 71; tenure litigation and, 72; as trustees, 150–51. *See also specific ethnic groups*

multiculturalism, 75, 207

National Abortion Rights Action League, 30

National Center for Educational Statistics (NCES), 37, 41, 49n, 50, 81–83, 102, 134, 196

National Commission on Excellence in Education, 134

National Commission on Teaching & America's Future, 134

National Council for Research on Women, 30

National Defense Education Act (1957), 37

National Education Association (NEA), 17, 25, 50, 58

National Organization for Women (NOW), 15, 17

national origin, 31, 71, 73

National Research Council, 41, 90, 202

National Survey of Postsecondary Faculty (NSOPF-93), 55, 58, 134

National Women's Party, 12, 14

National Women's Policy Institute, 30

National Women's Political Caucus (NWPC), 17, 19

Native Americans, 32, 43, 53, 149, 150–51; women, 106, 107, 175

Neumann, Anna, 148, 152, 153

New Hampshire, University of, 175–77

New Jersey, 18, 33, 62, 119, 177

New Jersey state university system, 16

New Right, 19, 31

New School for Social Research, 10–11

New York, City University of (CUNY), 6, 10, 11, 95; *Melani v. Board of Higher Education*, 95

New York, State University of (SUNY), 10, 80, 148; at Purchase, 3–8

New York City, 6, 10, 11, 120

New York State, 4, 6, 10, 14, 18–20, 177; Fleischmann Commission, 6; Taylor Law, 6

New York State United Teachers (NYSUT), 6, 62

New York State Women's Political Caucus (NYSWPC), 17, 18

New York University, 3, 6, 10–11, 116

Nixon, Richard, 9, 14, 15, 16, 24

non-tenure-track (NTT) positions, 135, 139, 196, 202; data trends in, 61–64; dual employment track and, 57–61; growth of, 65–66, 70; in law schools, 121; in medical schools, 68, 111–13; women in, 48, 50–55, 107, 112, 118, 178, 180, 181, 187, 198

Northeastern University, 124

Northern Arizona University, 173, 174

Northwestern University, 75, 129

nursing, 102, 104, 136, 138; business schools and, 129–30; salaries in, 38, 90, 117; women deans in, 153, 179

O'Connor, Sandra Day, 34, 127

Ohio, 78

Ohio State University, 182–83

Opportunity 2000 (network), 144

Oregon Board of Higher Education, 95

organizational culture, 139, 146, 187; faculty motivation and, 61, 63–64; feminism and, 207–8; male dominance in, 141–42, 145, 153, 164; temporary employment and, 154–55

part-time (PT) faculty, 48, 57–60, 67–68, 196. *See also* dual employment track

Penk v. Oregon Board of Higher Education, 95

Pennsylvania, University of, 71, 73–74, 76, 147; Law School, 125; Wharton School of Business, 73, 129

Pennsylvania State System, Women's Consortium of, 176–77

Pennsylvania State University, 181, 186

status professions (cont.)
    women in, 43, 101–4, 146, 153, 178, 196.
        See also business; engineering; law;
        medicine; professional fields
stereotyping, 29, 146, 167, 188; in the pro-
    fessions, 110, 114, 115, 119–20, 121, 127, 129
student advisement time, 56, 68, 173, 202
student services administration, 154, 156,
    196
SUNY. See New York, State University of
Supreme Court, U.S.: affirmative action
    policies and, 32, 34, 201; retirement ben-
    efits and, 97; salary discrimination
    claims and, 95; sexual harassment and,
    127; tenure and, 71, 74, 77; Title VII
    amendments and, 28; women on, 127
Survey of Earned Doctorates, 41, 42n, 103
Symington, Fife, 128, 174

Teachers Insurance and Annuity Associa-
    tion (TIAA-CREF), 39, 97–98; pen-
    sions, 39, 71, 97–98
teaching schedules, 90, 98, 116, 122; dual
    employment track and, 58, 61; faculty
    reappointment and, 56, 64; standards
    for, 70–71, 78; of women faculty, 55, 173
temporary employment, 38–39, 48, 61–64,
    154–55
tenure, 65–100; abuses in, 78; academic
    feminism and, 22, 23, 24; academic free-
    dom and, ix, 67–69; affirmative action
    and, 16, 57, 166, 197–98; age discrimina-
    tion and, 71, 76; barriers to, 124; benefits
    and, 98–99; campus commissions and,
    75, 176, 187, 201, 205; continuous, 62, 69;
    criteria for, 65, 67, 70, 74, 76–77; debate
    over, 67–91, 204; intervention in, 78–81,
    151, 191; legal action against, 71–77, 79,
    94, 203; male-dominated culture and,
    185, 198; peer evaluation and, 68, 74; re-
    structuring of, 202–3; salaries and, 66,
    67–68, 76; stop-the-clock, 112, 187, 205;
    three-track employment system and,
    196; trends in, 61–64
tenure-track positions, 41, 67, 110, 139, 202;
    decrease of, 92; in dental schools, 118–19;
    dual employment track and, 57–61; in
    law schools, 122–24; in medical schools,
    111–13, 115–16; women in, 50–55, 63,
    65–67, 172, 175, 178, 180, 181, 183–84, 196
term appointments. See contract employ-
    ment system

Texas, 29, 32–33, 62
Texas, University of, 32–33, 80
three-track employment system, 196
TIAA-CREF. See Teachers Insurance and
    Annuity Association
Title I, 4
Title II (Glass Ceiling Act), 143
Title VI (Civil Rights Act), 13, 28, 33
Title VII (Civil Rights Act), 14, 16, 33, 97,
    99, 101, 104; implementation of, 165–68;
    legal profession and, 126, 127; salaries
    and, 65, 93–95; tenure litigation and, 73,
    77
Title IX, 10, 16, 17, 23, 24–34, 57, 95; imple-
    mentation of, 165–68; passage of, 24–25,
    36; women in the professions and, 104,
    105; women's athletics and, 25–27
tokenism, 56, 103, 104, 115; in administra-
    tion, 141, 185; gender equity environ-
    ment and, 81, 205; in the professions,
    124, 204
trustees, women as, 149–51
tuition policies, 10, 151, 202
two-tier system. See dual employment
    track
two-year institutions: enrollment rates in,
    40; faculty data at, 48, 49–50, 66; salaries
    at, 81–83, 85, 88–89, 155; teaching sched-
    ules at, 56; women leaders at, 148, 151,
    152. See also colleges: community

undergraduate programs, 78, 131; women
    in, 40, 42, 67, 128, 175, 178, 195, 198–99
unionization, 60, 62, 79, 184; collective
    bargaining and, 6, 58, 168
United Federation of Teachers, 6
United Kingdom, 135, 144
universities: Carnegie classification of, 82;
    comprehensive (Category IIA), 55, 58,
    82–84, 86–87; corporate model of, 202;
    land-grant, 175–76, 181; master's level,
    58, 134, 152. See also doctoral-granting
    universities; research universities
University of Pennsylvania v. Equal Em-
    ployment Opportunity Commission, 71,
    73–74, 76
university presidents, 149–51, 178; campus
    commissions and, 168–69, 169, 170, 172,
    176, 182, 184–85; salaries of, 155; women
    as, 147–49, 153, 172, 185
university systems, 16–17, 70, 199, 205; aca-
    demic pipeline in, 65–66; affirmative ac-

tion laws and, 15, 90; expansion of, 37, 49; restructuring of, ix, 63, 186, 200
Utah, 28

Vanderbilt University, 17, 137
Varner et al. v. Illinois State University, 95–96
Vassar College, 76–77
Vermont, University of, 176
Vetter, Betty M., 77, 90
Virginia, University of, School of Medicine, 113
Virginia Commonwealth University, 96

Wang v. University of California, 76
Wayne State University, 97
WEAL (Women's Equity Action League), 15–17
Weiler, Kathleen, 189–90
Weinstock v. Columbia University, 74
welfare system, 38, 200
West, Martha S., 72–73
Westchester Community College, 3, 8, 25
Wilson, Pete, 31
Wisconsin, University of, 16, 186
Women at the Top (Hansard Society for Parliamentary Government), 144

women of color, 15, 42–43, 134, 154; as academic leaders, 149, 158–61; affirmative action debate and, 31–34; campus commissions and, 172, 178–79, 182, 184; faculty data on, 52–53, 55; in the professions, 106, 107, 123, 124, 127
Women's Bureau, Department of Labor, 13, 38
Women's Equity Action League (WEAL), 15–17
women's movement, 1, 22, 169; academic feminists and, xi, 189; backlash against women and, 29, 30–31; civil rights movement and, 30, 34–35; ERA defeat and, 18–20; progress of, ix, x, 12–18, 200
women's studies programs, 14, 23–24, 81, 147, 171–72, 180; campus commissions and, 168, 169, 171, 177, 184, 205; feminist pedagogy and, 190, 195
working conditions, ix, 21, 71, 115, 166, 176, 198, 202

Yale University, 10, 60, 63, 75–76, 116, 121, 147

Zahorik v. Cornell University, 72

The Library of Congress has cataloged the hardcover edition of this book as follows:

Glazer-Raymo, Judith.
  Shattering the myths : women in academe / Judith Glazer-Raymo.
    p.   cm.
  Includes bibliographical references (p.   ) and index.
  ISBN 0-8018-6120-9 (alk. paper)
    1. Women college teachers—United States—History.   2. Women
college teachers—United States—Social conditions.   3. Feminism and
education—United States—History.   4. Educational equalization—
United States—History.   I. Title.
LB2332.3G.53   1999
378.1′2′082—DC21   98-49542

ISBN 0-8018-6641-3 (pbk.)